Great Scenes From Minority Playwrights

Seventy-four scenes of cultural diversity

edited by

MARSH CASSADY

MERIWETHER PUBLISHING LTD.
Colorado Springs, Colorado

Meriwether Publishing Ltd., Publisher
P.O. Box 7710
Colorado Springs, CO 80933

Editor: Theodore O. Zapel
Typesetting: Sharon E. Garlock
Cover design: Tom Myers

Library of Congress Cataloging-in-Publication Data

Great scenes from minority playwrights : 74 scenes of cultural diversity / [edited] by Marsh Cassady. -- 1st ed.
p.   c.m.
Summary: A collection of scenes from Hispanic as well as Native-American, African-American, Jewish-American, and Asian-American theater; background information and discussion/analysis follow each scene.
ISBN 1-56608-029-0
1. American drama--Minority authors. 2. American drama--20th century. 3. Minorities--United States--Drama. 4. Young adult drama, American. 5. Acting. [1. Minorities--Drama. 2. Plays-Collections. 3. Acting.] I. Cassady, Marsh, 1936-
PS627.M5G65   1997
812'.5080920693--dc21
                                                       97-298
                                                        CIP
                                                        AC

1   2   3   4   5   6   7   8   9   99   98   97

To Mary Louise O'Hara

CONTENTS

THE DEVELOPMENT OF MINORITY THEATRE

Theatre in the United States is diverse in background and experience. Besides presenting plays that draw on dozens of cultures and backgrounds, America has made its own unique contributions to world theatre, often through the efforts of people from other cultures and backgrounds. In fact, in the last few decades, audiences of various backgrounds have attended plays that were written from minority points of view. More than ever before in history minority theatre is drawing wide attention.

Beginning hundreds of years ago, theatre of various sorts existed in what would become the United States. Native-American theatre existed before other races immigrated to America. Next to develop was Mexican theatre, which started in the Southwest four hundred years ago. Then came English companies and those from other European nations. Soon afterward African-Americans began to participate in theatrical activities.

Many different ethnic groups arrived in America from Europe, first largely from the Western half, and then from Eastern Europe. This latter group included Jews, many of whom had fled Russian oppression. Nearly all of these ethnic groups developed theatres based on the sort of productions immigrants had been used to in their homelands. As time went on, many of the directors and actors from minority theatres became important in mainstream theatre, based largely on English and other Western European models.

Last to develop was Asian-American theatre, which evolved differently from that of other minority or ethnic theatres in that there was a tendency for those of various Asian backgrounds to band together. A single company often included members from various countries.

How Minority Theatre Developed

A combination of causes led to ethnic theatre's becoming established. First, it helped minorities from other countries to cope with their separation from the language and culture of mainstream America. Thus, it often came into being to keep alive memories of homelands long left behind.

Another important reason was as a means of protest. David Henry Hwang, for instance, says he wrote *M. Butterfly* "as a plea to all sides to cut through our respective layers of cultural and sexual misperception, to deal with one another truthfully for our mutual good, from the common and equal ground we share as human beings."[1]

Ethnic and minority theatre allowed participants to move beyond stereotyping and to write and present truthful depictions of themselves and their culture. The civil rights movement of the 1960s brought about an increase in political activism and ethnic and racial pride, beginning with blacks but quickly embracing Hispanics, Asians, and Native Americans. From the 1960s on, there was an explosion of ethnic theatre into the mainstream.

> The black, the Indian, the Chicano, the Chinese and, in another area, the homosexual, had found their own lives reflected, if at all, only as stereotype, as comic caricature or simple villain. They were effectively excluded from national myths which turned on white supremacy. In the central plot of American history — that of the invention of a nation — they had been presented as either mere observers or dangerous impediments. The culture hero was on the whole Anglo-Saxon and male....[2]

[1]David Henry Hwang, "Afterword," *M. Butterfly* (New York: New American Library, 1989), p. 99.

[2]C. W. E. Bigsby, *A Critical Introduction to Twentieth-Century American Drama* (New York: Cambridge University Press, 1985), p. 374.

WORKING WITH THE SCENES

Great Scenes From Minority Playwrights was written to acquaint you with plays from as many minority groups as possible, and to give a good overall idea of what each play is like. For this reason the book is somewhat different in approach than most other collections of scenes. Instead of isolated cuttings from a large number of plays, there are a number of scenes from each play. The scenes are tied together with a short synopsis (except for those plays that are only unrelated monologs). This is to give you an overall view of each work so that you can better grasp what the playwright meant to convey.

Each play is different. Each minority group and each playwright within that group brings a different cultural background and personal perspective to theatre and drama. Many of the plays deal with prejudice of one kind or another, but even this subject is given a broad interpretation. Some playwrights see the tragedy in prejudice; some satirize it. Many of the plays show unique aspects of the culture from which they derived.

The book then can provide a stepping stone to further study of ethnic plays, perhaps a more complete investigation of a particular ethnic or racial group, or even investigation of other groups not touched upon. However, there is a common reaction in regard to minority writing that you should beware of and thus try to avoid. Often, an audience or a reader tends to assume that a member of a minority, in his or her writing, speaks for the minority as a whole. This simply is not the case. An excellent illustration of the difference is to examine the first two plays in the book, *Cherokee Night* and *Weebjob,* both of which were written by playwrights with Cherokee blood. The plays present vastly different situations, characters and attitudes, and are written in much different styles.

Equally as important as providing a stepping stone to a study of minority writing, *Great Scenes From Minority Playwrights* provides you with a variety of scenes for acting and directing practice. They range from less that two minutes to ten or more minutes. If you wish, you can begin with short scenes and later move on to those that are longer. Or you may decide to begin with monologs before planning scenes with others.

The plays are arranged in a modified chronological order

3

according to when a particular minority first presented theatre in America. There is some deviation. Mexican-American theatre developed much earlier than Cuban or Puerto Rican theatre. Yet, Hispanic cultures are somewhat similar. Thus Latino plays follow one another.

There are brief introductory sections before each play, one on the minority and the other on the playwright and play. They serve three purposes: to explain differences between minority and mainstream theatre; to provide background on the playwright, and occasionally to present special circumstances that influenced subject matter or style. Each scene also has an introduction which shows how it fits into the play as a whole.

Occasionally, within scenes appear three periods inside brackets. This indicates that anything from a word to several lines has been cut, sometimes to delete action or dialog that is inappropriate or irrelevant to the immediate action.

There is no single way of interpreting and presenting characters and scenes correctly. There are as many "correct" ways as there are actors and directors. Of course, there are certain rules you should follow most often. These involve such things as vocal projection, movement and placement. It would be "wrong" or at least ill-advised to ignore the necessity of playing to an audience. For one thing they want to see actors' faces as much as possible.

Preparing the Scenes

Since you will work with each scene for a week or more, try to make sure it is something you will continue to enjoy. Of course, you may be assigned scenes of a specific length or with a specific number or combination of characters. Still, you should be able to find cuttings you like. As a director, make sure to consider whether you have actors capable of filling each role.

Analyzing the Scene

From the Actor's Viewpoint

Questions like the following should help you analyze your character.

1. Figure out what the playwright wants to convey with the scene and with your character. What, in other words, is the central idea or theme? Then think about the best way of communicating this to an audience.

4

2. Figure out the mood and how best to convey it. Mood is not the same as the emotions your character feels. For example, a character could be angry, but the scene itself could convey a sense of helplessness.

3. Unless you are doing a monolog, you need to get together with your fellow actors and agree both on theme and mood. Then work out together the way to emphasize these things for an audience. Try to remain true to the playwright's intentions.

4. You need to analyze your character, as well as the scene. Consider:

   a. Present situation? Where does the character live? What country or area? What is the person's financial situation? Social status? How does all this affect what he or she is like?

   b. Origin? Where did the character grow up? Live most of his or her life? Is the culture vastly different from the one you are used to? How might all this affect the way a person thinks, feels, or believes?

   c. Age? If the character's age is different from your own, what can you do to make the person convincing?

   d. Major influences in the person's life? How do they affect occupation, beliefs, and outlook?

   e. Personality traits? Is the character jealous, greedy, stingy, loving, caring and so on? How do you know this? How does all this affect the way the person comes across in a scene?

   f. Likeable personality? How do you feel about the character? What makes you feel this way?

   g. Relationship with the other characters? How does the character interact with others, and how do they feel about each other? How do you know this? Why is the character friends with one person, enemies with another, lukewarm with a third?

   h. Goal to be reached? Every character has something he or she is working toward in each scene. For a minor character, it can be as simple as providing atmosphere. In *12-1-A*, for instance, characters often cross the stage on apparent errands, simply to provide the idea that the relocation camp is filled with people. Sometimes actors' goals vary from scene to scene. In Glancy's *Weebjob*, Sweet Potato wants to have a sense of belonging. To achieve this she often wants to hitchhike to Gallup, or to open a store with her mother.

Take into consideration what your character wants and why the goal is important. Then figure out how you might portray the character's needs or wants. In some of the scenes, incidentally, you can eliminate characters with only a line or two by skipping over them or just pretending they aren't there.

5. Next you should meet with your partners and agree on everything you've discovered. Sometimes you may need to compromise.

Take into consideration such things as hand and set props (including furniture) you will need and decide whether this will be all imaginary, all real or a mixture. Figure out where the furniture should be placed. Continue working together in planning the movement and gestures. If you are the type of person who normally uses a lot of gestures and movement in everyday life, you probably will use more in presenting your scene. But again consider whether your use of gestures matches that of your partner(s). Each person's style of acting should match that of the others.

You should be guided by several things in planning movement and gestures: 1) the type of person your character is; 2) how you interpret the emotional situation that either calls for more movement, as anger or nervousness might, or less movement as fright could, and 3) how comfortable you are with gestures.

6. Most likely, you will need to memorize the scene. Some people like to memorize the text before working out movement and gestures; others like to memorize everything at the same time.

Memorization is an individual thing, so that what works well for someone else might not work for you.

a. Be certain that you know the meaning of each word and phrase. Although this is important for every type of scene, you may have to do more investigating of the meanings of words and references in historical pieces.

b. Memorize the ideas and the flow of the scene, along with your cues, so that you have the outline or the ideas firmly in mind before you try to memorize exact words.

c. Work on memorizing the scene the last thing before you go to sleep at night; this helps you retain it.

7. Rehearse the scene as many times as necessary to feel confident that you and your co-actors are presenting it to the best of your abilities. This often means simply going over and over it until you

are sure you have it firmly fixed in your mind. If you have access to a video camera, you may want to have someone else tape the scene so that you can watch and listen in evaluating how it is coming across.

The analysis sheet that follows can help you because it often is better to write things out so you are sure you have covered everything important. But remember that you do not have to do the sheet in any particular order.

It might be a good idea for you to photocopy this sheet for each scene in which you are involved.

Analysis Sheet

Title of the Play:

Playwright:

Theme or Central Idea:

Secondary Themes:

Overall Mood:

My Character:

     Where From:

     Age:

     Environment (Time and Location of Scene):

     Major Influences:

     Personality Traits:

     Motives and Goals:

Interests:

     A. Jobs:

     B. Hobbies:

     C. Friends:

Relationship With Other Characters:

Brief Description of the Other Characters:

From the Director's Viewpoint

As a director, you should analyze each character, though not necessarily as thoroughly as each performer does his or her own character. A lot of the subtleties of interpretation can be left to the actor. This often includes gestures and facial expression, except, of course, if the actor is having trouble with them.

Whether the actors are directing their own scenes or there is a different director, there are several things that are important to know, besides those on the actor's analysis sheet.

Every scene in a play has to maintain the audience's interest. You need to figure out what in your scene would do so. Are the characters unique? The situation? The setting? Often the conflict or struggle maintains interest.

As a director, you need to figure out which lines are most important for the audience to know to be able to understand the struggle (these are called plot lines), and which characters are more important at any given second. This way when directors block the scenes (plan the movement), they can place the actors where they are the most prominent when they have important lines or actions so the audience is sure to focus on what is most vital.

For instance, an actor who is upstage, that is, closer to the back wall of the set, is most prominent. A single actor commands more focus than one in a group.

An actor who is either standing or at a higher level on the stage (on a platform, for example) will gain more audience attention than one who is seated or who is at a lower level. One who is the focus of attention for the other actors will also be the focus of the audience's attention.

It can be a big help to sketch the set as seen from above to be able to keep in mind, when planning the movement, where the furniture or other set props are placed.

You can fill out an analysis sheet like the one that follows.

Director's Analysis

Play:

Playwright:

Theme or Central Idea:

Characters' Descriptions:

    A. Character 1:

    B. Character 2:

    C. Character 3:

The Goals of Each Character:

Why Each Character Is Included:

How Each Character Advances the Scene:

The Basic Struggle or Conflict of the Scene:

The Needs of Each Character:

Diagram of the set, showing placement of set pieces, such as furniture, trees, rocks, and so on.

You should also prepare a prompt book, that is, the script photocopied in the center of a sheet of eight-and-a-half by eleven inch paper, so there is plenty of space in the margins to write anything important having to do with the movement or placement of the actors. This can be done with drawings of the set showing the movement or by written directions or even with a combination of drawing and writing.

Often you will want to go back and change things because they worked better on paper than in actuality, so it is better to write in pencil, rather than pen.

Native-American Theatre

Native-American Theatre

Native-American theatre is important not so much because of its effect on mainstream plays and performance theatre, but because the dramatic activities of Native Americans were widespread, including all the many tribes in North America.

Not much Native-American drama was presented commercially until the past few years since early performances were not the sort that would be likely to succeed in the kind of theatre with which most of us are familiar, the type which has its roots in Europe. Native-American theatre is tied more closely to storytelling, dancing, celebrations, and rites. Sometimes there is no separation between audience and performer since everyone takes part.

Usually, Euro-American drama progresses chronologically and has conflict. This was not generally the sort performed by Native Americans, although there are exceptions. The Aztecs of Mexico and parts of the United States presented both comedies and tragedies, much like European drama, and the plays, as those of Elizabethan England, were performed in verse.

Although Native-American tribes differ in religious belief and culture, they have one thing in common: Their theatre reflects the religious outlook and moral values of each group. At the core of most Native-American presentations are 1) the idea of nonlinear (nonchronological) time and 2) "the concept of a dimensionless sacred place, the center of the universe...." The ideas are similar "for each point in time or space is infinitely large, extending outward from the sacred event to include all creation, yet located around the event in a way that precisely fixes the position and assumes the security of all the participants." Sometimes the performances are given in a special location such as the rectangular platforms erected by the ancient Aztecs, or sometimes in a temporary location, "like the Sun Dance lodges of the High Plains. Sometimes the stage is the people's ordinary living space, like the Northwest Coast family houses, the Southwest village plazas, or the Plains lodges."[1]

Since it stemmed from religion, early Native-American drama often has greater significance for those involved than mainstream Western theatre has for its audiences. The drama is diverse, ranging from spellbinding storytelling to shamanistic improvisation to 100-

[1]Jeffrey F. Huntsman, "Native American Theatre" in *Ethnic Theatre in the United States,* ed. Maxine Schwartz Seller (Westport: Greenwood Press, 1983), p. 359-60.

hour long Navajo chantways that involve entire communities and are planned to the smallest detail.

Often the government, in the form of the Bureau of Indian Affairs, banned religious dramas, such as the Sun Dance, common to all the Northern Plains tribes. In 1923 the government even limited "Indian dances" (performances) to one a month, and declared that only those over the age of fifty could participate.

Playwrights and Companies

The first collection of plays of Native-American life by a Native American was not published until the latter part of the twentieth century. This was Hanay Geiogamah's *New Native American Drama: Three Plays* (1980), which "grew out of the author's desire to present Native Americans to Native Americans in ways that are vivid and compelling and free from the more pernicious of the Euro-American stereotypes of Indians."[2] Like many of the writers whose work is included in *Great Scenes From Minority Playwrights,* Geiogamah uses stereotyped characters to show how absurd these misconceptions are. His plays were first presented off-Broadway by the Native-American Theatre Ensemble.

Although Geiogamah's group was the most active, there were a number of other Native-American companies, including the Santa Fe Theatre Project, which between 1968 and 1970, performed at the Institute of American Indian Arts. Other companies included the Navajo Theatre directed by Robert Shorty and the Thunderbird Company in Ontario.

Successful in recent years is Spiderwoman, formed by three sisters, Lisa Mayo, Gloria Miguel, and Muriel Miguel (of Cuan/Rappahannock ancestry) who began working together in New York in 1975 in order to create theatrical performances free of "grandmothers and medicine women." They named their group Spiderwoman after the Hopi household god, Spider Grandmother Woman, who taught her people the art of weaving.

Using a technique called "storyweaving," Spiderwoman's first presentation, *Women and Violence*, was presented in 1976. The group "wove" stories from their own lives around that of a Native-American leader who fought for his people's rights while at the same

[2]Jeffrey F. Huntsman, "Introduction" to Hanay Geiogamah, *New Native American Drama: Three Plays* (Norman, OK: University of Oklahoma Press, 1980), p. ix.

time he brutalized women. Although the women deal with serious subjects, they weave slapstick humor into the plays.

Another company of sisters is Coatlicue/Las Colorado with Hortensia and Elvira Colorado, who are of Chichimec background. Although they grew up in Chicago, their parents came from Mexico. Their first performance was an original play called *Huipil*, named for a sleeveless garment worn by Mexican women. Similar to Spiderwoman, "the Colorado sisters weave their own huipiles, incorporating in the garment's decoration their experiences, stories, sorrows and dreams."[3]

For decades, there have been some playwrights of Native-American or mixed ancestry who have written mainstream plays that often dealt with Native-American themes.

---

[3]Luis Torres, "Sisters weave colorful tale in 'Huipil,'" *The Express News*, San Antonio, August 14, 1992, pp. 4-5.

CHEROKEE NIGHT

Lynn Riggs

Lynn Rollie Riggs (1899-1954) was a playwright, poet, journalist and screenwriter. Born outside Claremore, Oklahoma, then Indian Territory and one of the most isolated areas of the country, Riggs dreamed of becoming an actor, and, in fact, did work as an extra in films, as well as being a proofreader, a reporter, and a clerk before attending the University of Oklahoma. Soon he began having poetry published and in 1922 wrote his first play, *Cuckoo*. Nearly all his plays are folk drama. That is, they attempt to capture the character or qualities of an area, including general attitudes, beliefs, and outlook. Since he grew up among full- or part-blooded Native Americans and was part Cherokee himself, he often wrote about Native Americans. He is probably best remembered for *Green Grow the Lilacs*, upon which the musical *Oklahoma* was based.

Different in structure from most of his work, *Cherokee Night* is perhaps more similar to the nonlinear qualities of early Native American drama. The play is presented in seven "scenes," though each really is a separate one-act. Four couples from "Scene One" appear in various other segments. Yet the play is neither chronological nor does it have a continuing plot. The theme or central idea is that denying background or roots diminishes a person as a human being.

"Scene One" opens with the eight characters, all part Cherokee, on a picnic near Claremore Mound. An insane old man tells them of seeing long-dead Cherokees painted for war, belts lined with Osage scalps.

"And *more* – they was more than happened...they seen me. They looked at me. They come toward me down the mountain... One of 'em – the biggest one – in his war bonnet, he stood right in front of me. He looked th'ough me like I wasn't there!... "Jim Talbert," he said – "Now you've saw, you've been showed. *Us* – the Cherokees – in our pride, our last glory! This is the way we were, the way we were meant to be....

But that was moons ago;
"We, too, are dead.
We have no bodies,
We are homeless ghosts,
We are made of air.

Talbert symbolically foretells the disintegration of the lives of the four couples, as well as the Cherokee way of life.

Most of the scenes from this play are among the longest in the book. The scene is from Riggs's second section.

SCENE 1: ONE FEMALE AND THREE MALES

Bee, probably 20s

Art, 32

Sheriff, probably 50s

Guard, about 30

The sound of rain on a tin roof joins with the beat of a drum, which then fades away. The lights come up on two jail cells separated by bars. The Sheriff, the Guard, and Bee enter. The Sheriff is a "gruff older man," the guard, "a rough, dull, young man," and Bee "dark, strange, vivid." Bee stops, and the sheriff asks what's wrong. "I don't like it," she says. The sheriff tells her she can't back out. "I give you ten dollars and the promise of fifteen more.... Now git in the cell!" She holds out a ten-dollar bill and tells him to take it back.

"Aw listen, Bee," he tells her, "all you got to do is make him talk." "Whut'll it do to him, though?" she asks.

The sheriff admits it will lead to his hanging. "They's nuthin' like hangin' a man to make you feel good," she says with sarcasm. However, she agrees to be locked in a cell to make the situation appear convincing. The sheriff will say she's been jailed for public drunkenness.

The plan is to remove the prisoner and "give him the third degree" while Bee is taken to the cell. Thus, she'll be there when the prisoner is taken back.

This scene ends the second section of the play.

1. Why do you think Art hated his wife so much? If you were playing this role, how would you try to make this hate convincing?

2. Do you sympathize with Art? Why? Why not?

3. Why do you think Art agrees with Bee that he had a beating coming?

4. What does Art mean when he says, "How did I get here? What am

I doin' here?" Why does Bee then tell him he's talkin' crazy? What emotions do you think she is feeling here?

5. Why do you think Bee tells Art that no one will hear them talking? Does she believe that?

6. There is a reference to Art's once hitting Viney. This occurs in the first segment of the play where Viney is talking about her first job teaching school. One of her students was Hutch, a big boy who became really angry when she asked him to stay after school "'Cause you don't work your 'rithmetic... 'Cause you spit on the floor, and 'cause your overalls is filthy dirty, and your neck is not clean. And — 'cause you stutter!" Art asks why Hutch didn't sock her, and Hutch says he doesn't know. Art says he should have. Viney challenges him to do it, and he does. Why do you suppose Bee feels it was all right to slap Viney?

7. Why do you think Art married Clara if she really matched the description Bee gave of her?

8. What were Art's probable reasons for killing his wife? Why did he hate her so much?

9. What do you think Bee means by saying she understands Art's feeling of hate?

10. Why did Bee get close enough to Art to let him grab her? Why does she later tell the sheriff "not to get too close to a rope," because it might "jerk that head of yours plumb off?"

11. Why does Bee say she's a "good girl." Is she? Explain.

(The sound of the rain increases for a moment. Then the GUARD brings in along the corridor a young man about 32, shaken and troubled. His hair is in his eyes. But in spite of his distress, his eyes burn with a fierce wild venomous glow. It is ART OSBURN. He strides into the cell quickly, turns like a caged panther and snarls at the GUARD, who is busy with the door.)

ART: [...] *(He turns away again, walks once swiftly around his cage. Suddenly he sees BEE on the stool in her cell. He takes a step backward, sharply.)* **Who're you? What're you doin' here?**

BEE: *(Shortly)* **I'm not gonna bite you, little boy.**

ART: **Christ.** *(He turns away, muttering.)* **Scared by a chippy.**

BEE: **Who's a chippy?**

ART: *(Impatiently)* **You, you!**

BEE: **Yeah? Well, you're a murderer.**

ART: *(Fiercely, crazily, grabbing the bars between them)* **I didn't kill her, I didn't kill her! God's sake! I told you!** – I – *(His eyes fasten on the girl. His voice goes low.)* **I know you. You're Bee. Bee Newcomb.**

BEE: *(Levelly)* **I know you, too. Art Osburn.** *(His legs give way under him. He sinks to his stool, his arms sliding down wearily between the bars.)*

ART: **Jesus!** *(Weakly)* **They beat hell out of me.** *(She rises and for a moment makes as if to go toward him. Her impulse dies. She stares at him coolly.)*

BEE: **I guess you had it comin' to you.**

ART: *(Wearily)* **I reckon.**

BEE: **You orten't to a – killed that old Indian womern.**

ART: **I keep *tellin'* you –!**

BEE: **All right, all right. I don't keer whether you did or not. Kill a dozen, you cain't make *me* mad. Competition's fierce.** *(Looking at him)* **You look shot, all right. Crime don't pay, does it?**

ART: *(Helplessly, fiercely)* **Cain't you let up on it, cain't you?!**

BEE: **Sure. Sorry I mentioned it. I guess I better keep my mouth shut.**

ART: **You can talk if you want to.**

BEE: **I wouldn't know where to start at, I ain't saw you in so long. Us**

21

livin' in the same town, too. It's funny, ain't it?

ART: *(Strangely, in a dark absorption, his frenzy rising)* **How did I get here? What am I doin' here?**

BEE: *(Disturbed)* **You got me there.**

ART: *(Desperation and fear in his voice)* **What's the matter with me?** *(Turning to stare at her, crazily, half-rising)* **What're they tryin' to do to me, what're they tryin' –!**

BEE: *(Quickly, standing up, fiercely shouting)* **Shut up! You're crazy. You're talkin' crazy!** *(Her sharp strength overpowers him.)*

ART: *(Quieter)* **I feel that way.** *(He sinks back.)*

BEE: *(Remembering her mission, sitting again)* **You can talk all you want to, crazy or not. Nobody'll hear you.**

ART: I don't want to talk.

BEE: There ain't a soul in this end of the jail. Nobody but us. You and me.

ART: What're *you* doin' here?

BEE: I was drunk.

ART: I wish to God I was!

BEE: [...] *(Looking at him)* **We mighta been friends.** *(With real feeling, real bitterness)* **I ain't got so many. You remember Gar Breeden? He won't look at me no more, won't give me a tumble. He ain't even *looked* at me for five year. D' you know why? We had the same daddy, and what'd you think of that? Purty mess, ain't it?** *(He nods dully.)* **Listen, whatever become of Audeal?**

ART: Audeal?

BEE: *You* know. Audeal Coombs. The little fool. Bet you got good and t'ard of her. Somebody told me she run off to Springfield with a drummer. You musta h'ard him to take her off yer hands. *(A curious light comes into her eyes.)* You know – that time at Claremore Mound – you slapped Viney Jones? She had it comin', that one did. I'd a-kissed you fer that 'f I hadn't a-been skeered you'd give me a whack. *(With quiet scorn)* What I cain't understand – how a man like you could do that nen turn around and take up 'th that old witch of a Indian womern – Clara Leahy. Old enough to be yer own mammy! A lot of ready-made kids hangin' onto her. Nen to *marry* her! Bad enough to have her keep you's long's she did. *(As he does not answer)* Shore treated you nice, too, didn't she? Appreciated you. Yeah! Onct last winter I seen her come in the picture show and climb all over everybody and drag you outside a-cussin' the livin' daylights out of you – and you never said *Boo*. *(Harshly)* How much money'd she 'low you fer yer excitin' comp'ny, eh? Musta been a plenty to pay fer whut you tuck off of her! Yeah, but that's all over now, ain't it? You don't have to stand fer it now. *(Brassily, almost fiercely)* She's dead – dead as a door nail – drownded in the Verdigree River, 's fur as anybody can make out – Drownded! Dead and gone. And you got her money! Ain't you lucky?

ART: *(With absorbed concentration, a fevered excitement underneath)* Listen, I tell you – I ain't told nobody. When me and Clara got in the boat they was sump'n funny happened. That little girl of her'n come runnin' down to the river bank yellin', "Don't go, mammy! Don't go, mammy!" Musta felt sump'n was gonna happen. We was jist goin' acrost the river to see 'bout buyin' me a ridin' horse – that spotted cow pony of Bill Chambers'. We pushed out in the current 'th that kid standin' yellin' on the bank. We went upstream a ways till the kid was out of sight. I mean we had to go upstream, anyway. In clost to the bank, they was a lot of willer trees hangin' down. *(His eyes wide, seeing it, his hysteria growing, his speech rapid)* I couldn't help it when Clara riz up in the boat like she'd went crazy, could I? I couldn't help it when she jumped in head first right in the shaller water the way she did! She musta went plumb crazy! She cut her head wide open, her body shot downstream 'fore I could stop it! I tried to! *(Fearfully, in a swift, clear rush)* Her blood come up on the water the way oil does. She floated on down and drifted right in whur that kid was standin'! Her head was cut open from the rocks. The kid stopped cryin' long enough to yell at me that I killed her mammy! I *didn't* kill her! She *jumped* in! She hit her head on the rocks. I told the kid to shut up. I told her I'd kill her 'f she told anyone I killed her mammy! You *know* how sharp them rocks is! Boys is always

23

cuttin' their heads on 'em, you know that yerself – swimmin'. They wouldn't take that kid's word fer it, would they? They couldn't hang me like they said they would? I never killed her! Why – I was married to her – I –

BEE: *(Scornfully, brassily, in sharp snarling accusation)* **Yeah, and** *loved* **her, I reckon? Swore to pertect and cherish her till death did you part, didn't you? Death parted you, all right. And you got her money, too, didn't you? Don't cry! Don't weep for her! She's dead. Put up a swell tombstone! A weepin' willer tree over her grave! Dike yerself up in blue! Go callin' on the gals from here to Sapulpa!** *(Snarling in loud disgust as she jumps to her feet)* **Anh – You killed her! You hit her with sump'n! You killed her for her money!**

(When BEE rises, a sharp flooding spotlight is turned on them quickly. He rises, one hand out as if suspended, breathless, his head turning from side to side, crazily.)

ART: **No! Sh! Don't say – I tell you – You won't tell on me – Don't tell on me! I – No one cain't hear me, can they? I hated her. Don't you know what it is to hate?** *(In a rush)* **Her leathery old face, them eyes all bloodshot, her stringy hair, she hissed with her teeth when she talked, like a snake! You've saw her. I hated her. I wanted to kill her. I** *always* **wanted to kill her!** *(Fiercely)* **See the blood spout from her ugly face, see her quiver and shake and fight to keep from dyin'! You're a girl, you don't know the way it got me.** *(Softly, with mounting, horrible fervor)* **In the boat they was a hatchet – one of them little hatchets – sharp – sharp off the grindstone! I retch fer it. She grinned at me. I hit her and hit her, her grinnin' at me like a fool! Hit her seven or eight times, her clawin' to git away! Killed her, throwed her overboard! The blood come on the water like oil! Not fer her money, though, don't you think that! I wouldn't do that. I hated her, that's why,** *hated* **her, hated everybody –!** *(He is shouting now.)*

BEE: *(With savage joy, topping him in volume)* **Hate! Everybody! Me, too! Like me!** *(Almost hysterically)* **I won't – that's all right – I'll never tell – I won't give you away – I thought it was money – I**

thought – *(Darkly, terribly)* **Anh, that's different! I never had the nerve! Listen, that's the way I feel – All the men I'd kill! I can see how you felt.** *(Hypnotized)* **I can see her there in the boat – grinnin' up at you – her hair stringy, her eyes all bloodshot! Kill her!** *(Startled)* **There! Look there!** *(She is suddenly staring fearfully toward the back of his cell, her arm outstretched. On the wall past his shoulder something luminous is glowing in the darkness.)*

ART: **Bee! What're you doin'? You're crazy – you're –** *(He turns. The face of the dead woman grins down at him from the wall. His voice becomes a tense whisper.)* **It's Clara! It's her!** *(With fierce conviction)* **Anh, it cain't be! It's a trick. It's them! [...]** *(He grabs the picture of the dead woman from the wall. He jumps on it, stamping it, his voice crazy and jubilant.)* **You're dead, dead! I killed you! They thought they'd skeer me, did they, with a dead goddamned face on the wall – They thought they'd fool me – they –**

BEE: *(Sharply, a horrible realization of something further in her)* **Art!**

ART: **Whutta they think I am, anyway? God, what a bunch of lousy hicks – a school kid wouldn't be took in by it –! Grin at me, will you – Grin in hell where you're burnin'!** *(He gives a final fierce stamp.)*

BEE: **Art!** *(Pointing)* **What's that?**

(In the spot of light on the wall is a small black oval box-like projection. He looks. He backs away slowly, his eyes on it. When he speaks again his voice is low, with a taut and fearful excitement thrumming underneath.)

ART: *(Turning to her)* **Bee – What's that – D' you ever see a – They couldn't do that – Whut'd I say? I didn't say anything – It cain't be –!** *(Sharply)* **It is! It's a dictaphone!** *(He turns swiftly, clutching BEE through the bars. His face is livid, a cold sweat stands out on him; his voice is thick, his nostrils dilated.)* **It's you! You knowed it! You was in on it!**

BEE: **Art! Art!**

ART: **You got me to tell on myself!** *(His hands are on her throat, choking her.)* **I'll kill you, I'll choke you till yer eyes come out of yer head! You've killed me – you hear? – You've murdered me the way I murdered her! Anh! Before I die – they'll be another** dead 'un! What's another'n! What difference does it make now? *(A door clangs as he speaks. Feet run hurriedly along the corridor. The GUARD, the DEPUTY, and the SHERIFF burst into sight. The GUARD quickly unlocks the door, fumbling at it.)*

SHERIFF: *(Cutting into ART's speech)* **Open it! Open it! Don't let him –! Hurry up, there!** *(The GUARD and the DEPUTY spring into the cell and drag him away from the girl. He cries out wildly as they jerk him along the corridor. BEE has sunk down against the bars.)* **Are you hurt? Listen!** *(He shakes the bars.)* **Are you all right?**

BEE: *(Wearily)* **Go away.**

SHERIFF: **Guard! Smiley! I cain't get in! Bring me the key! Dyke can handle him! Come on here!** *(The GUARD comes in, running, unlocks the cell and goes to the girl.)*

GUARD: **Are you all right? D' he hurt you? Git up on yer feet.** *(He lifts her up, holding her.)* **We got here quick's we could. Here, Miss.**

BEE: *(Strangely, her eyes clouded)* **Leave me here. Go away.**

SHERIFF: *(Going into ART's cell)* **We didn't think he could git at you. I swear I thought: you had sense enough to – You orten't to a-got so close up to him. You knowed he was dangerous – I told you what he –**

GUARD: *(TO BEE, who has said something to him)* **What? What's that, Miss?**

BEE: *(Quietly)* **Leave me here. Slam the bolts to! What's the dif? I'm dead. Bury me.**

SHERIFF: *(Softly, alarmed)* **Bring her on out here.** *(The GUARD leads her out gently, her hat in his hand, her coat over his arm. The SHERIFF comes out.)* **You'll be all right. I'm shore sorry he went and done that. Go to Dr. Bayes. Tell him I sent you. He'll fix you up, all right. Here.** *(He hands her some money.)* **Take it.**

BEE: **What is it?**

SHERIFF: **It's your'n, what I owe you. You shore earned it. Take it.**

BEE: *(Wryly)* **Why not?** *(She takes it, puts it in her stocking.)*

SHERIFF: *(Delightedly)* **I shore am powerful indebted to you! He'll hang now! We got it all down – his own words. Why, his life ain't worth a damn! We'll rope that neck of his'n and jerk him so high he'll think a buzzard's got him. I shore do thank you!**

BEE: *(Harshly)* **You're welcome. It's a pleasure! Don't git too clost to a rope yerself, Mr. Sheriff! It'd jerk that head of yours plumb off! Yer wife ud have a hard time with no one to call her "Honey" – somebody swell like you.** *(Turning away, in disgust)* [...]

SHERIFF: *(Nonplussed)* **'F I can ever help you, in any way – The county shore owes you a lot.**

BEE: The county owes me a plenty.

SHERIFF: Well, good-bye, Miss Newcomb. *(Puzzled, he goes out along the corridor. She grimaces, turns to SMILEY, remembering.)*

GUARD: *(Softly)* **Good-bye – Bee.**

BEE: *(Smiling ruefully)* **Thanks.**

GUARD: Say –

BEE: What is it?

GUARD: *(Awkwardly)* **Say – is that the truth 'bout you wantin' to kill everybody?**

BEE: What!

GUARD: You know – what you said about all the men you'd kill –?

BEE: God, did that thing hear ever' word I said, too? *(With desperate irony, her voice harsh and troubled)* **It's a lie, Big Boy! I wouldn't hurt a fly! I go to church. I'm a good girl – I'm happy as hell. I love everybody. You'll see. You'll find out. When I was born, they wondered why I looked so sweet. Now they know why. I am sweet, that's the trouble with me. I cain't help it. I was born that way –** *(On part of the speech she crosses to him slowly, seductively. She puts up a hand on his shoulder.)*

(The sound of an organ, wheezing and reluctant, pours down the corridor, drowning out the sound of her voice, and the sound of the rain on the roof. The jail fades quickly from sight.)

SCENE 2: THREE FEMALES

Maisie, 17

Sarah, 50

Viney, 41

This section of the play follows directly after the preceding. The only continuing character is Viney, whom the audience met at the beginning of the play. The location is "a small room on the edge of Claremore, in the winter of 1931." It's "a sordid, miserable," place with little furniture except for chairs and a heating stove. "The principal object" is "a wheezing organ" where Maisie sits. "Pathetically thin and white, with stringy hair," she has been singing a hymn in a flat, tired voice. Sarah Pickard, Maisie's mother, is gaunt and dark, with high cheekbones that "stand out in her leathery, proud face." Maisie asks if Sarah would like to hear more singing. She says she would. Maisie notices that Sarah is in pain and asks what's wrong. "Nothing," she replies and then asks about the wood.

1. What message is Riggs attempting to convey to the audience in this scene? How do you know that?

2. Do you sympathize with Sarah and Maisie? Why? Why not? Do you like them?

3. What are some things you might do to convey Sarah and Maisie's poverty? Their feelings?

4. Why do you think Viney hasn't visited Sarah in ten years? Why does she visit now?

5. Why does Sarah not want to take the fifty cents?

6. Why does Viney make such a show of pointing out all her financial advantages and her status — the mansion, the daughter in a private school, her husband's serving as mayor?

7. What facet of Viney's character do you feel is most important? Why? How might you try to convey this to an audience?

8. Why does Viney not want to "show" that she's part Cherokee?

9. Why do you suppose Riggs used free verse instead of prose in two of Sarah's speeches?

10. Why does Sarah admit to Viney, whom she obviously doesn't like, that she has failed?

11. Why does Viney take "cruel delight" in tossing the money into the middle of the room?

12. What is the significance of ending this scene as it opened — with Maisie's singing?

SARAH: Is this all the wood they is left?

MAISIE: *(Soberly, looking down, shamefacedly)* **Yes. Less'n Roll gets some along Cat Crick as he comes by. Here.** *(She jumps up, picks up a rag rug off the floor and puts it around her mother's knees. Then she kneels by her.)* **Is the pain mostly in your knees again?**

SARAH: Oh, tain't much.

MAISIE: You'd ort to have some liniment to rub on.

SARAH: I don't need it. *(MAISIE suddenly bursts unaccountably into tears.)*

MAISIE: I don't see why – I don't see – !

SARAH: *(Compassionately)* **Maisie, honey –**

MAISIE: My own maw down and ailin' with rheumatism and pains, and we ain't got enough money to do anything about it – Cain't even keep her warm enough!

SARAH: Now, Maisie –

MAISIE: It ain't fair, it ain't fair!

SARAH: Don't talk like that.

MAISIE: I don't keer, it ain't! *(She stands up, quieter.)* **Maybe Roll'll get some money.** *(Protectively)* **He tries, he works hard!**

SARAH: Of course he does, He's a good man and a good husband to you. *(Soberly)* **Listen, Maisie – we've all done our best. It might not a-been right, but we done all we knowed how to do.**

MAISIE: To think we used to own our own farm and here we air like this – *(She crosses toward the organ stool.)*

SARAH: They's people worse off.

MAISIE: *(Turning toward the organ, dabbing her eyes)* **I'd like to know who?**

SARAH: Plenty of folks.

MAISIE: *(Unappeased)* **I don't see how they live, then.**

SARAH: *(Turning to look at her)* **Don't cry, Maisie.** *(Her eyes stop at the window as she turns back.)* **Maisie, is that someone comin' up the road?**

MAISIE: *(Going to her side, looking)* **Yes.**

SARAH: Who could it be?

MAISIE: She's all dressed up, whoever it is. I don't know. *(Suddenly)* **Maw! Why, it looks like Aunt Viney.**

SARAH: Viney?

MAISIE: Looks like her pictures.

SARAH: What on earth –? I ain't saw her fer ten years or more. *(She stretches aside in the chair to see.)* **It is Viney.**

MAISIE: *(Eagerly)* **Maw – maybe Aunt Viney'll help us. She's doin' well, ever'body says, up at Quapaw –**

SARAH: **Yes, maybe she will, Maisie, I never thought of –** *(Then, something strangely final coming into her voice)* **I couldn't ask her – I –**

MAISIE: **But if we was to starve! If we could just get a little ahead to see us through a few weeks, Maw. Roll'll get his money for teamin' maybe pretty soon –**

SARAH: *(Firmly)* **I wouldn't take help from Viney. Not after the way she – Here.** *(She takes the rug off her knees.)* **Put this back on the floor where it belongs. Straighten things up a little.** *(MAISIE obeys.)* **Maisie –**

MAISIE: **Yes, Maw.**

SARAH: **I'd ask Viney to help if I could.**

MAISIE: **Why cain't you? It's just pride, Maw, and you know it!**

SARAH: *(A flicker of amazing dignity and strength in her face)* **Pride? Maybe. When you've got nothing left in the world but pride, you're bad off.**

MAISIE: **You *will* ask her, then?**

SARAH: **Viney's my sister, Maisie – but I ain't got any claim on her. She's left me alone for ten year. Even one year makes people different. They go their own way, and it's fur apart. How do I know she ain't a stranger walkin' into my house?**

MAISIE: **A stranger – your own sister, Maw?**

SARAH: **Viney and me was always kind of strangers to one another.**

MAISIE: **How?** *(There is a knock.)*

SARAH: **Go to the door.**

(MAISIE opens the door. VINEY CLEPPER comes in. She is forty-one now, well dressed in small-town taste — she is unmistakably complacent, righteous and patronizing. But she feels for a second the constraint of the meeting.)

VINEY: **Hello, Sarah.** *(She crosses her, to SARAH's right.)*

31

SARAH: Come in, Viney.

VINEY: Is this Maisie?

MAISIE: *(Coming up close to her mother)* Yes. Howdy, Aunt Viney.

VINEY: I hear you're married now.

MAISIE: Yes'm. Roll Henley.

VINEY: Who's he?

MAISIE: Bob Henley's son. He's a teamster.

VINEY: Oh.

SARAH: Set down, Viney. What're you doin' in Claremore?

VINEY: *(Sitting down on the organ stool)* Just came down with Jack – on business. Thought I'd run out and say hello. How're you feeling, Sarah?

SARAH: Not very well.

VINEY: Rheumatism?

SARAH: Yes.

VINEY: *(In her old didactic manner)* You ought to get some liniment. There's a good kind called Vamos. Costs only fifty cents a bottle. You try it. Jack used one bottle and hasn't had an ache or a pain since.

SARAH: How is Jack?

VINEY: Oh, he's fine. You know, of course, he's got to be the mayor of Quapaw?

SARAH: I heard that, yes.

VINEY: We've sent Alma off this winter to a boarding school. That fine one in Kirksburg. She's a big girl now, fourteen.

SARAH: I wouldn't know her.

VINEY: I wouldn't have known Maisie, either. *(To MAISIE)* So you're married, honey? Pretty early, isn't it?

MAISIE: I'm seventeen.

VINEY: 'Course our mother married when she was sixteen. But that was different –

SARAH: *(Quickly)* Maisie, see about dinner, will you? Maybe Aunt Viney will stay.

MAISIE: Yes, Maw. *(She goes out, right.)*

VINEY: So Maisie married a teamster, did she? Is he working?

SARAH: It's Sunday.

VINEY: Where'd he team yesterday?

SARAH: *(Coldly)* It rained yesterday.

VINEY: Oh. I hope he gets enough work to take good care of you all. These hard times. Most people don't know where the next meal's coming from. I'm thankful to say that me and Jack are – Is it cold in here, Sarah?

SARAH: *(Looks at her sharply, then says simply)* Yes, it is cold, Viney.

VINEY: *(Drawing her fur about her)* You've used up your land allotment, have you, Sarah?

SARAH: The mortgage took it.

VINEY: How long since Ed died?

SARAH: Five years.

VINEY: Where've the boys got off to? I can't seem to keep up with you all.

SARAH: They're married and gone – long ago.

VINEY: Your oldest boy must have got Indian land, too, didn't he? He was born in 1898 about. What'd he do with it?

SARAH: He sold it when he was twenty-one.

VINEY: What was his name? I was trying to tell Jack. What was it?

SARAH: Who?

VINEY: Your oldest.

SARAH: *(Gravely)* You named him, Viney. You named him after Paw.

VINEY: Oh, I'd forgotten. *(She looks about the bare and dismal room. At sight of the organ, she gets up to get a good look at it; she is Downstage of organ.)* I see you still got Maw's old organ. I'd sell it and buy me a radio. *(Reaching in her pocketbook)* Oh, I brought you something. *(She brings it out, goes over to SARAH.)* A picture of our place in Quapaw. That's me and Alma on the porch. Here's Jack over here by the garage. And look! The maid stuck her head out the window so as to be in the picture.

SARAH: It's very nice.

VINEY: They call it The Mansion. *(She crosses, lays picture and bag on the upper end of organ, stands there.)*

SARAH: *(Gravely)* You've done very well, Viney.

VINEY: Well – Jack was the main one, I guess.

SARAH: And Hutch – whatever became of him?

33

VINEY: *(Viciously)* **I don't know and I don't care. It was Hutch that came close to ruining my whole life. That dumb Indian, that's all he was! You never could tell about him, couldn't get on to what he was up to!** *(Thoughtfully, half to herself)* **He didn't have any change in him, he was stuck someway. He was broody and sullen, he couldn't seem to get hold of himself, like a lot of part-Indians around here.**

SARAH: And what about you, Viney?

VINEY: What about me?

SARAH: You're more Cherokee than Hutch.

VINEY: Well, I'm thankful to say it doesn't show.

SARAH: *(Strangely)* **Every word you say shows. Everything you say shames you. You try too hard to deny what you are. It tells on you.** *(Harshly)* **You say Hutch didn't have any *change* in him. They's nuthin' else in you *but* change. You've turned your back on what you ought to a-been proud of.**

VINEY: *(Angrily)* **Being a part-Indian? What would it get me? Do you think I want to be ignorant and hungry and crazy in my head half the time like a lot of 'em around here? Do you think I want to be looked down on because I can't do anything, can't get along like other people? Do you think I want to make the kind of mess of my life *you* have – and live in a filthy hole like this the rest of my days – ?**

SARAH: You won't have to. The hole you live in is filthier, and it suits you down to the ground.

VINEY: *(Sitting down on the organ stool, fuming and disturbed)* **What do you mean?**

(The lights begin to go down strangely. A fantastic glow from the stove creeps into the room, blotting out its realistic outline, its encompassing walls, throwing SARAH's shadow, huge and dark, on the wall.)

SARAH: *(Fiercely, growing in strangeness, like an oracle)* **Mean? Listen to me. You're not my sister. Your blood ain't mine and never was! Change, change till doomsday – one thing'll stay! Your heart's as black as ever and hard as flint. Be mean and cunning and full of hate, like the Indian. Be greedy and selfish**

the way the white man is. None of what's good – let the good
things be! You're past 'em! Use the most shameful things you
got in you to get ahead. You'll get ahead, all right! *(Seeing it*
darkly, slowly facing front)
You'll come to a close tight place in the hills, between rocks.
The rocks'll get closer together!
They'll squeeze you dry.
Your flesh'll fall from you like feathers,
Your bones'll crumble!

You can't turn back:
You'll *want* to turn back!
You walkin', turrible, dried-up thing, you'll be crushed to a
gray powder!
Your cupful of ashes'll scatter on the wind!
One thing you can't do, you with your table full of meat and
furs around your neck:
You can't take a path you ain't meant to.
It'll take you to the jaws of wild animals,
It'll guide you west, to the rivers of quicksand,
It'll take you to jagged cliffs,
It'll lead you to death!

VINEY: *(Jumping up, crying out with febrile anger)* Yanh, I'm to stay
here and rot then! I'm not to be smart enough to keep meat on
the table and the cold wind outside! Oh, no! It isn't decent, it's
not the way to be! *(Her anger has carried her above the organ,*
facing front.)

SARAH: No. It's not the way to be. *(She has gone inward.)* The way to
be is to be humble, and remember the life that's in you. Our
Maw told us once the way we was meant to live. "Remember
it," she said. "Remember it and your days'll be food and drink.
They'll be a river in the desert, they'll be waving grass and
deer feeding." *(Quietly, like a prayer)*
"The man'll plow the ground," Maw said.
"And he'll plant and cultivate.
The woman'll have her garden and her house.

There'll be pork and corn dodgers, molasses from the cane
   patch, beans on the vine.
There'll be berries and fruit – blackberries, strawberries, plums.
The woods'll be thick with squirrels.
The woman'll go down to the branch with her apron full of
   corn and a pan of ashes to make hominy.
The nights'll come.
Children'll be born.
The gods of the earth things – the gods of the stone and the
   tree and all natural things
Will live by their side.
And the God of the Christians, too,
Will keep them from sin."
*(Crying out, as the vision and the memory have become slowly too
powerful, too painful)*
Maw! Maw! Where are you?
Where has the good life gone to?
It's got fur away and dim. It's not plain anymore.
I can't follow.
I tried ! I tried – !
(She relaxes weakly, miserably, her hand at her face.)

VINEY: *(Taking a step nearer)* **Sarah, what is it?**

SARAH: *(From her dark)* **I failed.**

VINEY: **You mustn't go on like that.**

SARAH: *(Lifting her head)* **I'm a failure, too – like you. We're both
failures. But I tried, and you didn't. I wouldn't trade places
with you.**

VINEY: *(Bridling)* **Well! You wouldn't? It's lucky you feel that way,
because I feel the same way about it. And let me tell you something, Sarah. As long as I've got money and a good home, and
am living right, I don't call myself a failure. And neither does
anyone else, but you. If you haven't anything better to say to me
after ten years, I'm going.** *(She gets her bag from the organ.
Turning slyly, cruelly)* **Oh! If your rheumatism doesn't get any
better, you'd better get that liniment I told you about. Vamos,
it's called. Here's fifty cents.** *(She holds it out.)*

SARAH: *(Fiercely)* **Get out!**

VINEY: *(Coolly, going to her)* **I'm giving you a little present.**

SARAH: *(Dangerously)* **Get out, Viney!**

VINEY: *(A cruel delight coming into her face. She goes to door, turns, her back almost to audience.)* **I'll go, Sarah. I may never see you again. And all the same, you may *need* fifty cents.** *(She tosses it into the middle of the room and goes out, quickly. Hearing the door close, MAISIE comes in.)*

MAISIE: **Aunt Viney gone? I thought she'd stay for dinner!** *(Seeing the money on the floor)* **Why, Maw, here's fifty cents on the floor!** *(She starts to stoop for it.)*

SARAH: *(Fiercely)* **Leave it alone, leave it alone!**

MAISIE: *(Astonished)* **Whut! Why, Maw!** *(SARAH bursts into tears.)* **Whut is it, Maw?**

SARAH: *(Wiping her tears away, wryly)* **Nuthin'.**

MAISIE: **Where'd this fifty cents come from?**

SARAH: *(With quiet despair at her dead pride)* **You musta dropped it, Maisie. Or maybe Aunt Viney did. Pick it up. We'll need it.** *(MAISIE picks it up, crying out joyously.)*

MAISIE: **I don't know how it got there, and I don't care! Look, Maw, it'll buy you some of that liniment Aunt Viney told you about, that's whut it'll do! It sure will!** *(She flies to the organ, and starts pumping gaily, and singing again, the last verse of "My Faith Looks Up to Thee.")*

SCENE 3: UNDETERMINED NUMBER

Henry, probably 30s or 40s

Abner, probably 30s or 40s

Rufe, probably 30s or 40s

People [The Congregation], all ages

Lize, probably late 20s or 30s

Annie, probably late 20s or 30s

Jonas, probably late 60s

The following is the beginning of the playwright's original Scene 5. As many actors as desired can play members of the People. This segment, which for acting purposes is split here into several scenes, actually is continuous from beginning to end and is one of the most powerful parts of the play. The ending is unexpected though believable since the People trust only in themselves and in their twisted idea of religion.

This scene, which occurs in 1913, two years before the play's opening and eighteen years before the scene with Sarah and Viney, can be challenging to direct since so many actors are involved. No exact number is specified, but there should be enough to suggest the congregation of a church. The scene begins leisurely and quietly with people meeting outside, probably in groups of two or three, and greeting each other before going into the building. The situation seems pleasant, and yet there is an undertone of danger and suspense in Henry's opening question: "No sign of trouble?"

Occasionally, Riggs gives a number of lines for the "People." These are meant to be delivered by different individuals in different groupings. There are, of course, occasional lines that need to be heard by the audience. However, the overall picture should be of people passing the time in a companionable or friendly way.

You may choose to cut certain parts of the scene or to present it as it is. You can eliminate the first part or skip the section with Lize and Annie. Actually, in the original scene, before Jonas enters, there is a section involving a seven-year-old girl named Ailsey. After talking with Lize, her mother, and Annie, she jumps up on the altar and says she is standing on the "rock." When Jonas enters, she presents Jonas with a handful of blackberries she's picked.

The action occurs "on Eagle Bluff, which overlooks the Illinois River and the town of Tahlequah, seat of the Cherokee Nation."

A bell begins to toll, and the lights come up to reveal a "primitive little church" standing near the edge of a cliff. At the front are an altar and a "tiny platform on which is a chair and a reading stand." A rope hangs down from the bell tower.

1. What is the purpose of the conversation between Lize and Annie?

2. Point out any hints you see of approaching danger. Explain why you chose these lines.

3. What sort of man is Jonas? Why do you think the People are willing to follow him?

4. The People obviously belong to a sort of cult, rather than a conventional religion. Which lines support this? In what way?

5. Why do the People mistrust others? Why do they want to remain isolated? Is this logical or believable? Why? Why not?

6. What does Jonas mean when he calls the People members of the Lost Tribe?

7. Suppose you were playing one of the members. What might you do to make this person fit in with the rest and still be an individual?

8. In the service, why do the People praise so many things?

9. What is the Man at the end implying when he answers Jonas by saying that God is the law of the mountain?

(Standing inside and near the left door of the church, an unshaven, rough-looking man, HENRY, is pulling the bellrope. ABNER and RUFE, in coarse jackets and corduroys, appear, ABNER from Up Center, RUFE from the left. HENRY finishes ringing the bell and comes forward.)

HENRY: *(With a wave of his hand, as he comes down)* **Mornin', Abner. Mornin', Rufe.** *(Softly)* **No sign of trouble?** *(RUFE has sat down on the fourth bench.)*

ABNER: *(Shortly, from a place near the pulpit)* **Ain't no trouble.**

HENRY: *(Philosophically)* **Well, I jist ask.** *(He goes out of sight.)*

RUFE: Reckon anything'll happen?

ABNER: What would?

RUFE: Oh, I don't know. People git sick and t'ard of havin' things stole off of 'em.

ABNER: *(Going to second bench, putting his foot on it, leaning closer to RUFE)* **Look, Rufe. Down there in Tahlequah, the land's good for farmin', makin' a good livin'. Up here on the bluff – why, this ole bluff and table land does ever'thing it *can* to keep from raisin' a form thing. Well, it won't hurt 'em none down there to help God's Chosen People a little bit, will it? We got to eat someway, ain't we?**

RUFE: You blame right.

ABNER: Ain't we one of the Lost Tribes of Israel? Ain't we God's favorites? Them ole Cherokees ort to be proud to furnish God's People a cow or a sack of corn or half a hog onct in awhile. Do 'em good. You heared what Jonas said this mornin' in meetin' –

RUFE: Yeah, I heared –

ABNER: Well, there you air.

RUFE: *(Getting up)* **Yeah, but – we had trouble *onct* – the time that Shuruff come up here from Tahlequah and –**

ABNER: Shet up about it! We don't know nuthin' about that! Besides, it'd be purty hard to climb up the bluff, you know.

RUFE: They could go around – and come up the long way.

ABNER: *(Lifting his rifle)* **What'd you think these here things are fer?**
(PEOPLE of the congregation – men, women and children – begin

to come in from every opening, casually, laughing and talking. They are ragged and unkempt, the women in old dresses and mother hubbards, some wearing sunbonnets. They begin to sit down, chatting. ABNER and RUFE disappear around the tabernacle.)

PEOPLE: Was a-skeered to chop no furder 'th old Butch runnin' around in the bresh liable to get fell on.

How'd you find bee's honey – most a bucketful?

Frankie! Frankie!

I'm gonna set clost to the door so's to spit ef'n I want.

The wind was on the prairies! Clouds clumb nigh up here with lightnin' showin' forked in the folds! Wish't it had stormed!

Put up or shet up. If you had no more'n that, I'd be shamed to tell it!

Where's Jonas at?

Ain't come out of his study yit.

Le's git set down.

(LIZE and ANNIE, two brown-faced, raw-boned women of the Tribe, greet each other down front. LIZE is much amused at something. She has come in at center, with others, caught sight of ANNIE who has entered left, and waved to her.)

LIZE: Listen, Annie. My man Luke went to the spring to git water. They was a big ole copperhead settin' there. *(She laughs.)* **Luke come on back with the bucket empty!**

ANNIE: Was he afeared of a ole copperhead snake?

LIZE: No, not a-tall, to hear him tell it. He says to me, "Lize," he says, "that snake's got as much right to git hisself a drink as *I* got." And he was right.

ANNIE: Pshaw! He was jist afeared.

LIZE: I 'spect he was, Annie. But he made out like he was jist bein' kind.

41

ANNIE: **Men'll do that.** *(She sits in the fourth row.)*

LIZE: **'Cause he 'spected that was the way he'd orter feel – kind-like. Luke – he's awful silly, Luke is.**

ANNIE: **Womenfolks won't lie to *their*selves.**

LIZE: **Not even if Jonas tells 'em. Jonas jist laugh if he knowed what Luke'd done.** *(She starts to her seat in the second row.)*

ANNIE: *(Chortling)* **Wouldn't he jist laugh!** *(Calling LIZE closer)* **Lize, come 'ere.** *(LIZE does so.)* **Sh! Jonas. He's ailin'.**

LIZE: *(Soberly)* **I noticed this mornin' in meetin'.**

ANNIE: **If he died, I don't know who'd lead us.**

LIZE: **We'd git along, I guess.**

ANNIE: **We'd *have* to git. [...]**

> *(JONAS has [...] come in from his study. The PEOPLE sit up, watching him respectfully, reverently. He is dressed in rough shoes, baggy trousers, and a faded blue shirt. His white hair and beard give him an air of ascetic nobility. But his eyes are strange, fanatic.)*

JONAS: *(Goes up on the rostrum, turns and surveys his audience. The PEOPLE lean forward expectantly.)* **People of the Lost Tribe. God's Chosen! Let us begin –**

JONAS and PEOPLE: *(In full round tones, like an organ)* **O Lord most high!**

JONAS: **O Lord in the heavens, hear us in this hour!**

PEOPLE: **O Lord most high!**

JONAS: **The day is half gone. The sun has climbed to its peak in the sky.**

PEOPLE: **You are the sun, O Lord!**

JONAS and PEOPLE: **O Sun most high!**

JONAS: **The clouds have scattered before you –**
   Sunlight descends.

JONAS and PEOPLE: **You are the sun, O Lord!**
   You are the rain and the snow!
   You are the hail descending!
   Hear us, be with us, O Lord!

   (Hands have begun to go up in ecstasy.)

A WOMAN: *(With a rapt, ecstatic look, as if praying, jumping to her feet)*

I went out this mornin' when the bees was about –
The bees was singin' where they flew about the flowers.

PEOPLE: Hear us, O Lord!

A MAN: *(Jumping up)* The cows knowed thy presence –
The calves leaped up for joy.

PEOPLE: Hear us, O Lord!

A WOMAN: *(Jumping up in front and turning back to the others)* The
f'ar burned most of itself when I struck the flint;
The peas is gettin' ripe and fat in their pods.

PEOPLE: Hear us, O Lord!

A MAN: *(Jumping up)* When I crossed the crick a-lookin' for my
coon dog,
He come a-runnin' and a-lickin' my face like he was happy.

PEOPLE: Hear us, O Lord!

A WOMAN: *(Jumping Up)* My sister in Caroliny sent a bolt of blue
calico –
And I'm a-restin' easy where I been ailin' so long.

PEOPLE: Hear us, O Lord!

(Exclaiming, outside the litany rhythm) Hear us, O
Lord! Praise Jesus! Bless his holy name! Halleluia!

A MAN: *(Jumping up)* Water flowed uphill I swear to my time! –
For me to git a drink of where it hadn't got muddy.

PEOPLE: Hear us, O Lord!

A BOY: Grapes was so green they puckered up my mouth so I'd
learn to whistle.

PEOPLE: *(Smiling)* Hear us, O Lord!

AILSEY: Toad-frog a-settin' right there on a rock
Jist looked at me and grinned all over.

PEOPLE: Hear us, O Lord!

A MAN: A-hoein' the corn my hoe got sharp in the sand-stones,
Blackie treed a squirrel for my wife to cook.

PEOPLE: Hear us, O Lord!

A MAN: *(Leaping to his feet, excitedly)* When I was a boy back in the
Ozarks, I used to go a-barefoot. And I'd steal apples. And sass
my Paw. I'd beat the ole cow. I'd be mean to my little sisters
and brothers. I wouldn't be thankful jist to be a-livin'. I was

always wantin' sump'n. *And* a-gettin' nuthin'. *And* a-cussin'.
And a-swearin'. And a-gettin' next to all the girls like a wild
hoss. And I was a-gettin' wickeder and wickeder when Jonas
come along, praise the Lord! And I follered him, praise the
Lord! And I lissened and heared him, praise Jonas! And I'll die
happy like I'm a-livin', praise the Lord on high!

A WOMAN: *(Rising, ecstatic)* My maw prayed for me to do better but I
wouldn't listen. I wouldn't churn or darn. Or sweep the floor,
and land knows it was always a-needin' it! I wouldn't cook. I
wouldn't mind no one. I was wild and crazy-like. And a-feared
of the dark. One day I heared Jonas a-callin' me. And I left off
my sinful ways. And I begin to do whut was right. Never a-
complainin', never a-sighin'. Always a-singin' like I'm singin'
now, praise the Lord!

PEOPLE: *(Shouting)* Praise Jesus!
Glory be to God!
Took away our sins, washed us clean!
Bless his holy name!

A MAN: I was a hoss thief and a mule stealer. And a wife beater. And
mean to my kids. And the stock and the houn'dogs. But no
more. Now I walk where the sun's at. And I praise the Lord!

PEOPLE: *(Beginning the litany rhythm again)* O Lord most high!
JONAS: O Lord in the heavens, hear our testimony!
PEOPLE: O Lord most high!
JONAS: The day is half gone. The sun is resting on its peak in the sky –
JONAS and PEOPLE: You are the sun, O Lord!
O Sun most high!
JONAS: The clouds have scattered before you –
Sunlight descends.
JONAS and PEOPLE: You are the Sun, O Lord!
You are the rain –
*(There is the sudden sound of a rifle shot. The PEOPLE stop their
chant raggedly, some continuing. JONAS stops a moment too, then
begins again.)*
JONAS: The clouds have scattered before you.
Sunlight descends.

JONAS and PEOPLE: You are the Sun, O Lord!
You are the rain and the snow!
You are the hail –
(ABNER, rifle in hand, bursts in Up Center.)

ABNER: *(Shouting)* 'D he come in here? A man! I think I got him –
climbin' up the cliff – I thought he run this a-way!

JONAS: No one's been here, Abner.

ABNER: *(Circling in front of people and going out Up Left as he speaks)*
He must be hidin' in the bushes back of the tabernacle! I'll git
him! Once I git a fair shot – *(He disappears. The PEOPLE
murmur among themselves uneasily. JONAS lifts his hand.)*

JONAS: Here! Is this going to interrupt your worship? God is our
protection – *(With a smile)* – and we've got plenty of guns, you
know.

A MAN: But it might be the law, Jonas!

JONAS: *(Fixing on him a sharp hard stare)* The law? Who is the law of
this mountain?

A MAN: *(Grudgingly)* Well, God's the law – I guess.

SCENE 4: THREE MALES, PLUS
UNDETERMINED NUMBER OF PEOPLE

People, all ages

Jonas, probably late 60s

Abner, 30s or 40s

Gar, 17 or 18

This scene comes directly after the preceding. Again, when different lines are attributed to the People, they should overlap, with two or three characters perhaps speaking at the same time.

1. Why would Jonas and the others want Gar to be dead? Is it logical that Abner try to kill him in cold blood? Explain.

2. Do you think it is logical that Gar came to the mountain? Is it believable that he did? Can you think of reasons why anyone might approach a group such as this?

3. Why do you suppose Gar suddenly appears in desperate agony?

4. What reason could there be for Jonas's wanting to be alone with Gar?

JONAS: **God is the law of this mountain. God is the ruler, the preserver. On Him the burden of our safety and peace lies easily. Nothing can disturb His calm: let nothing dismay His people. Peace be to you as to Him!** – *(There is another shot back of the tabernacle and GAR BREEDEN stumbles in from the study door, closing it after him. His shirt and trousers are dirty and torn. His hair is awry, his face streaked with blood where the briars have scratched him. Instantly, there is a wild confusion. Most of the PEOPLE scramble back, but some advance threateningly. There are screams of dismay.)* **Wait! Stand back!** *(They stand back a little.)* **Who are you? What do you want here?** *(GAR looks from the PEOPLE to JONAS and back.)*

GAR: **Don't let him shoot me!**

PEOPLE: *(Muttering)* **What's he doin' here – bustin' in? Come breakin' in the tabernacle this-a-way... Spyin' on us, I reckon! Shoot him, that's what we'd orter do with him!**

JONAS: **Stop it! Luke! Charley! Hear what he's got to say.** *(To GAR)* **What is it?**

GAR: **I climbed up the cliff here – I – I'll go.** *(He turns as if to go out the back. ABNER bursts in quickly at the left, running right to about third row and down front.)*

ABNER: **There he is! I thought I'd run him – !** *(He puts his gun to his shoulder as if to fire.)*

GAR: *(To JONAS)* **For God's sake! Give me a chance, can't you?**

JONAS: **Go away, Abner! Put your gun up.**

ABNER: **Stand back, Jonas! I'll shoot him – the skunk!**

JONAS: *(Going toward him)* **Do as I tell you! You've done enough shooting.** *(ABNER relaxes, rebelliously. Turning to GAR who is now at his right)* **Now, tell me what this – Wait a minute. Are you hurt?**

GAR: **No. He missed me.**

JONAS: *(Puzzled)* **Missed you? Abner did?**

GAR: **Twice.**

JONAS: **I don't understand that.** *(Smiling)* **Abner, you'd better go and sit down.**

ABNER: *(Muttering)* **If I'd a-had fair shot** – *(He sits down, disgruntled, on the fourth row.)*

JONAS: Abner's the best shot on the mountain.

GAR: He hasn't any business shootin' at me.

JONAS: You haven't any business on the mountain.

GAR: *(Hotly)* This is a free country, ain't it? You don't own this mountain, do you? What right has he got to shoot at me for climbin' up the cliff? *(ABNER jumps up. Several men rush threateningly toward GAR.)*

PEOPLE: *(Angrily)* Why, the young snappin' turtle!

He cain't talk that-a-way to Jonas. By God, I'll –

Shet up yer talk, you!

Abner'd orter shot him in the back.

Give me a chanst, and he won't git away!

JONAS: *(Silencing them)* Here! I'll attend to this. *(To GAR)* Where'd you come from?

GAR: Down below here.

JONAS: From Tahlequah?

GAR: Yes, Tahlequah. *(Something in the question and answer reminds him of a forgotten distress. His present anger dies. He speaks as if far away, lost in his isolated despair.)*

JONAS: Came up to spy on us, eh?

GAR: No.

JONAS: What's your reason, then?

GAR: *(After a moment of hesitation)* No reason.

JONAS: Oh, you just came to look at us, is that it? *(Scornfully)* Heard we were a strange lot of religious fanatics, didn't you?

GAR: Yes.

JONAS: *(Scornfully)* So you came to look us over, so you could go back and boast how you'd been here and seen terrible goings-on, and come away unharmed – though you were shot at by the crack marksman of the Tribe? Is that it?

GAR: No.

JONAS: No? Do I look especially stupid or ignorant?

GAR: *(With a little surprise)* No.

JONAS: Then perhaps I might understand. *(GAR, suddenly, unaccountably, puts a hand to his forehead, in violent and unbearable agony. He slumps. His voice becomes choked, his words almost indistinguishable, as he cries out against an inner desperation.)*

GAR: Christ! Where – where – ?

JONAS: *(Quickly)* **Abner, Annie – all of you. Go outside. Wait there.**

ABNER: Now, Jonas –

JONAS: You hear me. Outside, go on!

ABNER: What're you gonna do?

JONAS: Never mind. Do as I tell you. Abner – keep your ears open.
Is Rufe on the bluff?

ABNER: Yes.

JONAS: Keep your rifles ready.

SCENE 5: TWO MALES

Jonas, probably late 60s

Gar, 17 or 18

The action here continues uninterrupted from the preceding scene, except that the People have filed out of the church. Gar refers to the death of his father, Edgar Spench. This actually happens later, in the final segment of the play. And the circumstances are somewhat similar in that Edgar feels he's lost, that he can't help what he does — and he has done many wrongs, including murder.

1. Why does Jonas tell Gar it will help to talk?

2. Why do you think Gar confides his feelings and problems to Jonas?

3. What sort of person is Gar? Why do you think he feels he doesn't fit in at the places where he's been?

4. What kind of help do you think Gar has been seeking?

5. Why is Jonas so fanatic in the speech in which he tells Gar to talk to heaven. Since he has never previously met Gar, why does Jonas offer him the leadership of the People?

6. Is there any justification in Jonas's saying Gar is a coward for not wanting to be shot in the back? Why does he say this?

7. Since Gar knows his life is in danger, why do you suppose he argues with Jonas and says the People really are crazy? Is his arguing believable in this sort of situation?

8. Why does Jonas imply that God would kill Gar? What does he mean by this? Do you think he really believes what he says? Explain.

JONAS: *(Crosses a little to left and Upstage of benches, as if to be sure everyone is out. Then he turns back to GAR, his face full of concern and cunning. He comes down.)* **Now, then. What's troubling you, son? You can talk to me if you want to. What is it?**

GAR: *(His voice agonized)* **Why should I talk to you? Anyone!**

JONAS: It'll help.

GAR: *(Lifting his head, violently)* **Listen! It's all shut up in me, it's drivin' me crazy!**

JONAS: Talk.

GAR: Knowed they wasn't no use comin' to Tahlequah – No use anywhere!

JONAS: Try to be calm.

GAR: *(Intensely)* **Let me out of here. Let me go!**

JONAS: Quiet – take it easy –

GAR: Old men, settin' in the square!

JONAS: Here, sit down. *(He leads him forward, puts a stool in the clear place between benches and rostrum.)*

GAR: *(Drooping, sitting)* **I'm t'ard.**

JONAS: *(Still left of him)* **You'll be all right.**

GAR: *(With more composure)* **Sorry to bust in – I – little crazy.**

JONAS: If you'd like to tell me –

GAR: *(Darkly)* **Why not?** *(His head droops. He stares at the floor.)* **I'm not from Tahlequah. I just came down from Claremore. Run away.**

JONAS: Why?

GAR: Had to do sump'n. Listen, you're a good man, ain't you? They say down below here you're all crazy, 't you steal and are no-'count. You don't look crazy. I come up to see. I come up to find out.

JONAS: To find out what?

GAR: *(In a jumbled rush)* **They's no place for me anywhere, see! Mr. Ferber wanted me to be educated, like him. He's my guardeen. He sent me to A. and M. I played football, made the track team. Didn't study. Didn't want to study. I got kicked out. I didn't belong there. Don't belong in Claremore. No place for me anywhere! Come down to Tahlequah yesterday to see if – to see – I thought this bein' the head of – Listen, I'm half Cherokee. I**

51

thought they could help me out here, I thought they – Old men
sittin' in the square! No Tribe to go to, no Council to help me
out of the kind of trouble I'm in. Nuthin' to count on – !

JONAS: *(A gleam in his eye)* You're just a kid. Seventeen or eighteen
at most. You need guidance, guidance of the spirit. This Mr.
Ferber you speak of –

GAR: He's my guardeen. My pappy's dead. He was Edgar Spench.
They killed him down on Spunky Creek – a year after I was
born.

JONAS: And your mother?

GAR: She's dead, too.

JONAS: *(A fanatic intensity growing in him)* You're alone, then. Lost!
No one to help. What your guardian wants you to do is not for
you. You tried it, didn't you? There's no help from the
Cherokees. They're dying out. They're hardly a Tribe anymore.
They have no order of life you could live. Their ways are going.
Their customs change. That part of you can never be fulfilled.
What's left? You must look to heaven! Like us! *(A terrific inten-
sity and power, almost hypnotic, has gathered in his voice. The
lights everywhere begin to go down, except a concentrated glow on
GAR and the fanatic old man. GAR begins to feel the strangeness.
The valley and the colored fields have disappeared. Claremore
Mound's faint outline no longer stands up on the horizon.
Somewhere in the speech, JONAS crosses, mounts the rostrum,
hypnotic, queer, powerful.)* Our eyes on the hereafter! Our feet
in the Now! We walk here on the mountaintop away from the
world and its wickedness. We lay up treasures in heaven.
Listen to me! After I worked my way through college, I went up
in the Ozarks all alone. I worked out a way of life all by myself,
far from civilization. It had work in it, and prayer, and simple
delights. Others joined me – men and women sick of the life
they had known. Mostly ignorant people. We built us a church.
But civilization crept up on us, forced us out. Back in the
nineties we moved to Oklahoma. But not to the towns. We had
seen the ways men called Christian. And that is why we
preferred the peace of this high mountain. *(Rapt, quietly*

ecstatic) **We rise before the sun rises. In the hushed hour, all is gray and quiet. We touch the rocks. We lift a hand as a tree lifts its branches. We are a part of wild, growing things. The sun rises. We are exalted and stirred. We work, struggle, sweat at our daily toil. But there is no strife and no anger. For the peace of the morning goes with us – till the sun is gone, and we sleep again. Or perhaps there is storm. Lightning cracks across the sky. The heavens open. The voice of God speaks to us from the tempest. We lift up our heads to hear His words. We lift up our hands to receive the power He looses above us.**

GAR: *(His eyes on the old man)* **Let me go!**

JONAS: *(Coming down, touching his shoulder)* **Listen to me. I'm getting old. Year by year I can feel death creeping up on me. And in all the Tribe there's no one to take my place. I've tried to train men – Abner, Rufe – many others. They're not good enough. They're not only ignorant, they are crude souls, who understand only the simplest things.** *(He goes left toward benches, crossing in front of GAR, in his anguish.)* **I can't go away and leave these people without a leader, surely you see that! They're children who must be watched and guided. Through all the years, there has been only one hope I clung to: someone must come from outside – someone who has courage and insight. What if I offered you this? You could join the Tribe. You could work to become worthy. In time you'd become worthy –** *(He has gone toward GAR, rapt, mad.)*

GAR: *(Getting up)* **Let me go.**

JONAS: *(Back a step, brought back to reality)* **Go?**

GAR: *(Watching the old man, in alarm)* **You've never seen me before. You'll never see me again! Let me go!** *(He goes Upstage, harassed, turns back.)*

JONAS: *(Cunningly)* **You want to go? Go, then.**

GAR: They'll shoot me.

JONAS: Are you so afraid of bullets? Are you such a coward?

GAR: *(Intensely, unable to endure the strangeness, as if stating a creed)* **Listen! I don't want to die with a bullet in my back! I'm lost, yes! We're all lost. We don't know where we are. We've never**

even lived. But if I have to die, I want to face the direction death's coming from, do you hear me! I want to see what he looks like! I want to find out why we're afraid of him. In that moment, I'll be alive, alive! – no longer afraid of death, do you understand! Call off your men. Let me out of here!

JONAS: *(With a dangerous smile)* I said you could go.

GAR: And get shot in the back!

JONAS: Suppose you stay, then. Of your own free will. This is God's house. It's safe here. *(He holds up his arms, as if benignly.)*

GAR: *(Fiercely)* God's house! Den of cow thieves and madmen. What you offer me is crazy! They were right about you down below. You touch the rocks, yes! You are exalted and stirred, O God yes! Let me go!

JONAS: *(His voice sharp with anger and hate)* You scorn our religion! You mock our way of life! You refuse bread offered you when you're starving. All right! You're not the first. Look! Do you see that post? *(He indicates the post, standing in the clear space in the back.)* Once a scoffer stood there, too. Chained to that post. *(With a vicious smile)* Would you like to know who it was? Sheriff Johnson.

GAR: *(His voice low)* You killed him.

JONAS: *(With mad delight)* Oh, no, I wouldn't say that. He came up here, as you did. I talked to him as I talked to you. I thought he'd been sent by the Almighty to take my place. He grew violent. We chained him there. He sprang at me, tried to kill me. Abner shot him – to save my life. It was God's will. We wouldn't want God to kill you, too – you so *young* – !

SCENE 6: FOUR MALES, ONE FEMALE, PLUS UNDETERMINED NUMBER OF PEOPLE

Jonas, probably late 60s

Abner, probably 30s or 40s

Gar, 17 or 18

Rufe, probably 30s or 40s

Lize, probably late 20s or 30s

People, all ages

The action is continuous from the last scene to this one.

1. Why is Abner so gleeful at the thought of killing Gar? What does this tell you about his character?

2. Do you think Jonas would have let Gar go if the posse hadn't arrived? Explain.

3. Is it believable that the People continue with the worship service in light of what is happening to Gar?

4. Do you like this scene? Why? Why not?

5. Are any of the characters sympathetic? Explain.

6. What is the point of the Klaxon at the end? Do you think this would be effective?

(There is a loud hammering at the left door. ABNER bursts in, crosses in front of benches to center.)

ABNER: Jonas! They's a whole crowd a-horseback comin' to the foot of the cliff!

JONAS: A crowd?

ABNER: Ten or more – headin' straight this way!

JONAS: *(To GAR, angrily)* It's a trick. You've been lying!

GAR: I don't know what you – I don't know what you're talking about.

JONAS: Listen! Some things were stolen at Tahlequah last night. Don't tell me you didn't know it! They sent you up here to spy on us! I might have known!

GAR: I don't know anything about it!

JONAS: Now a posse is coming. Let 'em come! If they fire on us, it'll be too bad for you! Abner –

ABNER: We'll sneak down and open f'ar on 'em, Jonas!

JONAS: No, wait. They won't come up the cliff. *(RUFE and HENRY burst in, left. HENRY stops at back of seats. RUFE runs to Upstage of benches.)*

RUFE: Jonas! They're turned! They're goin' plumb round the mountain to come up on the other side!

JONAS: I thought so. It'll take several hours to get here. In the meantime we'll –

ABNER: You want us to go and meet 'em, Jonas? You better let us! They'll shoot up the place.

JONAS: No. But keep an eye out for 'em.

ABNER: *(Protesting)* Jonas.

JONAS: Watch them – some of you. But don't shoot – unless I tell you.

ABNER: *(In consternation)* They'll come up here – plumb up here, Jonas!

JONAS: Warn everyone to stay in the enclosure. Bar the gates, Rufe.

RUFE: Well, it 'pears to me –

JONAS: *(With violent command)* Bar the gates!

RUFE: But if *he* gits away and tells – nuthin'll stop 'em! They'll f'ar on us! They'll burn us out! They'll be hell to pay!

JONAS: I'll take care of that. Go on! *(He crosses to the platform. RUFE* *goes out.)* **Abner – in the study there – you'll find hanging on a nail, by the door –**

ABNER: *(Grinning)* **I know, Jonas.** *(He goes swiftly in.)*

JONAS: Henry, call everybody in. *(HENRY begins to toll the bell in the corner.)*

ABNER: *(Entering with lock and chain)* **Here y'air, Jonas.**

JONAS: All right – over there –

ABNER: *(With relish)* **I know what to do, all right, all right!** *(He starts putting the chains on GAR's wrists.)*

GAR: You can't do this.

ABNER: *(Gloating)* **Oh, we're jist a-treatin' you nice. Wait'll you find out what's a-goin' to happen to you!**

JONAS: Abner, stop that talk! Put the lock on. *(ABNER does, and ties GAR to the ring in the post. JONAS has gone to the pulpit; the PEOPLE come in and take seats. The bell tolling stops. The PEOPLE mutter about GAR, excited, whispering, gesturing. JONAS lifts his hand for silence. The excitement of the morning seems to have left him unmoved. Majestically)* **Let us begin –**

LIZE: Where you left off, Jonas?

JONAS: Let us begin at the beginning –

JONAS and PEOPLE: O Lord most high!

JONAS: O Lord in the heavens, hear us in this hour!

PEOPLE: O Lord most high!

JONAS: The day is half gone. The sun has climbed to its peak in the sky.

JONAS and PEOPLE: You are the sun, O Lord!

(GAR breaks out suddenly with decisive and loud anger, while the chant goes on.)

JONAS and PEOPLE:
   O Sun most high!
JONAS: The clouds have
   scattered before you.
   Sunlight descends.
JONAS and PEOPLE:
   You are the sun, O Lord!
   You are the rain and the
	GAR: I won't die this way! I'm
	tied up here, yes. But some
	day I'll get loose. You won't
	kill me! You can't kill me!
	I'm going to live. Live! And
	I'll burn your God-damned
	tabernacle to the ground!
	Do you hear me? Your God-

snow!
You are the hail descending!
Hear us, be with us, O Lord!

damned tabernacle to the ground!

(The voices go on into the darkness. The angry repeated sound of a motor Klaxon thrusts itself sharply into the litany.)

(The final section goes back once more in time and involves GAR's father being shot and killed, reenforcing the play's theme.)

SPENCH: I tried ever'thing. Tried to farm. Too restless. Cattle herdin', ridin' fence. Sump'n always drove me on. The bosses! Burned down their barns, rustled their cattle, slept with their wives. Shot the bastards down – ! Sump'n inside – no rest, I don't know – Bad blood. Too much Indian, they tell me.

GRAY-WOLF: *(The revelation growing in him from what SPENCH has said)* Not enough Indian.

SPENCH: How – !

GRAY-WOLF: *(With troubled compassion)* I'm full-blood Cherokee. I live peaceful. I ain't troubled. I remember the way my people lived in quiet times. Think of my ancestors. It keeps me safe. You though – like my boy. He's dead. He was half white, like you. They killed him, had to kill him! Not enough Indian. The mixture. *(He sits on the stool again.)*

WEEBJOB
Diane Glancy

Although Diane Glancy, the author of *Weebjob*, is also part Cherokee, her play, first presented in 1987 or about fifty years after *Cherokee Night,* presents a much different facet of Native-American life. A college instructor, Glancy says that she got the idea for the play, her first, when she looked across Highway 380 in New Mexico and saw the valley there. Several other ideas came together then to add to this. She actually had seen a place where a man kept putting up signs on his property, and once while driving to a poetry conference, she imagined a woman's hitchhiking. Of course, this became her character Sweet Potato.

In the character descriptions, the playwright describes *Weebjob* (pronounced with long "e"s and "o") as based on the biblical Job and "beset with problems." He has a friend "Pick Up, who isn't much comfort."

> Weebjob is a holy man, a Mescalero Apache. He's stern and unyielding, a little impracticable, yet likeable. Weebjob always seems to be at a crossroads in his life. He lets rich land lie fallow. He paints signs and hangs them on fences. Signs that say: "He hangs the earth on nothing, Job 26:7," "Rodeo/Albuquerque," "Behold the behemoth. He eats grass as an ox. He moveth his tail like the pines, Job 40:15, 17," "Vote/Olfred for Chief."

There is somewhat of a similarity between *Cherokee Night* and *Weebjob* in that Suzanne Long Chalk (Sweet Potato), like Gar and many of the other characters, "is unhappy with life because she doesn't know where she belongs." Thus she keeps running away to hitchhike to Gallup. Such a feeling is common to many members of minorities from newly arrived immigrants to those who perceive themselves as different. Even Glancy says that "I was born to a mother of a different race than I was. (Her mother was English and German.) I came out looking and acting like my father's family, much to her disappointment and dismay. It wasn't long before I realized much of the world would feel the same way."[4]

A collection of Glancy's plays entitled *War Cries* was published in 1995.

[4]Diane Glancy, "Artistic Statement," in Perkins, Kathy A. and Roberta Uno, *Contemporary Plays by Women of Color: An Anthology* (New York: Routledge, 1996), p 168.

SCENE 1: TWO MALES AND ONE FEMALE

Weebjob, 48

Pick Up (Percy Willingdeer), 43

Sweet Potato, 21

The following scene opens the play, which is set in "the Salazar Canyon in Lincoln County, New Mexico." As the action begins, Weebjob "is in his squash patch when he hears a truck. He turns to the road, but finishes digging before he walks to the house," which is small, constructed of mud-brick. On the porch are a wooden table and four chairs.

1. Why do you think Weebjob spends so much time in the squash patch staring at the mountains?

2. What is the overall mood of this scene? Do you think Glancy meant it to be serious, humorous, satiric, or something entirely different? Why? How would you try to convey the mood to an audience?

3. What type of person is Weebjob? Is his character realistic? What are his most important traits?

4. What is Weebjob implying when he says he was born in a different culture?

5. Why does Pick Up say Sweet Potato is bitter?

6. In what way is Weebjob being melodramatic in this scene? Point to lines that show this and explain why you think they do.

7. What does Weebjob mean when he says, "I can remember nothing without Sweet Grass."

8. There is a lot of humor in this scene. Find examples and explain why you think they're funny? What might you do to try to convey them to an audience.

9. What sort of relationship do Sweet Potato and Weebjob have?

10. Why does Sweet Potato call her hitchhiking to Gallup a pilgrimage?

11. Why do you suppose Weebjob doesn't work his fertile land? Why does he even let his squash patch fail to produce?

12. Is Weebjob's faith realistic? Justifiable? What does he mean when he refers to it? Would you enjoy playing the role of Weebjob?

Why? Why not?

13. Why do you think the playwright gave some of the characters such unconventional names?

PICK UP: *(He enters.)* **Ola, Weebjob.**

WEEBJOB: **Ola, Pick Up.** *(There's the sound of the truck door slamming.)*

PICK UP: **I've returned with your daughter, Sweet Potato.**

SWEET POTATO: **My name is Suzanne!** *(She sits on the steps of the house.)*

PICK UP: **I saw her on the road hitchhiking to Gallup. I told her I would bring her back to her father.** *(SWEET POTATO sits on the steps and doesn't look at them.)*

WEEBJOB: **What have my days come to?** *(Pause)*

PICK UP: **She didn't want to come.**

WEEBJOB: **The young are restless as the pines.**

PICK UP: **She says you do nothing but read the Book and sit in the squash patch and stare across the jaundiced hills.**

WEEBJOB: **She overestimates me! And they're mountains, not hills.** *(SWEET POTATO still does not speak, but lies on the porch step with her feet sticking off the side.)* **We, who were raised in the old reservation boarding schools, know tolerance, persistence, perspicacity.**

PICK UP: **Pardon?**

WEEBJOB: **Discernment.**

PICK UP: **Ah! Horse sense.** *(SWEET POTATO turns her backside to the men.)* **You learned the Book well at school.**

WEEBJOB: **Every word.**

SWEET POTATO: **And not a word of it got through.** *(She sits up.)*

WEEBJOB: *(Looking at SWEET POTATO)* **You misunderstand. I was raised in a different culture...I have trouble understanding... Come on, Sweet Potato. Dismount. Your mother is at her sister's, not to return for a few days. I'm hungry. See what's in the kitchen and I will break my fast.**

SWEET POTATO: **Nothing's in the kitchen if mother's not here.** *(Impatiently)* **You're busy making philosophy to the pines and religion to the mountains. You print signs and hang them on the fence by the highway. You read the Book. And yet the garden grows nothing but squash vines. Not one word of your Book changes anything!**

PICK UP: **I believe the child is bitter.**

WEEBJOB: *(Ignoring PICK UP)* **Sweet Potato, my daughter, tuber of my soul, see what's in the kitchen for your starving father, Weebjob. I shall relinquish my fast.** *(Pause)*

PICK UP: *(Looking at WEEBJOB)* **She does not move.**

WEEBJOB: **I see that she does not move! You need not tell me, Job's friend. She is stubborn and recalcitrant.**

PICK UP: **You're too kind with your words.**

WEEBJOB: **I'm grumpy as thunder. Like Mighty Warrior, my dog. Like my wife two weeks at her sister's and nothing to eat.**

PICK UP: **It must come with age.**

WEEBJOB: **No, the daughter has it too.**

PICK UP: **And sons.**

WEEBJOB: **Enough! I'm reminded of my plight. Deserted in the desert. No loaves and fish.**

PICK UP: **That doesn't sound like you, Weebjob. I've never heard you talk that way.**

WEEBJOB: **I'm at a crossroads in my life.**

SWEET POTATO: *(Rising from the steps)* **Mutton. I've heard that all my life. You're always at a crossroad.**

PICK UP: **You've always lived by the words of the Book you've committed to memory.**

WEEBJOB: **I remember nothing. What memory? I can remember nothing but war.**

SWEET POTATO: *(Almost rests her arm against PICK UP, but decides against it)* **You've never been in war. You were too young for one, too old for another.**

WEEBJOB: **To get up in the morning is war.** *(As WEEBJOB makes this speech to the heavens, PICK UP brushes SWEET POTATO's arm.)* **To wrestle with the day, and with my work, is war. To have three children with minds of their own is war.** *(Turns to his daughter.)* **See what there is to eat, Sweet Potato! Your name makes hunger come to me.**

SWEET POTATO: *(To WEEBJOB and PICK UP)* **I'm going to continue my pilgrimage to Gallup.**

PICK UP: *(Turns his head.)* **Another crusader in the Long Chalk family.**

WEEBJOB: I shall continue to meditate on the passages of the Book. I'll stand with my feet on the holy ground of Canaan. *(Nods his head to indicate his squash patch.)* I will sit in the squash patch, *(Waves his arm toward it)* see the Thunder Hawk *(He looks to heaven)* and fight holy wars. *(Turns tenderly to his daughter.)* I need you, Sweet Potato.

PICK UP: *(Agrees with WEEBJOB.)* Gallup is a long way.

WEEBJOB: Three hundred miles.

SWEET POTATO: *(She walks back to the steps. Stands there with her hand in her hip pocket.)* It's because nothing happens here. You live in the fertile Salazar Canyon, the greenest in New Mexico. *(She raises her arms.)* You could have sheep, but you won't fence your land. You could have crops. James makes you an irrigation ditch, but what do you grow? *(She slaps her hands at her sides.)* Nothing! You put up signs where our road runs into the highway. You makes more signs. They say, "Canaan." Whatever that means. They say, "The devil and I do not speak." *(She looks at WEEBJOB fiercely.)* Whatever that means. When I go in to Old Lincoln they ask at the general store if I've come for more paint. *(Pause)* Once in a while you sell gourds and squash at the roadside stand. You sell mother's blankets in Old Lincoln when we're desperate. What good ever comes from this? *(She shrugs as though giving up, and stands with her hands on her hips again.)*

WEEBJOB: Yes, I have nothing. I'm proud to have nothing! The prophets of the Book had nothing. It's work to have nothing, Sweet Potato. I should have sent you to the Female Seminary where your mother went. Then you wouldn't have these ideas...

SWEET POTATO: *(Under her breath)* Shit.

WEEBJOB: Then you would understand that I grow visions –

SWEET POTATO: *(With her hands over her ears)* Heaven above. This is your harvest? I've seen you sitting in your squash patch in some kind of trance. Holy God. You look like you're talking to yourself. Is that the culmination of your life's work?

WEEBJOB: I won't have irreverence on my land. Someday you'll understand what "Canaan" means. For now, get me something to eat! *(More definite now)*

SWEET POTATO: I thought it was your meat to do the will of the father.

WEEBJOB: It is. And to finish the work I've begun. The fields are white with harvest. This is what I'll do until I hear my name called from beyond the mountains.

SWEET POTATO: Your fields and desert look brown to me. You interpret the Book to fit your purpose.

WEEBJOB: Not so, Tuber. Indeed, I'm the man you see before your eyes, and I'm not appreciated. There may be things you don't know. I have faith that the desert is white with harvest, and will blossom by faith. I have seen the Thunder Hawk, Sweet Potato, what else can I say to you? *(SWEET POTATO walks reluctantly toward the house. The men watch her until she enters the front door.)*

SCENE 2: TWO MALES

Weebjob, 48

James, 23

This scene occurs a little later in the first act. In the meantime, Pick Up has told Weebjob that he could beat his sword into a plowshare (a biblical reference). He says Weebjob cannot expect his kids to understand his ways, that his two sons already have left him, his wife is away at her sister's, and Sweet Potato keeps trying to leave.

Weebjob says his sons return at times and his wife is only visiting. In other words, he refuses to accept that he leads a strange life.

Sweet Potato has gone to look for food but finds only a turnip and a hard crust of bread. Weebjob's son James stops by and immediately Weebjob accuses him of not keeping in touch enough. Sweet Potato says James would have gotten further in life (he works for the highway department) if Weebjob had let him get a college loan.

James lives with his girlfriend Hersah but says he thinks she's more Sweet Potato's friend than his own. Again Sweet Potato says Weebjob should try to make a living keeping sheep. Pick Up says that in the Bible people were shepherds. "I've considered that," Weebjob answers.

Pick Up and Sweet Potato leave for town to buy food.

1. What sort of person is James? How does he differ from Sweet Potato in his feelings about their father?

2. Why do you think Weebjob doesn't work, fish, or drive?

3. Why does Weebjob become upset at the thought that Pick Up comes to Socorro to see Sweet Potato? In his place, would this bother you, do you think? Why? Why not?

4. Why is James being accusatory in mentioning Sweet Grass's being away from home?

5. How would you describe Weebjob's reaction to the letter?

6. What does Weebjob's final speech here mean? What do you think he's feeling? If you were acting this role, how might you try to show this?

7. Is James a likeable person? Why? Why not? From reading this scene, what can you determine about his character?

WEEBJOB: I feel badly, James.

JAMES: Why, Dad?

WEEBJOB: Sweet Potato told me that you wanted to go to college.

JAMES: I'm doing fine with the highway department. I'm getting an education from the horticulturist just the same as if I were in school. And I'm getting paid for it.

WEEBJOB: When she said that, it made me think how I have stayed here and not helped any of you.

JAMES: I like my job. Don't worry about Sweet Potato. William has done all right too. Sweet Potato just gets down on everything. Didn't William finish law school?

WEEBJOB: Yes, because his wife's family helped him.

JAMES: *(He takes WEEBJOB's shoulders in his hands with care.)* We do what we must.

WEEBJOB: What's wrong with her?

JAMES: I don't know. She can't find anything she wants to do. *(He lets go of WEEBJOB and puts his hands in his pockets.)* Weebjob, I could bring you some Spanish bayonet of agave for your garden. I could bring you some vegetables and show you how to care for them, and how to cultivate the squash you already have. Then you could harvest a crop to sell in Old Lincoln each year.

WEEBJOB: I don't know.

JAMES: You've done nothing with the land, Father. You don't even have a fishing license. A driver's license.

WEEBJOB: I don't need a license to fish on my own land.

JAMES: The land deed — Your will —

WEEBJOB: I could think I was talking to William. Has he put you up to this?

JAMES: *(Sarcastically)* No, Dad. I actually thought of it on my own.

WEEBJOB: I don't seem to know all I need to know either. *(The puzzled look returns to his face.)* What's going on in Socorro that you didn't know Sweet Potato was going to run away to Gallup?

JAMES: Am I supposed to know everything she's thinking? I'm gone sometimes several days on highway department work. She and Hersah talk. Ask her. All I know is that I heard them fighting one night.

WEEBJOB: The girls?

JAMES: No, Father. Pick Up and Sweet Potato.

WEEBJOB: Pick Up comes to Socorro?

JAMES: You didn't know?

WEEBJOB: Didn't know what? There's nothing to know.

JAMES: Pick Up comes to Socorro sometimes to see Sweet Potato.

WEEBJOB: Pick Up goes to Socorro to see Sweet Potato? He's my friend, not hers! He's old enough to be her father. I expect you to be your sister's keeper and you let something like that happen! He's almost as old as I am. The fool! *(WEEBJOB grabs JAMES'S shirt.)* Why is he bothering Sweet Potato?

JAMES: *(Takes his father's hands in his own.)* I don't think she minds it.

WEEBJOB: *(Pulls his hands away from JAMES. Hits his thighs in anger. He picks up a stick and chucks it in the ditch Off-stage.)* Chew it to bits, Mighty Warrior. *(He looks questioningly to heaven.)* WORSE than what I feared has come upon me. *(Looks to JAMES.)* Why am I not told anything? That old man bothering my daughter! What's wrong with –

JAMES: *(Interrupts his father.)* I came for another reason also, Father. Now that I know Sweet Potato is here, I see that Mother is gone. You didn't tell me. A letter came yesterday from Hobbs. She's at her sister's and assumes I know. Why am I not told anything?

WEEBJOB: You got a letter from your mother? Let me see it! *(JAMES takes it from his pocket and WEEBJOB grabs it from him. WEEBJOB opens the letter and reads.)* "Your father, as you know, is a difficult man to live with." *(WEEBJOB looks at JAMES.)* She writes you this? *(JAMES looks away from WEEBJOB.)* "He is not a practical man, but is caught up in his ideals. I thought I would stay at my sister's for a month, but I think continually of Weebjob, and how he is getting along without me to cook his meals and clean his house. I think I will finish the visit with my sister soon, and return to Salazar Canyon with Weebjob. I'll ride the bus as far as Roswell and William will bring me home..." *(WEEBJOB looks to heaven.)* William knows too! *(Reads* *again.)* "I don't like to be away from Weebjob after all..."

JAMES: How long has she been gone?

WEEBJOB: *(Regains his composure.)* Fifteen days.

JAMES: How did she get to Hobbs? It must be two hundred miles –

WEEBJOB: I took her to the junction in Carrizozo and she caught the bus.

JAMES: That was nice of you. Why didn't you make her walk to the junction? I don't like her riding the bus. I would have taken her to Hobbs if I knew you two were quarreling.

WEEBJOB: We're not quarreling! She simply wanted to see her sister. And it isn't any business of yours.

JAMES: Yes, it is.

WEEBJOB: The letter she wrote to you is hard for me to accept. I got Sweet Grass at an Indian Female Seminary. She would hardly look at me, much less speak anything to me. Now she tells you all this? *(He reads the rest of the letter in silence.)*

JAMES: I suppose she wrote so that I would understand why she wasn't here when I came.

WEEBJOB: Mutton. You used to be too young to know anything. Now you're told all. *(He crumples the letter and hands it back to JAMES.)*

SCENE 3: ONE MALE AND ONE FEMALE

Sweet Potato, 21

Pick Up, 43

Weebjob and James continue talking. Weebjob is feeling betrayed both because his wife is gone and because Sweet Potato and Pick Up are seeing each other. He becomes angry when James says that Sweet Potato was gone for a week. James thought she had gone with Pick Up. Instead, she had gone to Gallup (where the previous summer she'd worked in a restaurant). Weebjob begins to complain that Sweet Potato and Pick Up should have been back from the store by now. James says they hardly have had time yet to get to Lincoln.

1. Why does Sweet Potato say she doesn't want to speak of Pick Up's caring for her.

2. When Pick Up says, "You're more than Weebjob's daughter to me," Sweet Potato gives a flippant answer. Why do you suppose she does this?

3. What is the significance of the "I remember you..." speeches. Why does Pick Up say he should have let Sweet Potato drown?

4. Why does Sweep Potato then acquiesce and ask if Pick Up could call Weebjob Father?

5. Though Sweet Potato has argued with Weebjob, she says, "He's a better man than any I've known." What can you tell about her feelings for him from this line?

(The stage is dark except for a spotlight in the corner which falls on SWEET POTATO and PICK UP in the truck.)

SWEET POTATO: Why are we stopping? I need to get back to feed Weebjob.

PICK UP: Let him wait.

SWEET POTATO: I'll hear him bellering in the valley if we don't get back soon... He'll be painting another sign for the fence by the road... *(PICK UP touches her face.)*

PICK UP: Where were you for a week?

SWEET POTATO: You already asked me, and I told you I was on the road. *(Folds her arms.)* Why did you bring me back to him? You know I didn't want to come.

PICK UP: You can't run away, Sweet Potato.

SWEET POTATO: My name is Suzanne Long Chalk.

PICK UP: I'll call you what I please. I can't have you hitchhiking on the road for anyone to pick up. You shouldn't be out on the road alone. It's not good. What would you do in Gallup?

SWEET POTATO: Get a job. I can cook, wait tables. I worked there last summer, if you remember.

PICK UP: Yes, it's the first time I came to see you...I don't want you to go back there.

SWEET POTATO: You sound like my father.

PICK UP: It's not as your father that I'm speaking. Work at the Civil War in Old Lincoln if you must have a job. Let the men gawk at you. Wait tables. *(He pauses and looks at her.)* I care for you, Suzanne. You know that. *(Pause)* More than as a father. I didn't come to Socorro to see James.

SWEET POTATO: I told you I didn't want to speak of these things.

PICK UP: I didn't for many years. But now I can't wait any longer. You're more than Weebjob's daughter to me.

SWEET POTATO: Maybe we could be like cousins.

PICK UP: I want you as a close friend.

SWEET POTATO: We are close friends, Pick Up, my father's friend.

PICK UP: Yes, I'm his friend.

SWEET POTATO: You wouldn't be if he heard you speak to me

like that.

PICK UP: **I know.** *(He touches her face again.)*

SWEET POTATO: **I remember you, Pick Up, when you used to have a brown Volkswagen, and looked like a prune driving it down the road.**

PICK UP: **I remember you, Sweet Potato, in a round purple coat, like a plum on narrow legs, with skinny braids sticking out from beneath your cap.**

SWEET POTATO: **I remember the night you got drunk in the Civil War Bar in Old Lincoln and came to our house and quoted poetry to the weed-clumps.**

PICK UP: **I remember when the faintest bit of snow blew into the valley and you ran into my truck on William's bicycle and sprang the tire.**

SWEET POTATO: **I remember** – *(PICK UP puts his hands over her mouth.)*

PICK UP: **I remember when you fell into the stream. I should have let you drown.** *(He kisses her.)*

SWEET POTATO: **Would you call him Father?**

PICK UP: *(He rolls his head back.)* **I would rather have a buffalo for a father-in-law.**

SWEET POTATO: *(She takes up for WEEBJOB.)* **He's a better man than any I've known.**

PICK UP: **I know.**

SWEET POTATO: **Wise and goodhearted. Quick tempered. A little harsh with words and his head too much in the Bible, but a good man.**

PICK UP: **I don't know what to do, Suzanne. I want you, and I wonder why. I'm almost as old as your father. How could I think of you as a wife? How could you think of me** –

SWEET POTATO: **Don't talk about it.**

PICK UP: **Marry me, Suzanne.**

SWEET POTATO: **I can hear Weebjob roaring about it now.**

PICKUP: **He will be all right. Think about me, Sweet Potato.** *(He kisses her again.)* **Marry me.**

SWEET POTATO: **Maybe it's what you deserve.**

SCENE 4: THREE MALES AND ONE FEMALE

Weebjob, 48

Pick Up, 43

James, 23

Sweet Potato, 21

After this scene ends, the action switches back to Weebjob's place where he and James still are talking. "Ah! Here come Rumpelstiltskin and Juliet now," Weebjob says as Pick Up and Sweet Potato return. James tells him to be kind. Weebjob becomes angry when James says Pick Up is doing a better job with Sweet Potato than Weebjob is doing with Sweet Grass (his wife). Weebjob accuses Pick Up and Sweet Potato of having taken too long to go to town. He then asks Pick Up to step inside. Angry, Sweet Potato asks James what he has told Weebjob.

1. Why does Weebjob call Pick Up a failure?

2. Where is the humor in this scene? Explain.

WEEBJOB: It's not clear to me why I have such a jackass for a friend.

PICK UP: Nor do I understand why I put up with you unless it's for your daughter. *(WEEBJOB jerks PICK UP's shirt collar, ripping it.)*

JAMES: *(Rushes to the men, takes his father by the shoulders.)* **Gerald Long Chalk. You're a man of peace!**

WEEBJOB: *(He comes to his senses, and bows, formally.)* **Forgive me, Pick Up.** *(Stiffly)* **I forgot myself for a moment and wanted to smash your head.**

PICK UP: I understand, friend Weebjob. *(WEEBJOB holds up his hand to PICK UP as though protesting that he is his friend, but SWEET POTATO interrupts. She looks at the torn place on PICK UP's shirt, would like to pull it together, but decides to go into the house.)*

WEEBJOB: It's too soon to call me friend again, Pick Up. I must go to the squash patch for a while. *(He goes to the garden. JAMES and PICK UP remain on the porch. PICK UP pulls his shirt together.)*

JAMES: Another trip to the Holy Land. *(JAMES watches his father for a moment, then he puts his hand on PICK UP's shoulder to comfort him. PICK UP looks at the ground, shakes his head. They are uncertain at first what to say to one another. While WEEBJOB is in the squash patch, they talk, inaudibly.)*

WEEBJOB: *(Chants, then begins his prayers.)* **Great Spirit. Father of Fathers. Forgive me for anger, and in turn make me forgive Pick Up. Every rock has its flat side. He is taken with Sweet Potato. Maybe it will pass. He has always liked her, but I didn't expect this! Never this!** *(Shrugs.)* **Is it my new burden? Is this the catastrophe that comes even before my wife returns? I need her to soothe me. Bring her back quickly. I'm angry that my son-in-law is nearly as old as I am. I'm angry he's done nothing all his life. More flies than arrows. Wait until Sweet Grass hears about this! Make me forgive him and keep him from marrying my daughter.** *(He chants until SWEET POTATO calls him.)*

SWEET POTATO: *(She calls JAMES and PICK UP and hands the plates through the window to them. Then she comes out of the house and calls her father.)* **How now, Father. Your hamburger is**

ready. *(She holds her arm forward in an Indian salute.)*

WEEBJOB: *(He quickly finishes his prayers, bids the Great Spirit adieu.)* **Whuoah!** *(He joins JAMES and PICK UP at the table on the porch.)* **I see you waited.**

PICK UP: Ola, Weebjob. Have a seat.

WEEBJOB: On my own porch? You tell me to be seated. Thank you, kind friend.

SWEET POTATO: Peace, Father. Eat your meal. *(The four of them sit at the table.)*

WEEBJOB: *(Asks the blessing on the meal.)* **Great Spirit, we are grateful for the food which you provide.** *(SWEET POTATO and PICK UP look at one another.)* **Now help us to eat this meal in peace. Amen.**

PICK UP: Amen.

SCENE 5: THREE MALES AND ONE FEMALE

Weebjob, 48

Pick Up, 43

James, 23

Sweet Potato, 21

Sweet Potato wants to move the table and chairs inside. Weebjob says he's head of the house and wants them to remain where they are. The men talk, and then Pick Up asks why Weebjob won't raise sheep so his wife and Sweet Potato can open a store to sell blankets. He says he has a letter from Sweet Grass, which mentions the store.

1. Why do you think Weebjob hasn't known how Pick Up feels about Sweet Potato?

2. What is Weebjob's objection to the marriage? Do you think he's justified in opposing it? Why? Why not?

3. What is the significance of the last speech in the scene?

WEEBJOB: *(Pounds the table.)* **Mutton!** *(Rises, nearly tipping the table.)* **You have a letter from Sweet Grass?** *(PICK UP pulls the letter from his pocket and hands it to WEEBJOB, who reads it with disbelief.)* **"I am in Hobbs with my sister, Mary Jane Collar. I don't know how long I will be here. I have not seen her in a long time and she is old and alone. There's much to do. We talk of weaving and clean her small house. We put up cactus jelly for winter and speak of many things. I leave Weebjob to himself for a while."** *(He looks to heaven.)* **"I understand him as a man; sometimes it is easier to bear, sometimes not."** *(He sits in his chair. Reads more quietly now.)* **"I've been wanting to write you. I know how hard it is for you to feel about Sweet Potato as you do. Break it gently to Weebjob when the time comes!"** *(His voice rises again as he finishes reading his wife's letter to PICK UP.)* **"Tell Sweet Potato I'm fine..."** *(He pounds the table again, rises to his feet.)*

PICK UP: *(Angry now)* **Let me ask you something, Weebjob. I've known Sweet Potato since she was a child. I think it was me who first called her Sweet Potato.**

WEEBJOB: *(Angry also)* **It might have been.**

PICK UP: **That was twenty years ago. I have seen her nearly every week since then. I have loved her for years. Tell me, Weebjob, Gerald Long Chalk, holy man of Salazar Canyon – Why are you the only one who doesn't know? Are you so buried in *your* work, you don't know when your friend is in love with your daughter?**

WEEBJOB: **You as a son-in-law. No, by thunder. I won't have it.** *(Bangs the table again.)* **How old are you, Pick Up?**

PICK UP: **Forty-three, and Sweet Potato is twenty-one. It's as though I've always been waiting for her.**

WEEBJOB: **Bull crackers. You just don't want the responsibility of a wife and family.**

PICK UP: **That might be right. I saw you snorting about it so much through the years, I thought it couldn't be much fun.**

WEEBJOB: **It's a responsibility to have a wife and raise children.**

PICK UP: **So it would seem, listening to you.**

WEEBJOB: **Have you asked her to be your wife?**

PICK UP: Yes, and she almost agreed.

WEEBJOB: She doesn't know what else to do with herself. She hasn't even been able to make it to Gallup again. Maybe that's why she almost gives in to you. *(With his fist to PICK UP)* How many young girls are there in the valley? Why my daughter?

PICK UP: I would love Sweet Potato no matter what her age. I want her to be my wife and I don't want any old crank standing in the way. *(He pushes his chair away from him with his foot. PICK UP and WEEBJOB stand facing one another.)*

WEEBJOB: I'm not having an old Poker for a son-in-law.

PICK UP: You will if Sweet Potato agrees.

WEEBJOB: Mutton.

JAMES: Break it up, Weebjob. How silly to see two old bulls ready to fight.

WEEBJOB: Even if one of the old bulls is going to be your brother-in-law?

JAMES: That's up to Sweet Potato.

WEEBJOB: It's up to me to give permission.

SWEET POTATO: It's up to me, Father. I don't have to have your permission.

WEEBJOB: *(Looking up to heaven)* My father, Seewootee, never would have believed this!

PICK UP: Sweet Grass would return sooner if she knew you were close to a wedding.

WEEBJOB: There's not going to be a wedding yet! *(Pause)* I think she wrote to everyone but me...

SWEET POTATO: She hasn't written to me either. I've tried to be like her. But I am not my mother. I can't be her. I know she's sweet and gentle. And I'm not any of that...

PICK UP: *(He goes to SWEET POTATO, puts his arm around her.)* Let's walk up the road. *(He draws her off the porch.)*

WEEBJOB: *(Lowers his head, looks at them with a scowl.)* Such patience it will take for me to see him living with my daughter. Maybe they will move to Gallup, James. But I know they won't. I'll probably have them here with me in "Canaan"...

JAMES: *(Laughs.)* I doubt that.

WEEBJOB: Sweet Grass will return and weave behind my house. I will watch her make the roaming antelope design, bringing the pattern to a point, a place of finish. Her weaving is resolution. William will come with his wife, with their baby, and Hersah will still be unhappy that she's going to have another. She'll cry and I will hear her blow her nose into her handkerchief. *(Pause)* **Pick Up for a son-in-law!** *(Hits the table.)* ***MUTTON!***

SCENE 6: ONE MALE AND ONE FEMALE

Pick Up, 43

Sweet Potato, 21

In the next scene, Sweet Potato says she probably will marry Pick Up and then says that nothing she can think of right now would prevent its taking place. Pick Up asks if she is saying this because she has nowhere else to go. She says she could stay with James and Hersah, or she could go to Gallup again and work in a restaurant. Pick Up asks if she minds that he was the age she is now before she was born. She says she doesn't and then asks if he minds that she's so young.

1. Why do you thing Sweet Potato is afraid of committing herself to the marriage?

2. Is Pick Up being unreasonable in what he says he wants from the marriage to Sweet Potato? Why? Why not?

3. Why does Sweet Potato say she wants to be married in "Canaan"?

4. Do you think this marriage will work out? Why? Why not?

5. Why does Pick Up not want to get married in the squash patch?

6. What do you think makes Sweet Potato finally give in and say that she will marry Pick Up?

SWEET POTATO: Can't we get married in the old Indian way?

PICK UP: No.

SWEET POTATO: You could give Weebjob some horses, and I would just move in with you. If it doesn't work, I will put your bed-roll by the door and you can move out.

PICK UP: No.

SWEET POTATO: You'd want the horses back?

PICK UP: I don't have any horses.

SWEET POTATO: Your truck, then?

PICK UP: Yes. I don't want to lose my house and truck both. And I don't want you to be able to get out of it that easily.

SWEET POTATO: I don't like complications.

PICK UP: You don't want responsibility, Sweet Potato. I am going to marry you by law and in the Old Lincoln Church. And I want you in a dress. I'm going to have you as my wife, Suzanne. I expect you to clean the house, cook my suppers, wash the dishes and clothes. You aren't going to run off whenever you feel like it. You can visit James and Hersah in Socorro. Do what you like. But I will have your attention. Otherwise, don't marry me. You aren't coming to see if you like it. You are making a commitment I expect you to keep. I won't have it any other way. I'm from the old school too.

SWEET POTATO: And in trying to get away from Weebjob, I come to someone like him? *(She shrugs her shoulders.)*

PICK UP: I expect you to come to me as a wife who wants to live with me. I expect you to sacrifice your burning ambition to hitch-hike to Gallup. I won't have it. I'm old enough to want a wife that I know I'm not going to find on the highway with her thumb up.

SWEET POTATO: And what do I get in return for my unending subjection to you?

PICK UP: I'm taking you off Weebjob's hands. He should be giving me the horses. I'm giving you a chance to come where you will have respect as a person, and a chance to be on your own, to do as you want —

SWEET POTATO: As long as it isn't making sudden trips?

PICK UP: That's right. I will give you a chance to open your wool store with your mother in Old Lincoln, if that's what you want. I'd even buy you some sheep. Or you can wait tables at the Civil War if you like. I would rather that you didn't, but you are your own person, Sweet Potato. And I know you're struggling to find something that will satisfy you. I'm not taking you away from that. I'm giving you what you haven't had —

SWEET POTATO: It sounds like "Canaan" to me. Except — *(She puts her hands to her face.)* Unless I find I don't have any place I belong.

PICK UP: *(He holds her.)* Then you can be satisfied to be my wife. I'm making a place in my house for you.

SWEET POTATO: One concession, Pick Up.

PICK UP: What?

SWEET POTATO: No wedding in Old Lincoln Church, and not in a dress. Father's zeal has always made me shudder in church. I want to be married here — in "Canaan."

(Here the stage lights come back. WEEBJOB is in his squash patch. JAMES is in the house washing the pots and pans at the sink.)

WEEBJOB: Humbleness of mind, meekness, long suffering. *(He is on his knees praying.)* Forbearing one another, forgiving one another. *(He makes a fist toward heaven.)* Could you make this any harder?

PICK UP: *(He and SWEET POTATO return to the front porch.)* No – not there. *(He looks to the squash patch.)*

SWEET POTATO: Then the front porch, or outside somewhere – in the pines? But I have always liked the yellow blossoms.

PICK UP: Weebjob would never allow a wedding there. That is holy ground to him. I don't want to be married on his place anyway.

SWEET POTATO: And I don't want to be married in a dress!

WEEBJOB: *(Loudly)* Huah! Huah!

SWEET POTATO: He is plugged in again. Yes. I will marry you, Pick Up. I am sure.

SCENE 7: TWO FEMALES

Sweet Grass, 45

Sweet Potato, 21

Pick Up tells Weebjob that it's settled. He and Sweet Potato will marry. William, the elder son, brings Sweet Grass home. She has written to everyone except Weebjob. She didn't write him, she says, because she didn't know what to write. She says she was afraid to tell him about Sweet Potato and Pick Up. She tells Sweet Potato she wants to talk to her.

1. Why do you think Sweet Potato feels there's no place for her?

2. Is it logical that Sweet Grass questions Sweet Potato so much about what she really wants? Why does she do this?

3. Why does Sweet Grass say that Weebjob doesn't fall short most of the time? Which lines show that Sweet Grass loves Weebjob? As an actor, how could you try to convey her feelings to an audience?

SWEET GRASS: Are you sure, Suzanne, you want to marry Pick Up?

SWEET POTATO: No, I'm not.

SWEET GRASS: Do you love him?

SWEET POTATO: Yes, I always have. I feel like I belong with him. I'm not excited or bored with him. He's just there.

SWEET GRASS: But you can't go running away, as you have from us.

SWEET POTATO: I know. He's said as much.

SWEET GRASS: Is there anything you'd rather do?

SWEET POTATO: Yes, but it's unattainable. I don't like school. I can't be like William and go to college. I barely finished high school. And I wasn't in the right place like James when he found his job. That desert clodhopper. He just happened to apply for a job and the horticulturist took him!

SWEET GRASS: He always liked the squash patch and cactus.

SWEET POTATO: I've looked and seen things I've wanted, but I could never have them. There's never been any place for me, Mother. I don't want to go to school. I don't really want to wait tables. I'm happy when I'm on my way to Gallup. There isn't any room for me here on "Canaan."

SWEET GRASS: Yes, there is. You're our daughter.

SWEET POTATO: But I'm not your child anymore.

SWEET GRASS: Just so Pick Up isn't a father to you that you'd resent like Weebjob.

SWEET POTATO: *(She looks at her mother.)* No. He's one of my friends, though he's older.

SWEET GRASS: He's more like a brother?

SWEET POTATO: No. He's not like William or James to me. He's not Weebjob to me either. How could they have been friends for so long? They're different from one another.

SWEET GRASS: They complement each other somehow.

SWEET POTATO: Pick Up also asks me why I want to marry him.

SWEET GRASS: What do you tell him?

SWEET POTATO: What I tell you.

SWEET GRASS: You don't know what else to do so you're going to try marriage?

SWEET POTATO: Pick Up accused me of that also, but it isn't true.

I do want to be with him. I think I always did, but was afraid it would look ridiculous. Now I might marry him. We could live in Old Lincoln and drive to Socorro to see James and Hersah on the weekends. Maybe...I could have a wool store. I even have a name for it.

SWEET GRASS: What?

SWEET POTATO: "The Spinners." I might even be able to have sheep on Pick Up's place.

SWEET GRASS: Will you finally let me teach you to weave?

SWEET POTATO: Maybe. You'll be supplier of the blankets I sell.

SWEET GRASS: There isn't anyone else you want to marry?

SWEET POTATO: There have been others. But they married someone else, or went off, or weren't interested in me. One was so worthless I knew the marriage would never work.

SWEET GRASS: What if someone came...more your age?

SWEET POTATO: I would still be Pick Up's wife. I do want to be with him, Mother. He's a friend – I want him to be my husband.

SWEET GRASS: *(Puts her arm around SWEET POTATO.)* I've always liked Pick Up, though if I'd known he would be my son-in-law, I might have kicked about it at first. But now I feel differently. I can see him as your husband. I can understand why he loves you.

SWEET POTATO: What is it like to be a wife?

SWEET GRASS: It probably feels differently to every wife. To me it feels right to be Weebjob's wife. I see him as the man he wants to be, even when he falls short of it.

SWEET POTATO: Which is most of the time.

SWEET GRASS: No, it isn't. He's a good man. I like to look at him, feel him against me, listen to him. I shouldn't be speaking of these things to you. But I must be with him. Even if he is in the squash patch, sometimes I go out just to watch him work. Sometimes I hear his prayers, his chants. When he has visions of the Thunder Hawk, I leave him to himself. He's my companion. I don't know what I'd do without him. I suppose I'd go live with Mary Jane Collar and we'd can cactus jelly and paint her back steps. He's all I thought about in Hobbs...

SCENE 8: ONE MALE AND ONE FEMALE

Sweet Potato, 21

Pick Up, 45

Sweet Potato and Sweet Grass continue to talk; Weebjob enters and asks if marrying Pick Up is what Sweet Potato wants. He finally tells her, "God's blessing on your marriage, Suzanne Long Chalk." He adds, however, that Pick Up hasn't yet asked his permission for the marriage to take place.

Sweet Potato and Pick Up converse, though the audience cannot hear them. Yet it is apparent that she is telling him to talk to Weebjob, who at first says he denies permission for the two to marry. Then he agrees to it.

1. Why does Sweet Potato tell Pick Up how she feels about herself? What does she mean by saying that while on her way to Gallup, she's *Indian*.

2. Why does Pick Up say that there might be more on the road than he can give her? What is he feeling here?

3. Why doesn't Sweet Potato admit to seeing the danger in hitchhiking? What does hitchhiking symbolize for her? Explain why you think this?

4. Why does Pick Up say she could teach? What made him think of this?

5. What emotions do you think the two characters are feeling in this scene? Explain.

PICK UP: Weebjob has consented, and I didn't injure him before he did.

SWEET POTATO: You have shown patience.

PICK UP: Now, when can we get married?

SWEET POTATO: As soon as you like. But I won't wear a dress.

PICK UP: And I will *not* be married on "Canaan." *(He holds her in his arms.)* See that bright spot in the desert where the sun comes through the clouds and makes a ring of light?

SWEET POTATO: When I'm standing on the road with my thumb up, the heat trying to take my breath, the fear of passing cars pounding in my chest, I feel one with the land. The shrubs speak to me like children. The dry river beds may be without a trickle of water. I wash in the heat and feel alive on Interstate 40 West. Not straining for existence any longer, but filled with meaning.

PICK UP: But what's in Gallup?

SWEET POTATO: Nothing, I guess, but getting there. I forget I'm a reject of this world. When I'm on my way to Gallup, I'm *Indian.* I like these worn hills with wrinkles like an old man's face, and with sand as brown as our skin. The divided highway is not like 380 through the canyon. Wind plays with my hair and the heat laughs...The terrible heat that pulls one into itself, and windows of the skin are open and we are running with the heat. Not hardly anyone knows but us. I like the morning sun on my back and the long fingers of the evening shadow across the highway. I want to go again across the Cibolo County line to Gallup.

PICK UP: I believe you do, Suzanne.

SWEET POTATO: Palomino rocks. Mountains and plateaus. Sometimes I sit in the shade of a bush and listen to the cars pass. *(PICK UP looks away from her a moment. It's hard for him to listen to part of what she says, especially when he realizes there is danger in what she does.)* I don't ride with anyone who stops. I look them over first. There are white men who would use me...

PICK UP: *(Turns away from her.)* Indians, too.

SWEET POTATO: That's why they can't see and feel the life of the desert, and can't hear the Great Spirit walking in the heat – in the midst of the fiery furnace. See, I know some of the Book too. *(PICK UP walks away from her.)* **Pick Up?**

PICK UP: Go to Gallup. Maybe you have more there on the road than I can give you.

SWEET POTATO: When I get as far as Mesita I know I'll make it. Rock slides where the highway cuts through the plateaus. Payute. Cubero. James goes up into the Piños Mountains, but I have to go farther.

PICK UP: All the way to Gallup!

SWEET POTATO: What's wrong with hitchhiking to Gallup?

PICK UP: It isn't for a woman.

SWEET POTATO: It's exactly for me. Every place speaks my name and I know what to call them in return. The cactus and hills and arroyos.

PICK UP: I don't want you on the highway for another man to see. I don't want you misused, Sweet Potato. You can understand that. I want to protect you – *(He looks at the ground.)* I want to consume you myself.

SWEET POTATO: Last week before I left I kept thinking of El Morro. San Rafael. Quemado. I don't ride with anyone. Sometimes it's like they're dead already when I look at their eyes. They look like a lava rock to me. *(She touches PICK UP.)* I'm glad you worry about me. It's always been me who saw others look at you. I remember the women who wanted you – Why didn't you ever marry after the first time?

PICK UP: I never found anyone I really wanted to marry. But you've caught me, Suzanne. You have a sweetness, too, like your mother. You get a little rusty sometimes, like the desert water in my well – but you're not so tough, Miss Long Chalk. I won't tell anyone, though.

SWEET POTATO: Sometimes the jack rabbits hop right in front of me. *(She ignores him.)* Pick Up, I'm alive on the road to Gallup.

PICK UP: It's suicide for you to hitchhike, Sweet Potato.

SWEET POTATO: I've run into the bad ones before... *(She looks at PICK UP.)* There was a man who tried to pick me up once. He followed me along the highway for a while, but I wouldn't get into his car.

PICK UP: *(Angry with her)* **God, Sweet Potato.**

SWEET POTATO: **I always got away from any trouble.**

PICK UP: **But you might not always...How can I let you go? I remember when you had to sit on books to reach the supper table. And now you're hitchhiking? Why do you want to go to Gallup?**

SWEET POTATO: **For the thrill of passing Ozanbito. The army depot and cathedral. The Outpost Restaurant where I worked that summer on my own. I used to cross the street and eat in the cemetery. The handmade grave markers. A picket fence like a playpen. The little weeds that jumped at my feet.**

PICK UP: **The street corner crowd at Indian capital? The "No Loitering" sign at the cemetery?**

SWEET POTATO: **On Sundays I walked up to the Cathedral.**

PICK UP: **You could teach, Sweet Potato. You aren't too old to go back to school. The children at Indian missions need teachers...**

SWEET POTATO: **I don't know –**

PICK UP: **I remember you in a little pinafore with the straps crossed on your bare back. They made a big white X and I knew then you were one I could probably wait for –** *(SWEET POTATO pushes PICK UP away when he tries to kiss her.)* **I have to go – I might have some calls for my tow truck...** *(He kisses her.)*

SCENE 9: ONE MALE

Weebjob, 48

Weebjob, as usual, is being obstinate and disagreeable. When Sweet Grass disagrees with what he says, he tells her she shouldn't contradict him. "Haven't I always been free to offer an opinion?" she asks. He tells her that's true so long as it does not go against what he says. Sweet Potato enters and asks if Weebjob is threatening to send Sweet Grass back to the female seminary. This leads to Sweet Potato's saying she always failed in school. Sweet Grass tells Sweet Potato, "I remember how I felt when I saw Weebjob. I didn't have time to love him. He just decided I would be his wife. But later...those feelings always remained unspoken."

Sweet Potato turns to her father and tells him that for once he's being quiet. You can cut, "Ah! Yes, I am" since the monolog would make more sense without it, if given by itself.

1. In this speech, what do you think the playwright really is saying to the audience?

2. What is Weebjob feeling here?

WEEBJOB: Ah! Yes, I am. I was listening to Sweet Grass, and didn't know what to say. I remembered when I went to the Female Seminary for a wife. I had a friend who I went to see, and all the girls out on the lawn made me think it was a place to get a wife. I was thinking of the boarding school for Indian boys... *(Pause)* I like this time of evening. I remember the fingers of the sun across the yard of the boarding school from the canyons and arroyos as evening reached from the parched desert. We couldn't ignore it. We woke up in the morning sweating with the heat. It only intensified during the day. We couldn't ignore the poverty of the school. The dreariness of the land. Our heritage was rich with tradition, and it was taken from us. We had to learn a new way, dry and dull, against our reasoning. I longed for Indian ways just as the others. Christianity wasn't enough. And nothing came to fill the particular hunger we felt. Others grew bitter, later drank and wasted their lives. But I have always felt the closeness of the Great Spirit, and that he would manifest himself to me. Why would I have the hunger if there was nothing to fill it? And in the desolation of the nights, when I could hear other boys cry or moan with nightmares, the vision of the Thunder Hawk came, not the vision, for it was the Thunder Hawk himself. A magnificent bird from the spirit world full of light like a blue, stained glass window in a cathedral. The vine at the window in the winter also reminded me of him. When the land was even deader than it was in summer. The dry vine rattling at the window was like the wings of the Thunder Hawk coming to me right through the walls of the boarding school for Indian boys. It was like the sweat lodge I heard about from the old Indian men before we were taken to school. It seemed to me to be "Canaan" that was talked about in the Book. And this place, too, here where I've lived all these years, where I can do what I want without fear or interference. It is "Canaan." I see the Thunder Hawk to this day. He has never left me. Great Spirit, how can you merge with us, who are mortal in our flesh and bound with error and filled with

weakness? I must go to the squash patch for a while. I feel the wind over me like the presence of the Great Spirit...like the hot shower in the motel in Roswell when William got married and I stayed until the water ran cold and Sweet Grass called for me to get out. *(SWEET GRASS laughs. WEEBJOB goes to the squash patch.)*

Much of the rest of the play shows the wedding, which ends with a wedding guest asking Pick Up where he is taking Sweet Potato for their honeymoon. Pick Up answers: "We're going to hitchhike to Gallup."

Hispanic Theatre

Mexican-American Theatre

Even though the first Spanish-language performance in America probably occurred in a mission in 1567 near what would become Miami, Spanish-language plays became established first in the Southwest beginning in the late 1500s.

Professional theatre began in the early 1800s when Mexican and Spanish actors appeared in the port cities of California and northern Mexico. Even during the Depression, Los Angeles and San Antonio had a number of successful Mexican-American theatres. However, the greatest success in Hispanic theatre in the Southwest was the appearance in 1965 of El Teatro Campesino, the Farm Workers Theatre, which later grew to include Broadway productions. Soon other Mexican-American theatres, playwrights and performers began to gain renown.

Cuban-American Theatre

In the last decade of the nineteenth century, theatre was becoming established in Tampa, catering to immigrants who had entered the country due to the turmoil created by the Cuban War of Independence.

Spanish melodramas and *zarzuelas* were presented regularly in New York and Tampa by Cuban (and other Hispanic groups), later exceeded in popularity only by the Cuban *teatro bufo*, a form of burlesque with stock characters and African-Cuban music and dance. For the most part Cuban theatre consisted of various forms of comedy. The Cuban Revolution of 1959 brought more immigrants to south Florida and other parts of the United States, spawning a type of theatre that dealt with problems in adjusting to a new culture.

In 1966, a group of seven Cuban Americans and Puerto Ricans founded INTAR, (International Arts Relations) to develop new playwrights and present their plays.

Puerto Rican Theatre

Modern theatre began in Puerto Rico in 1938 when the Ateneo Puertorriqueño (Athenaeum or cultural center), under the leadership of Emilio S. Belaval sponsored a contest for plays by Puerto Rican playwrights on Puerto Rican themes.

René Marqués, a member of the group, provided a transition between drama in Puerto Rico and New York. In 1949, he received a

Rockefeller Foundation grant to study playwriting in New York but later returned home to Puerto Rico.

The Spanish Civil War brought many immigrants to New York, and the Puerto Rican population increased as well, giving rise in the late 1960s to what has been referred to as "Nuyorican" theatre. Soon there was also an enormous increase in the number of Hispanic theatre companies and productions. There was also a movement toward *teatro popular*, a type of street theatre that argued for social causes.

Within the last few years, there have been a number of successful Hispanic plays in mainstream theatres. Cuban-American Eduardo Machado's *Floating Islands,* a six-hour long presentation of four interrelated plays, has been particularly successful, as has been José Rivera's *Marisol.*

RANCHO HOLLYWOOD

Carlos Morton

One of the most highly regarded Chicano playwrights is Carlos Morton (his immigrant father took the surname from a billboard advertising Morton Salt). His best-known play is *The Many Deaths of Danny Rosales* (1983), a quasi-documentary, based in part on the 1975 shooting death of Richard Morales at the hands of the Castroville, Texas, sheriff.

Morton also wrote a number of farces, such as *Rancho Hollywood,* which parodies Hollywood's stereotyping of Latinos, blacks, and Native Americans. It is similar in style to Mel Brooks's *Blazing Saddles* in that it involves the making of a movie, which then becomes entwined with "real" life.

In *Rancho Hollywood,* history moves quickly from the early Mexican settlement of California to the present. Characters change into other characters to keep up with the passage of time. Rufus, the slave, becomes Marcus (bringing to mind Marcus Garvey, a black nationalist leader who lived from 1887 to 1940) and later Malcolm (suggestive of militant Black Muslim leader Malcolm X who, in the 1950s and 60s, called for achieving racial equality by "any means necessary").

The play satirizes the idea of stereotypes, and the derogatory terms it uses for people of differing racial backgrounds is meant to make fun of the people who use these terms. It is not by any means meant to make fun of the minorities.

Rancho Hollywood is more important in what it says — that blanket prejudice against minorities is ridiculous — than in its story-line, which is held together by the idea of a movie company's filming a piece called "Ye Olde California Days."

Since it was written in the early 1980s, a few references to television commercials are somewhat outdated. Since characters often change and later become other characters, no ages are given for any of them. We can only guess at approximate ages.

Some of the words and phrases are in Spanish. If you don't know Spanish, maybe a friend can help you with translations and pronunciation.

SCENE 1: THREE FEMALES AND FOUR MALES

Sinmuhow, late teens or 20s

Director, probably 30s

Joaquín, probably 20s

Cameraman, probably 20s

Victoria, probably 40s

Rico, 40s to 50s

Ramona, late teens or early 20s

The play opens with the principals "preparing themselves for their entrances." They are Ramona, a "fiery Latina type"; Joaquín, "a young man dressed as a peon"; Sinmuhow, "a Native-American woman"; Victoria, "an older matronly type, Spanish looking"; and "Rico, a dark debonair older Mexican male." The director is trying to get started with the shooting of a "balcony" scene. Various characters wander in. The following occurs about a page into the script.

1. List all the stereotypes you can find in this scene.

2. What makes this scene humorous? Do you like this sort of humor? Why? Why not?

3. Why does the director want Victoria to enter making a tamale? Why does he ask Ramona to speak with a stronger accent?

4. Of course, none of the action is to be taken seriously. How can you tell that?

5. Do you think it would be more effective to play this scene very broadly or to underplay it as though it were true to life? Why?

6. Amid the humor, Morton is making some important statements. What are they?

SINMUHOW: I am Sinmuhow. *(Entering)*

DIRECTOR: Oh, you're Native American. Look everybody, a real honest-to-goodness Indian! We're going to have such good karma! *(He hugs her.)* Now then, this part calls for a Mexican, but I'm sure you can pass. At the very start of the scene you walk on undulating your hips like so. *(He walks across the set undulating his hips.)*

JOAQUÍN: Yes, and that's my cue. I lift the brim of my sombrero, stick out my tongue, and pant.

DIRECTOR: Good. *(To CAMERAMAN)* Couldn't we put some fruit on her head? You know, then she could do the cha-cha-cha.

CAMERAMAN: That's old hat.

DIRECTOR: All right, forget it. Who's next?

CAMERAMAN: Victoria the maid. *(Enter VICTORIA)*

VICTORIA: I was under the impression I was supposed to be her *[Ramona's]* mother.

DIRECTOR: You are, dear, but you're also the maid. Aren't all mothers? Johnny, what is she supposed to be doing?

CAMERAMAN: *(Reading script)* It says here, "enter making a tamale."

DIRECTOR: Oh, how ethnic. Well, where's your tamale? You little hot tamale you! *(Laughing at his own joke)* Cut to a long shot.

VICTORIA: *(Pulling out a fake tamale)* Ay, que ridículo.

DIRECTOR: Great! You speak Spanish! Throw in a few words every once in a while. Doesn't matter what you say, just as long as it sounds good. Give me your line.

VICTORIA: Ay Ramona, forget that no count Cisco, he is no good for you!

DIRECTOR: More accent!

RAMONA: Ay Mamá, I lub heen, he sets my heart on fi-errrrr.

DIRECTOR: What happens then?

CAMERAMAN: Her debonair, slightly greying Spanish grandee father enters cracking his whip and drinking tequila.

DIRECTOR: Father! Father! Where's the Father?

RICO: Ay voy, I'm coming!

DIRECTOR: These people! *(To CAMERAMAN who nods in agreement)*

You'd think this was the land of mañana! *(JOAQUÍN gets up to stretch.)*

VICTORIA: He's here!

RICO: Excuse me, I was getting made up. *(He enters with an excess of white powder on his face. The DIRECTOR does not really see him.)*

DIRECTOR: Let's go! We have a tight schedule! [...]

CAMERAMAN: Places! Places! *(JOAQUÍN squats back into place.)* Quiet! Quiet on the set! "Ye Olde California Days," take one.

DIRECTOR: Lights! Camera! Wait. *(He runs up and places a plastic rose between RAMONA'S teeth.)* Action! [...]

RAMONA: *(Stamping her feet and clapping her hands)* Olé! O, dis can nut go on. Wear es my sultry Cisco? [...]

VICTORIA: *(She drops her tamale as she enters.)* Ramona, forget dat no count Cisco, he es no goot for you.

RAMONA: Ay Mamá! You dropped your tamale. But I love heem, he puts my hard on fi-eerrrrr.

VICTORIA: Well, put de fi-errrrr out! He es un bandido, un deses-perado! If your Papá finds out he weeel keeel you!

RICO: *(Enters cracking his whip and drinking tequila from a bottle.)* Andale! Andale! Arriba! Arriba! *(Like SPEEDY GONZALEZ, like TRINI LOPEZ trilling and shouting)* Ajúa! Trlllllingg!

DIRECTOR: Cut! Cut! *(To Cameraman)* Has Central Casting gone color blind! I asked for a white Spanish grandee and they give me a dark farmworker!

VICTORIA: ¡Qué insulto!

RICO: Por eso me tardé tanto. Me pusieron todo este polvo.

DIRECTOR: Hey, no offense, fellah, but you don't look very Spanish. You're supposed to be Ramona's father, the Spanish grandee.

RICO: Sir, I don't understand, even if I am as dark as a Moor, I could still be Ramona's father.

VICTORIA: That's right, Ramona is a mestiza.

DIRECTOR: A what?

VICTORIA: A mestiza. Half and half. If I, as her mother, am fair, and the father is dark, then the child is like café con leche.

RAMONA: I've never been described that way before.

VICTORIA: Yes, but that is what the Mexican people are, a mixture of Spanish and Indian.

RICO: And Arab and Jewish and African....

DIRECTOR: That is very quaint, that is very informative. But this film is supposed to be about the Spanish Californios!

RICO: Mr. Director, with all due respect, I am afraid you have little conception of the Californio reality. The people of that time were Mexican, not Spanish.

RAMONA: Jed, honey, listen to these people, they're trying to tell you something.

CAMERAMAN: It says here in the script that Ramona's father is "a Spanish grandee type, representative of the early aristocratic Californios."

RICO: But did you know that many of the founding families of the City of Los Angeles were black? The last Mexican governor of California was a mulatto. His name was Pio Pico.

RAMONA: Who told you that?

RICO: I read it in a history book. They showed photos of him.

VICTORIA: That's right. All that stuff about the Spanish is pure bunk!

RICO: Look, I'm sure if you approached this film a bit more realistically, by doing some research, you'd find I could do this part.

DIRECTOR: All right! Have you all had your little says now? If you people ever want to work in this town again, you'll play your parts exactly the way I tell you to. Or you will never work anywhere in Hollywood again! Let's go! *(He exits followed by the CAMERAMAN.)*

SCENE 2: TWO FEMALES AND ONE MALE

Victoria, probably 40s

Rico, 40s to 50s

Ramona, late teens or early 20s

The actors say they're tired of playing demeaning roles. Victoria says that the old times must have been wonderful. Rico agrees but says the people then were living on borrowed time; the Indians were attacking the settlements. But, Victoria says, that would be solved in time since "we would all become one race." Maybe so, Rico agrees, but still there would be constant bickering between those in the North and those in the South — as shown in his dislike of Joaquín. Victoria is referring to Ramona and Joaquín in the opening line.

1. What is the main source of conflict or disagreement among the characters in this scene? What is at its basis?

2. Why do you suppose Rico looks down on Joaquín?

3. Why is it important to Rico to be thought of as Spanish? What sort of general attitude is this satirizing?

RICO: [...] [H]e is not to set foot in this house again!

RAMONA: Why do you dislike Joaquín so much? Aside from the fact he is from the North?

RICO: I'll tell you why. He drinks, swears, reads suggestive books, shoots his pistols in the air, duels and plots insurrections. Is that enough?!

VICTORIA: *(Aside to RAMONA)* Just like your father did when he was young.

RAMONA: Good God in heaven!

RICO: And there she goes, using the name of God in vain again!

RAMONA: Why don't you admit the real reason you dislike him is because he is in the forefront of steering a new and independent course for us Californios.

RICO: There she goes, using that word again – Californio!

VICTORIA: But Rico, it's just a word the young people use to describe themselves nowadays.

RICO: Not good enough to call themselves Mexicanos como sus padres.

VICTORIA: Don't you remember we used to call ourselves "Criollos" to distinguish us from the Españoles?

RICO: That was yesterday. Today we are Mexican. And we shall always remain Mexican. To call ourselves anything else is treason. I am the governor of this territory and I refuse to hear that word in my house!

VICTORIA: You are as unbending as a mountain; no wonder all the youth are rebelling.

RAMONA: There's some other reason why Papá hates Joaquín so much. Why don't you come out with it!

RICO: Mira, Mira! Don't speak to me in that tone of voice. For one thing, his people are barely gente de razón. They are but one generation removed from the savages.

RAMONA: Papá, with all due respect, you claim to dislike Joaquín because of his lower-class origins, yet mother tells me your grandparents were poor shepherds of the humblest class.

(VICTORIA is making frantic gestures and shaking her head "no.")

RICO: So, your aristocratic mother, descendant of the conquista-

103

dores, told you that, eh?

VICTORIA: Your father comes from good stock, dear, good sound stock.

RICO: Yes, there's no comparison between myself and that young rogue. Why, he's practically a coyote, a half breed.

RAMONA: You're calling him a coyote! What are you? What am I?

VICTORIA: Ramona, show your father more respect!

RAMONA: I see now, you dislike him because he is not "Spanish."

RICO: He's also the black sheep of the family, he is, esa bola de indios...

RAMONA: Well, let me tell you something, that "indio" asked me to marry him and I said "yes!"

VICTORIA: Why, Ramona, how improper! You know that the parents have to be consulted before a girl receives a proposal of marriage!

RICO: You will do no such thing!

RAMONA: Yes I will!

RICO: Get me a switch! I will beat her within a very inch of her life! Listen to me, young lady, you will marry only within your own class! You will marry someone of pure Spanish blood.

RAMONA: What difference does it make! You're not Spanish, I'm not Spanish!

RICO: Yes you are. Call yourself anything else and no gentleman will ever ask for your hand in marriage. Ramona, you don't know prejudice like we do.

VICTORIA: Listen to your father, he means well.

RICO: When I married your mother in Mexico City, her relatives looked down on her because I looked like a Moor!

VICTORIA: It's true, hija, that's why we came back to California.

RICO: I don't want the same thing happening to you!

RAMONA: My God, don't you see, you're being a hypocrite!

RICO: *(Raising his hand to slap her. Victoria restrains him.)* **Why can't you be like the little girl I once knew, who used to sit on my knee and listen to stories of why the sea is salty, or why the full moon has the face of a rabbit.**

RAMONA: I don't want to hear any more stories!

RICO: I used to tell her the reason people got dark is because they drank too much chocolate. But you're right, those days are past. Still, I have the final word in this house. You shall not see Joaquín again. I shall banish him to the farthest corners of this territory.

SCENE 3: FOUR MALES AND THREE FEMALES

Director, probably 40s

Cameraman, probably 20s

Tonta, late teens to 20s

Ramona, probably late teens to early 20s

Joaquín, probably 20s

Victoria, probably 40s

Rico, 40s to 50s

Victoria says that no matter who Ramona marries, her children could be black. Then she says to Rico: "You never told her your grandmother was a mulatto, did you?" He asks why he should tell her of inconsequential matters concerning her lineage. He says he never denied his origins. "My grandmother may have been a mulatto but my parents were mestizos. I, in turn, have become a gente de razón, a citizen with all the rights and benefits thereof." Victoria answers, "Where else but California could you begin life as a Negro and end up as an Español?"

Tonta announces the arrival of a clipper ship, and Victoria decides that they should invite the captain for dinner and dancing. In an aside to the audience Tonta says, "A mulatto, his grandmother. I knew it! That woolly headed old vieja was as black as Cleopatra!" The director breaks into the scene saying he "loves it!" The cameraman replies that the father seems "somewhat of a racist."

The director then decides he'll play the role of the captain, who is the star of the show and that the Cameraman will be his slave Rufus (later Marcus and then Malcolm). The Cameraman suggests that Jed (the captain) begin by singing a popular song of the day. He sings "Oh, Susanna," changing the destination to "Californee."

Jed then teaches Rufus "important" Spanish words and phrases such as "bajas intereses de crédito" (low-interest rates on credit). This is because Californios love buying on credit, Jed says. They are "all show" and love bright colors. He warns Rufus, however, to be careful because the people will "steal you blind." Rufus answers, "Just like you, eh, Massa Jed?"

Jed says the people, the California Mexicans are lazy and stupid, depending "almost entirely on Yankee clipper ships." He reads a passage from Richard Henry Dana's *Two Years Before the Mast,* which says: "The Californio men are generally indolent." He reads further that they "are of a harmless disposition, fond of spiritous liquors, [and] care little for their children. The women have but little virtue..." Jed calls the people "greasers" and Jed asks why. While combing his own greasy hair, Jed answers, "'Cause they got greasy hair and they eat greasy food." He says "They are a mixture of Spanish and Aztec, the latter of whom ripped the hearts out of their victims, made sandwiches of them and sold them on street corners." He warns Rufus that this is the reason "you have to be careful what you eat" or you'll end up with "Montezuma's revenge" (diarrhea). Jed then promises that if he makes enough money on the trip, he'll give Rufus his freedom.

If you wish, you can eliminate the first four speeches and begin with Tonta's second speech, "Pinche gente!..."

1. Why do you suppose so much of the movie is "ad-libbed"?

2. In what way is this scene exaggeratedly melodramatic? How might you try to play this sort of thing?

3. Why do you think Joaquín says Rico cannot be a bigot?

4. What is the point of Joaquín's hiding in the way that he does?

5. Why does Rico want to leave loose change in the bowl? What is Morton's reason for including this?

6. Why does Rico demand that Ramona dance? Why does she not want to?

DIRECTOR: *(Voice Off-stage)* **What's the next scene? Where are we?**

CAMERAMAN: Back at the Rancho. The gay Californios are preparing for the night's festivities. *(Voice Off-stage)*

TONTA: Californios didn't prepare anything. We servants did it all. *(Entering)*

DIRECTOR: Okay, Okay. Pretend you're making tortillas or something. And, uh, talk to yourself, complaining.

TONTA: *(Improvising)* **Pinche gente! Puras parrandas! They have to have a fandango every night. Why they hardly pause for an earthquake and continue right on dancing when it stops!** *(TONTA stops, hears voices off to the side, sees JOAQUÍN and RAMONA entering the garden, stops to listen.)*

RAMONA: Joaquín! I'm so glad you're here, querido!

JOAQUÍN: Your father has banished me to a military outpost in Sonoma.

RAMONA: Take me with you, I will go with you this very night!

JOAQUÍN: Out of the question. It's too dangerous. Russians to the north, Yankees to the east, British pirates.

RAMONA: Well, then we'll leave the country. We'll go to Mexico or Europe. Someplace where we can be together.

JOAQUÍN: I will never leave California. It is my home.

RAMONA: Well then...Joaquín, I thought we were going to elope tonight. I even packed my bags!

JOAQUÍN: Ramona, mi amor, we must respect your father's wishes. I will work very hard and rise up through the ranks. I will repel the invaders from our land. Then he will respect me.

RAMONA: He will never respect you, Joaquín. You see, my father dislikes you because of your skin color, because you look like an indio.

JOAQUÍN: Ramona, how can you say such a thing about your father? That's preposterous! Your father may be an old crustacean because of his politics, but a bigot he is not.

RAMONA: Joaquín, I'm speaking the truth. Listen to me, we must leave him and start our own lives. *(TONTA starts walking towards them.)*

JOAQUÍN: Shhh, someone is coming. I must go! Promise you'll wait for me!

RAMONA: Yes, I will, of course, but don't you see...my father will never have anything to do with you because you are not Spanish.

JOAQUÍN: Shhh, not another word. We are all the same raza. We will work things out. We always have before. *(He starts to leave but rushes back to RAMONA.)* ¡Ay Ramona, no voy a poder vivir sin ti! *(He turns to go and crashes into TONTA.)*

TONTA: Oye! If Don Rico sees you he'll make chorizo out of you!

JOAQUÍN: I'm leaving! I'm leaving! Querida, adiós. *(JOAQUÍN hears footsteps coming in the direction of his exit.)* Who's that? One of the guests?

TONTA: By the sound of the footsteps it is Don Rico himself! He's probably loading his revolver!

RAMONA: Quick! Hide! My parents are coming! *(JOAQUÍN makes desperate motions.)* Behind the pillar, under the table, anywhere! *(Depending upon the set JOAQUÍN can become a statue, lamp, fountain, etc.)* Tonta, cover for us, please!

TONTA: Why should I? You live in a dream world. Your life is full of intrigues and little masquerades. But who do you think gets stuck with all the mierda?

RAMONA: Tonta, ¡por favor! *(RAMONA sees that JOAQUÍN has tried to turn into a statue. She grabs him and exits opposite RICO and VICTORIA's entrance.)*

RICO: *(Entering)* Who were you talking to?

TONTA: Nobody. You know me. I'm a little loca. Sometimes I talk to myself.

VICTORIA: *(Who was not fooled)* Tonta, be sure to prepare a room for the captain of the Yankee clipper ship. He may stay the night.

TONTA: Shall I leave the pile of loose change in a bowl in his room as customary?

RICO: Yes, yes, of course. Show him some of that famous Californio hospitality!

VICTORIA: But I thought we were in debt!

RICO: Oh, this is just small change. Tonta, call my daughter to the living room. I want her to dance for our guests.

TONTA: Si, Señor.

RICO: **Ah, I see that my guests have arrived.** *(RICO goes off into the wing and welcomes the guests in the next room.)*

VICTORIA: *(Taking TONTA aside)* **What did they say?** *(While VICTORIA and TONTA are talking in private to the side, RAMONA enters with JOAQUÍN dressed in a ludicrous disguise. They kiss, he exits.)*

RICO: *(Voice Off-stage)* **Welcome! Welcome all to Rancho Madera Acebo!** *(Music starts playing, RICO enters On-stage.)* **Ah, Ramona, there you are. I'm glad to see that your spirits have lifted. Come, dear, dance for our guests.** *(Applause is heard, shouting.)*

RAMONA: Oh, no, Papá, please!

RICO: Yes, you will! *(Lights out except for spot on RAMONA. She dances to taped music, with the audience being the guests.)*

SCENE 4: ONE MALE AND ONE FEMALE

Tonta (Sinmuhow), late teens or 20s
Rufus, probably 30s

As Romana performs a dance, Jed and Rufus enter and are welcomed by Rico. Jed and Rico speak in a combination of Spanish and English, with Jed often using pseudo-Spanish words. Ramona agrees to translate until Rico learns English, which, Jed says, should be "any minute now."

When Rico asks why Jed is in California, he says to sell some beads and do some sightseeing. Rico asks Jed why he hasn't beaten his poor slave. Jed says, "Why, el como mi sono," ("Why, he is like my son" — in pseudo-Spanish) and Rufus says in an aside, "We probably related along de way."

Rico asks if Jed would like something to eat, "salt carne" (meat)? Corn pan (cornbread)? Jed asks about the availability of a Taco Bell. Rico then inquires about how long Jed will be in California. He answers, "What year is this? 1842? Oh, a couple of centuries, at least."

Rico declares the party over, angry, he says, because Jed apparently asked in a "tone of derision" "why there were so few white people like us in the territory." Besides, Jed is from Texas, "the same Tejas they stole in 1836" and "which now is a slave state." Victoria tells Ramona she knows Joaquín has been there and she should put him out of her mind.

Tonta has been asked to show Rufus where to sleep.

1. What provides the parody and humor in this scene?
2. Is the use of recent slang effective here? Why? Why not? Do you understand Rufus's reference to becoming mayor of Los Angeles?
3. Do you like this scene? Would you enjoy playing one of these roles? Why? Why not?

TONTA: This is the barn, this is where you sleep, Mr. Nigaro.

RUFUS: My name isn't "Nigaro," it's Rufus.

TONTA: Isn't that what the white man called you, "Nigaro"?

RUFUS: Yes, but don't you call me that. My real name is Rufus, Rufus Smith.

TONTA: Smith, isn't that the white man's name?

RUFUS: A slave doesn't really have a choice. Your last name is what your master's name is. I've been bought and sold three times. My last name was Jefferson, but I was born with the name Washington. Come to think of it, I may be related to the father of the United States. Say, I heard them calling you "Tonta." What kind of name is that? Indian name?

TONTA: No, it's a Spanish name.

RUFUS: Are you an Indian? What kind of Indian are you?

TONTA: I am a Kemyia.

RUFUS: Keem-aaa-yaaa?

TONTA: Kemyia. People who hunt by the cliffs in the morning.

RUFUS: How come you aren't hunting in the cliffs anymore?

TONTA: The white man came.

RUFUS: Oh. What does Tonta mean?

TONTA: *(Ignoring the question)* Long ago, when my people dwelt on this land, my grandfather, Chacupe-Chanush was the chief. We lived in wickiups and gathered berries and netted fish from the sea.

RUFUS: That sounds very familiar....

TONTA: But then the Holy Fathers came and converted us to Christianity. Are you a Catholic, or do you still believe in the mumbo jumbo?

RUFUS: No, girl, I'm a Protestant.

TONTA: A Protestant! Oh, good night! *(Turning to leave and crossing herself)*

RUFUS: Say, wait a minute, stay here and talk a bit, we have a lot in common.

TONTA: Oh, no, you're a Protestant! And besides that, you're a slave. I'm a free woman!

RUFUS: Now, now, now. Don't you put on no fancy airs with me. I suppose you cook and clean for them Californios from morning until night because you love them so much. You slave just like I do!

TONTA: No! Slavery is no more. Don Rico, how do you say, "abolished" it?

RUFUS: There are different kinds of slavery. Maybe you don't call it the same thing, but it doesn't make it any better. Huh, just because they made a Negro like Don Rico the governor, don't mean nothing.

TONTA: Don Rico is not a Nigaro. He is Spanish.

RUFUS: Girl, you are pulling my leg. Your Don Rico is blacker than my black fanny and you're telling me he's Spanish! Oh Lord, don't make me laugh! Besides, what do you care what he is, he still treats you like a dog!

TONTA: Very well, Mr. Rufus, have it your way. Perhaps you'll stay around California and become governor yourself someday.

RUFUS: Well, maybe I will. But first I'll start by becoming the mayor of Los Angeles.

TONTA: But for the time being, Señor Alcalde, here you sleep...with the mules!

RUFUS: Dang blast it! Can't get no respect! *(Getting ready his bedroll)* I'm not going to be sleeping in barns all my life, no Ma'am. Matter of fact, right after this trip, if I make Master Jed a whole pile of money, I'm going to be free. He promised! He promised.

TONTA: Don't believe a word they say, Rufus. I worked all my life for Don Rico, but I'm still just a dumb maid to him. You know what Tonta means? I'll tell you. Tonta means stupid. That's what they call us. Don't let them make a tonto out of you, Rufus! *(She exits.)*

SCENE 5: ONE MALE AND ONE FEMALE

Jed, probably 40s

Ramona, probably late teens or early 20s

This scene follows directly after the preceding.

1. Why do you suppose Morton mixed up the past and the present so much in this scene?

2. Why does Ramona ask Jed if he's ill?

3. Parts of this scene are meant as irony? Which are they? What makes them ironic?

4. What sort of person is Jed? Ramona? Of course, they are exaggerated, but which traits would you try most to emphasize if you were playing either of the two in this scene? Why?

JED: *(On another part of the stage, RAMONA is seen standing on her balcony, dreaming of JOAQUÍN. JED approaches her.)* **Buenas noches, Señorita.**

RAMONA: Oh! Good night, Mr. Smith! *(Turning to leave)*

JED: Please, don't go inside yet! I have been trying to orient myself geographically. Could you tell me the name of the mountains to the north there?

RAMONA: Las Montañas de San Bernardino.

JED: Saint Bernard. And what's the name of the valley down there?

RAMONA: El Valle de San Fernando.

JED: Saint Ferdinand. There was an unusual amount of smog today.

RAMONA: Esmog? What is esmog?

JED: Smog is what you get when General Motors, Firestone and the oil companies buy up the Electric Trolley Car system.

RAMONA: Oh. *(Not wishing to appear unworldly)* **We are very isolated from the rest of the world, Mr. Smith. We have no, uh, electric systems, yet. We do have the natural beauty of the terrain.**

JED: Oh, yes, I can't wait to go to Disneyland. Señorita, how far are the pyramids from here?

RAMONA: Oh, Señor, you are mistaken. We have no pyramids here in La Cuidad de La Reina de Los Angeles del Rio Porciúncula.

JED: Is that the full name of this city? Is it not rather long? Why don't you just call it Los Angeles or L.A.?

RAMONA: [...] Los Angeles, the city of the Angels, sounds heavenly.

JED: The city of Angels...the Lost Angeles! My God! I see it all now!

RAMONA: What do you see?

JED: It's the City of the Lost Angels, smoldering, there in the dark, the poisoned fumes, embers burning, the maws of Hell!

RAMONA: Hell?

JED: There amidst the metallic skyscrapers, smoke! And over there, in the east side, fire!

RAMONA: I see nothing! No smoke, no fire!

JED: [...] Can't you hear the noise, that awful droning, the machines whining, sirens howling...and men, the lost angels, battling each other like demi-gods!

RAMONA: Mr. Smith, are you ill? Shall I call for a physician?

JED: My mind! My mind! It's burning!

RAMONA: What shall I do? What shall I do?

JED: Water! Water! *(RAMONA dumps water from a flowerpot on JED's head.)* Thank you, I needed that.[1]

RAMONA: Are you well?

JED: Yes, yes, just a momentary burst of apocalyptic prophecy. I'll be all right. I have fits, er, visions.

RAMONA: You certainly possess a fertile imagination.

JED: I'll be okay.

RAMONA: Tell me, Mr. Smith, what vision or future do you see for yourself here in our fair city?

JED: I want to see commercial possibilities, not scenes of destruction.

RAMONA: We have need of more capital.

JED: All I want is a little piece of land. Orange County. I'll develop, but modestly, in harmony with the environment. A few condominiums, 7-11s, Dunkin Donuts....

RAMONA: We have a very liberal immigration policy, there being but six thousand of us Californios, and so much land for the taking. My father, the governor, has given many land grants away quite recently.

JED: Your father, what does he think of us Yankees?

RAMONA: He likes Mexicanized Yankees the best. Many of your people have come here and adopted our ways.

JED: I'll get me a sombrero and serape.... [...]

JED: Say, what does your father think about California uniting with the United States?

RAMONA: God forbid! Don't let him hear you say that. He's a staunch Mexicano all the way. But I know that someday California will be free to decide her own destiny.

JED: You need help, you need someone to stand by your side.

RAMONA: We can handle our own affairs.

JED: No you can't! There's too many wolves and bears around. Look at the Ruskies, why they're already in Alaska. Next thing you know they'll be in El Salvador. You need the old Red and White

---

[1]A line used in a TV commercial for shaving lotion.

and Blue beside you.

RAMONA: What can your country offer us?

JED: Uncle Sam can give you security and prosperity. Unite with us and you'll have apple pie and rock 'n roll, Mickey Mouse and the L.A.P.D.

RAMONA: We have no need of these things. We have our land and livestock, our stately churches and our merry fandangos, all of this here in Rancho Madera Acebo.

JED: Rancho Mad Era Azebo? What does that mean?

RAMONA: Literally, in English, the Ranch of the Wood Holly.

JED: Wood Holly? Woody Holly? Holly Woody. Hollywood! Hollywood! I see it all now!

RAMONA: Are you having another momentary apocalyptic fit?

JED: Hollywood and Vine! Grauman's Chinese Theatre. The Brown Derby! Motion pictures! Panavision!

RAMONA: Should I get more water? Your eyes, they look like shooting stars!

JED: Stars! Stars! Movie stars! I'll make movies.

RAMONA: Un momento, por favor, slow down.

JED: *(Climbing up on her balcony)* **Let me explain.** *(Pulling out a photograph)* **See this photograph of my mother, someday we'll be able to run thousands of these together into moving pictures. We'll project them on a screen and be able to control millions of people's minds!**

RAMONA: This is your mother? Where was this photograph taken?

JED: In Europe, her name was Goldie, she's dead now. I'm her only son. Promised I would carry her picture around with me forever, but that's another story.

SCENE 6: THREE MALES AND TWO FEMALES

Rico, 40s to 50s

Jed, probably 40s

Rufus, probably 20s

Victoria, probably 40s

Ramona, probably late teens to early 20s

Jed asks Ramona to marry him. She says she is promised to Joaquín, but Jed says he still wants a kiss. She pushes him over the balcony.

On another part of the stage, Rico is writing to the Mexican president, telling him he fears invasion from the United States of the North. At the same time Jed appears at another writing desk and announces that the people of California cannot defend themselves, and so the area could easily fall "into the hands of the Anglo-Saxon race." He tells the audience: "Therefore, I say, let us strike now and free this blessed country from Mexican tyranny."

1. Do you find this scene humorous? Why? Why not?

2. What sorts of stereotypes are being presented here?

3. Who do you side with in this conflict? Why?

4. Why does Rico change his mind about Joaquín?

5. This scene ends the first act of the play. Do you think this is an effective ending? Why? Why not?

RICO: *(To the audience as well)* **The Departmental Treasury is exhausted. We have no standing garrison other than volunteers. Please, send money, men, and material at once. God and Liberty, Rio Rico, Los Angeles, California. May 25, 1846.**

JED: **We'll take the capital, Monterey, and then by ship secure San Diego Bay.**

RICO: *(To Jed)* **By what right do you have to do this?**

JED: **Manifest Destiny!**

RICO: **Thievery!**

JED: **You stole it from the Indians.**

RICO: **You shall not have it! Do you intend to pursue your insidious goal of establishing slavery in California like you did in Texas?**

JED: **No! California will be free! Rufus! Rufus!** *(RICO and JED are face to face.)*

RUFUS: *(Running in with a rifle, followed by TONTA)* **Here I is!**

JED: **Cover my back, boy. Make sure it's a fair fight. You stick with me and you're free, hear?**

RUFUS: **I hear you.**

JED: **August, 1846.** *(To the audience)* **We've met little resistance.**

RICO: **Mexicanos! Mexicanos! Do not fail your country now! Death to the invaders!** *(VICTORIA and RAMONA enter.)*

VICTORIA: **¡Rico, estamos contigo!**

RICO: **Ramona, send word to Joaquín. Tell him to come quickly!**

RAMONA: **Papá, will you let him marry me?!**

RICO: **Of course! He's one of us. He's a Californio.** *(RAMONA kisses her father, then goes to whisper a message in TONTA's ear. Exit TONTA.)*

JED: **Very well, shall we commence?**

RICO: **After you.** *(The two combatants stand back to back, pistols in hand. There is a very dream-like quality to this scene, performed to a slow minuet.)*

JED: *(As they pace away from each other)* **Quite obviously, my dear sir, you are incapable of governing this territory.**

RICO: **Excuse me, but what do you know of civilization? We founded universities in Mexico City before you landed your motley crew on the Mayflower.**

119

JED: Yes, my dear sir, but we wrote the book on democracy. You merely copied us, and a cheap imitation at that.

RICO: You deceived us in Texas. We welcomed you as equals and you stabbed us in the back.

JED: Remember the Alamo!

RICO: Racist!

JED: Half breed!

RICO: Gringo!

JED: Greaser! You're done fur. General Kearny, who just took all of New Mexico without a fight, is on his way to San Diego.

RICO: Wrong! Kearny was stopped at San Pasqual by my brother's California Lancers, the best horsemen in the world. Kearny's steers. The rest are besieged and are forced to eat their mules!

JED: No! Everyone knows greasers are afraid to fight!

RICO: *(Shooting him down)* What do you think of Mexican cowardice now? Get back from whence you came, Yanqui!

JED: Not so fast. You may have won the battle...but look, look! All around you!

RICO: I see nothing. *(William Tell Overture)* What's that?

JED: Listen! Listen! *(Confusion on the Mexican side as jets roar overhead)* Up there, in the sky, it's a bird, it's a...Stealth Bomber! *(Jets shake the set.)* It's the United States Air Force!

RICO: Air Force?

JED: Oh, you primitives! If only you knew the glory that awaits us! *(Bombs drop. Everyone but JED runs for cover.)* Surrender! Surrender! Or face total annihilation! If you stand in the way of progress, we'll drop the atom bomb, so help us God! *(Aside)* After all, they'se only colored people!

RICO: *(Dazed and confused, RICO hands over his pistol.)* ¡Mi pistola!

JED: At last! She's mine, all mine! California! *(While VICTORIA consoles RICO, JED grabs RAMONA.)* California!

RAMONA: No, no, no! Let me go! Let me go!

RICO: You can't have my daughter!

JED: I do believe I've taken her already! *(Handing him a document)* Sign, sir, sign the surrender at Cahuenga Pass, January, 1847. *(After which he carries RAMONA away kicking and screaming)*

California, here I come! Right back where I started from!
(He exits.)

RAMONA: **My name is not California! It's Ramona!** *(Exits.)*

RICO: **¡Dios mío, qué desgracia!**

JOAQUÍN: *(Rushing in)* **Don Rico, Doña Victoria, the gringos...**

RICO: **We know. We lost the war.**

JOAQUÍN: **Where is Ramona?**

VICTORIA: **The gringo took her!**

JOAQUÍN: **Oh, my God! Which way?** *(They point; he exits.)*

SCENE 7: THREE MALES AND TWO FEMALES

Jed, probably 40s

Rico, 40s to 50s

Ramona, probably late teens or early 20s

Victoria, probably 40s

Joaquín, probably 20s

The second act opens with Joaquín telling Rico that "we have lost the myth" of the unconquerable "conquistadores." The difference, he says, is that the Spaniards brought a statue of the Virgin de Guadalupe to California, but the gringos brought the dollar. Before leaving, Joaquín says that the next time he appears he will not be wearing sheep's clothing.

Victoria tells Rico not to be despondent and suggests they look for gold. He says there is none, but Victoria finds a nugget. Shortly afterward Jed and Ramona enter.

1. Why does Ramona at first not recognize her parents?

2. There is a lot of exaggeration in this scene. What can you find that is exaggerated? In what way might you try to point this up if you were playing one of the characters?

3. What is the point of Joaquín's coming back as "El Zorrillo"?

4. Why do you suppose Ramona has stayed with Jed after he kidnapped her?

5. Do you like this scene? Why? Why not?

JED: *(Pulling out a gun)* **All right! All right! The Miner Forty-Niner and his Darlin' Clementine run the claim jumpers off their stake!**

RICO: *(Not recognizing them)* **I beg your pardon, Señor, but we found it first.**

JED: **I don't care, you are a foreigner. Only natives can mine here.**

RICO: **I beg your pardon, Señor, my family has been here for over three generations.**

JED: **Clementine, what's he look like to you?**

RAMONA: **Faintly familiar....**

JED: **Well, he looks like a damn greaser to me!** *(Cocking his gun)* **Now, for the last time, if you want to mine here you have to pay a Foreign Miner's tax.**

RICO: **But I told you, I am a native Californio.** *(JED points the gun at him.)*

JED: **You still look like a greaser from Sonora or Chile to me.**

RICO: **Señor, I want no trouble. I will pay the tax.**

JED: **That'll be three hundred dollars per month.**

RAMONA: **Three hundred dollars! But we won't be able to make a profit!**

JED: **Exactly.**

RICO: **This is our claim! We won't leave without a fight!**

JED: *(Shooting at him)* **That's okay with me, greaser!**

RAMONA: *(As RICO shoots back)* **Help, help, help! It's an insurrection!**

JED: **Don't give it any legitimacy! Your line is "help, the bandidos are robbing us!"**

RAMONA: **Oh, yes, "kill the Frito Bandido!"**[2]

RICO: **I am not a bandido. But you are turning me into a revolucionario!**

JED: **Kill the terrorists!**

RICO: **¡Viva Villa!**[3]

RAMONA: **Wait, Jed, I know that man....**

JED: **Don't worry, we've got 'em surrounded. We'll starve them out!**

RICO: **I have run out of ammunition! Estamos perdidos.**

---

[2]Refers to a cartoon caricature of a Mexican bandit in a TV commercial; many objected to the portrayal on the grounds that it was racist.

[3]Pancho Villa was a Mexican revolutionary leader.

VICTORIA: Is there no one who can save us from this fate?

RAMONA: No, don't shoot! He's my... *(Just as JED is about to shoot RICO we hear the strains of "Zacatecas.")*

VICTORIA: Could it be? *(Enter JOAQUÍN dressed like Zorro.)*

JED: Who is that?

RICO: El Zorro!

RAMONA: The fox!

JOAQUÍN: No, it is I, El Zorrillo!

JED: El Zorrillo? What's that mean?

RAMONA: Run! Run for your life! *(Running in the direction of her parents)* **El Zorrillo means...**

JOAQUÍN: *(Throwing a skunk at JED)* **Take that...you stinking Gringo!**

RAMONA: Skunk!

JOAQUÍN: *(As he exits through the audience)* **¡El Zorrillo! ¡El Zorrillo!**

JED: Oh, my God!

RICO: Who was that masked man? He saved our lives!

SCENE 8: ONE MALE AND ONE FEMALE

Marcus (Rufus), probably 20s

Gerónima (Tonta), late teens or 20s

The action switches from the last scene directly to this one.

1. Why does Morton have the characters change names in this scene? Why do they not know each other at first? Why have they changed so much?

2. Point out the characters' use of sarcasm in this scene.

3. Why does Marcus trust Gerónima enough to give her a rifle? Why does she then turn on him?

4. Why do you suppose Morton included the line, "I had no choice. I had no job, it was the only thing I could do" in answer to Gerónima's accusation that he killed her people.

GERÓNIMA: Black man, what is your name?

MARCUS: Marcus.

GERÓNIMA: My name is Gerónima. Let us not fight each other. Get back on your horse and leave these hills.

MARCUS: I don't know...

GERÓNIMA: Oh, I see. Did Kemosabe promise you forty acres of OUR LAND?

MARCUS: No, yes, I mean he did, but that ain't the reason...

GERÓNIMA: Is Kemosabe going to free you like Lincoln again?

MARCUS: You pretty damn smart, for an injun!

GERÓNIMA: What is that supposed to mean? Just because I am red and did not go to Booker T. Washington University, you think I am stupid?

MARCUS: All right, look. I'm going to put down one of my rifles and just walk out of here.

GERÓNIMA: Thank you. We will make good use of that rifle.

MARCUS: I hope some day we can talk under more pleasant circumstances. You know, there was a time once in the Florida Everglades when the Seminoles and some runaway slaves got together... [...]

GERÓNIMA: *(During this time GERÓNIMA has managed to come up and over to surprise MARCUS.)* Hold it, soldier!

MARCUS: Oh, Lordy!

GERÓNIMA: *(Cocking her pistol)* One move and you go to the sacred grounds.

MARCUS: Look, I had you cornered, but I let you go. I gave you a rifle!

GERÓNIMA: I want to see how black you really are. Take off that uniform. Go on, strip! Black or white, soldier, you killed many of my people.

MARCUS: *(Taking off his clothes)* I had no choice, I had no job, it was the only thing I could do! *(MARCUS throws his clothes in GERÓNIMA's face and attacks her. They wrestle to the ground with MARCUS on top.)*

GERÓNIMA: Rufus!

MARCUS: Tonta! It's you! I almost killed you. What are you doing out here?

126

GERÓNIMA: I ran away to join the free tribes. Rufus, they're killing all of my people, just like the buffalo.

MARCUS: God, I'm so sorry! Did I hurt you? I'm so glad I found you again. Gerónima, I like that much better than Tonta.

GERÓNIMA: What are you going to do now, Marcus? Take me back to the white man?

SCENE 9: TWO MALES AND TWO FEMALES

Jed, probably 40s

Rico, 40s to 50s

Ramona, late teens or 20s

Victoria, probably 40s

Jed asks Rico to sign the Treaty of Guadalupe Hidalgo. Rico asks if Mexicans will be accorded the same rights as other citizens. Jed says they will, so Rico swears to uphold the Constitution of the United States.

Rico agrees to Jed's request of Ramona's hand in marriage, and they are married immediately. Rico is about to leave when Jed stops him and asks him to sign a document, the Law of 1851, "under which the burden of proof is placed on the land owner to defend the title to his land." Jed has once more taken advantage of Rico who will have to fight a lengthy court battle if he wants to retain his land. Or he can write to his congressman who just happens to be Jed.

Jed then hands Rico a registration form. When he is ready to sign, Jed says he can do so only if he owns land. But you stole it, Rico says. Jed answers: "That's showbiz!"

Jed erects a new sign calling the place Rancho Hollywood. Rico tries to strangle Jed but is restrained by Ramona and Victoria. Marcus enters and Rico tells him that Jed stole his land.

"Just like you stole it from the Indians," Marcus says. "Excellent, Rufus," Jed tells him, "you are learning well. Marcus says that Rufus is no longer his name. Jed replies: "My goodness, are we moving through time that fast?" He then asks Marcus if he's handled the Indian problem. "I sure did," Marcus replied, "I married her."

Jed says he'll have Marcus's stripes for marrying a squaw. Marcus replies that he's a free man, and he and Gerónima are going to "raise us a whole lot of black and red children." Jed tries to cajole him into staying, finally telling him, "I'm your Daddy!" Marcus does not react kindly to this. Rather he tells Jed if he ever sees him "around me or mine again, I'll kill you."

1. Why do you suppose the characters are longing for the good old days?

2. Why do you think Morton included all the silly lines about cele

brating the old days?

3. In what way are the "script" and the lives of the characters becoming mixed up here? What is the purpose of this?

JED: It's the dawn of the twentieth century, time to usher in a new era of peace and prosperity.

RAMONA: Do you really mean it? No more war, no more killing?

JED: Oh, maybe just a little charge up San Juan Hill....

RICO: The twentieth century already? Why, it seems as though we just settled California yesterday.

VICTORIA: And Mexico the day before.

JED: Come, come, you already said those lines. We're going to have to find you some new ones.

RAMONA: Jed's right, Mamá, we Mexican-hyphen-Americans can't be living in the past.

RICO: Mexican-hyphen-Americans now, are we?

RAMONA: Papá, I've become a child of both cultures. And my name is not Ramona anymore, it's Ronny.

RICO: Roni? Ay, Ramona, ¡cómo te has perdido!

VICTORIA: Everything is changing so fast! I wish we could go back to the old days; life was much simpler.

RICO: There was order, family, tradition.

VICTORIA: Yes, and the fiestas and ferias....

JED: Wait a minute! I just thought of something!

RAMONA: Jed, are you having another vision!

JED: Yes! I see how we can use the past to find our future. Why don't we have an **Old Spanish Days Fiesta** and celebrate your Spanish heritage!

RAMONA: Married, doesn't that sound like a grand idea?! *(VICTORIA is not convinced.)*

JED: See those old run-down adobes and missions? We'll restore them, by golly. Start a Native Sons of the Golden West Club. Dress up like Spaniards and ride through downtown Santa Barbara. Name a baseball team the "Padres." Don Rico can be the grand marshal.

RAMONA: You can wear your charro suit, Papá.

JED: Doña Vicky can ride side saddle in her mantilla.

VICTORIA: Ramona, help me fix my hair. *(RAMONA does so.)*

RICO: I could do a few rope tricks with my lasso. You know that many things western, like rodeos and the lasso, came from the

Mexican. We were the original vaqueros, what you call "buckaroos."

JED: Exactly. We'll have sangria, flamenco dancers, Taco Bells! Olé! Olé! We'll haul in tourists by the busloads. Real estate values will soar! We'll even make a movie out of it!

RAMONA: Ye Olde California Days, take two!

JED: No, well call it...RANCHO HOLLYWOOD! Ronny, I am going to make a star out of you!

SCENE 10: THREE MALES AND ONE FEMALE

Jed, probably 40s

Joaquín, probably 20s

Malcolm, probably 20s

Ramona, probably late teens or early twenties

Jed once more becomes the director and says the balcony scene will be shot again. Jed now will play "the male lead." "But you're anglo," Rico tells him. Jed says he'll wear brown contacts. "No, no, no!" Rico says. "We were everything, white, black brown..." "Black?" Ramona asks. "Me! Blonde Ronny Rico, star of the stage, screen and the Great White Way, black?" Rico tells her it's nothing to be ashamed of, but she feels that if Jed finds out, it will ruin her career.

Rico asks if he will have a role in the movie. A nonspeaking role, Jed tells him. He is insulted and quits. Once more there is an intermixture of "reality" and "script" when Ramona says, "But Papà, where will you go, what will you do?" "No importa," he says. "I'll go back to being a ranchero." Jed corrects him to say "ranch hand, Rico, I mean 'pobre' [poor one; a reversal of fortunes since the word "rico" means rich]. I own the land."

"At least it's honest work," Rico says.

"Goodbye, Mamà. Goodbye, Papà," Ramona says as she hugs them. They leave. "My parents, they're gone!" Ramona says.

Jed wants to begin shooting the scene. This time, Ramona will be "Ronny Rocket, Latin spitfire, the hottest thing to hit Hollywood since Carmen Miranda." This time the movie will be triple X-rated. Ramona refuses. Jed leaves to find another actress, whom Ramona says will be a "gringa."

Joaquín tells Ramona they could form their own company. Now Sinmuhow and Rufus (who is now Malcolm) come to audition. Jed asks Malcolm if he's had any experience. He says he's played many parts: "slave, worker, soldier, invisible man," the latter because white people never look at him. Jed asks him to play a "Mexican half-breed type" and tells him "he could probably pass." But he should wear a bandana to cover his Afro. He asks if that's like whites wearing blackface (as they did in minstrel shows).

When Malcolm asks about a role as a revolutionary, Jed says he has nothing at present but maybe can work him into something like "Shaft vs. the Maraudering Mau Maus."

Sinmuhow tells Jed she is a "Spirit Woman, woman who knows many things." He tells her he doesn't need anyone like that. He wants a silent sexy Latina. She says she is real and could not play "a wooden Indian." When he suggests they play cowboys and Indians, she says only if "we play Custer's Last Stand."

In the following scene, Morton hits on just about every ethnic stereotype possible.

1. What is the significance of Jed's saying "We're equal opportunity employers."

2. Why do you suppose Morton brings in all the different ethnic and racial groups, showing all these stereotypes of them?

3. Do you see humor in this scene? Explain.

4. Who is Morton poking fun at in this scene?

5. This scene really is the climax or high point of the play. Can you explain why this is so?

JED: Who's next? We're equal opportunity employers.

JOAQUÍN: I am. Don't you remember me? I'm one of the latest in your long line of stereotypes. I am your combination sleepy peon, Frito Bandido, Zorro, Cantinflesque, vato loco, wetback.

JED: Hey, how about a little gang exploitation film set in the smoldering East Los Barrio, huh? No? Well then, Kunta, how about a Bojangles movie? Let me see you dance, I know you got rhythm. *(JED dances; the rest of the players remain silent as they close in around him.)* Mr. Booooooo-jangles, dance, dance, dance. Sinmuhow! How about a nice wholesome maize commercial, huh? You know: "Our ancestors scalped settlers and at the end of the day were rewarded by the golden goodness of maize."[4] *(Hopping around on one foot)* Whooop! Whooop! Whooop!

MALCOLM: I have a better idea, why don't we do a "kill whitey" film.

JED: No, no, that could be labeled communist propaganda. Besides, who would pay to go see it?

RAMONA: The liberals.

JED: That's right, make them feel ashamed of being white.

RAMONA: Jed, don't you see, these distortions have twisted the minds of generations of children. Is this really how you see us?

JED: You too, huh? I always knew you were one of them.

RAMONA: That's right, I am. I am black and brown and white. And I'm proud of it.

JED: Oh, yeah, well let me tell you something. I'm a minority too. I'm part Jewish, just like Barry Goldwater. My grandmother Goldie, remember? We've been persecuted for over two thousand years just because they say we killed Christ, Jesus!

JOAQUÍN: Ladies and gentlemen, we are gathered here today to roast a great American filmmaker over the coals.

JED: Please, please! You're all taking this much too seriously. After all, it's only make believe!

JOAQUÍN: We, the assembled representatives of all the so-called minorities, although we are actually in the majority now, want

---

[4]A parody of a commercial for corn oil.

to pay homage to you, Jedediah Goldbanger Smith....

JED: Wait a minute, aren't you missing someone? Where's Charlie Chan? Where's our slant-eyed little nip? *(Assuming martial arts stance)* **Toyota! Datsun! Sony! Mao! Chop suey!**

JOAQUÍN: Jed, thank you, from the bottom of our hearts, for the creation of such memorable stereotypes, for the advancement of collective inferiority complexes, for the maligning and desecration of our cultures and for the loss, theft, and distortion of our history.

JED: Don't forget the wops and the micks and the polacks and the frogs and the...

JOAQUÍN: *We hereby present you with this mask as a token of our esteem.* *(They ceremoniously hand JED a redneck pig mask.)*

RAMONA: Jed, you really must change your image!

JED: My image? My image! Oh no, I couldn't accept this, really. I just want to thank all of those hardy pilgrims and pioneers for making all this possible. I'm afraid this doesn't really fit me! Wait! Cut the scene! Cut the scene! Cut! Cuuuuuuuuuuutttt!

(Blackout)

SCENE 11: FOUR MALES AND TWO FEMALES

Victoria, probably 40s

Rico, 40s to 50s

Sinmuhow, late teens or 20s

Malcolm, probably 20s

Jed, probably 40s

Joaquín, probably 20s

This scene comes directly after the preceding and continues till the end of the play.

1. What do you think is the purpose of this final scene?

2. What is the point Morton wants to make in having Malcolm and Sinmuhow talk about their investments?

3. Beyond what is said in the script, why does Jed ask Joaquín about the world of art?

4. Why does Morton bring in all the "causes" here — equal rights, affirmative action, and so on?

5. What is Morton satirizing when he has Jed say he has decided to run for president of the United States?

(On another part of the stage, RICO and VICTORIA exit as though from a movie theatre, dressed in evening clothes.)

VICTORIA: God, wasn't that a fantastic movie! Variety called "Rancho Hollywood" the most profound statement ever made about the history of California.

RICO: I still can't believe that Joaquín, Malcolm, Jed, Ramona, all worked to make this project a success.

VICTORIA: Oh, and wasn't Ramona wonderful? I bet she gets nominated for an Oscar. Oh, how I wish we could have stayed on to work in the film.

RICO: Don't worry, I hear there might be a sequel. Well, there's the reception. Good thing we have our passes, otherwise we'd never get past security. Everybody who is anybody in Hollywood is here tonight.

VICTORIA: *(As they enter the central area, showing an imaginary guard their passes)* **Oh, there they are! Drinking champagne.** *(We see the others partying.)*

RICO: Don't be obtrusive, let them enjoy the limelight.

SINMUHOW: The Executive Producer of Programming for CBS told me he wants to do a series based on "Rancho Hollywood."

MALCOLM: Is that so? An agent for the Shuberts told me they want to stage it on Broadway.

JED: Hey, aren't you glad we buried the hatchet and got down firme? Hah! Ha!

JOAQUÍN: Orale, especially since we are all equal partners in the production.

RAMONA: I was just told: "Rancho Hollywood" has seven Oscar nominations!

JED: Why not? It grossed twenty million in the first two weeks.

JOAQUÍN: Let's drink to that! *(They all toast.)*

VICTORIA: *(To RICO)* I can't believe this, I'm so proud of them.

RICO: Everything we worked for has come true.

SINMUHOW: *(To MALCOLM)* You know, all of a sudden I have all this money I don't know what to do with.

MALCOLM: I put my bread back into the ghetto. I bought a controlling interest in a chain of liquor stores.

SINMUHOW: I know what you mean. I went back to the reservation and started looking into prime investment properties –

RICO: Liquor stores? Buying land on the reservations?

JED: Well, Joaquín, how is the world of art these days?

RAMONA: Oh, he's been painting some beautiful murals a la Orozco, Rivera, Siqueiros.

JED: Public art?

JOAQUÍN: Not exactly, man, those pinche homeboys keep spray painting my murals.

JED: Like I always said, the masses don't really appreciate these things.

JOAQUÍN: So now I do mostly interiors, you know, the Bank of America, Hilton Inn, places like that.

RICO: Victoria, this doesn't sound right....

RAMONA: Well, my broker is E. F. Hutton. And E. F. Hutton says...[5]

(Everybody but RICO and VICTORIA freeze.)

RICO: Have they forgotten everything? Wake up! ¡Despierten! *(Speaking to deaf ears)* **Don't think only of your own greed and profit! You have a powerful tool at your disposal, use it!**

VICTORIA: Rico, it's no use, they can't hear you.

RICO: All the social gains we made in the past...in danger of being swept aside. Listen to me, we, the elderly, the poor, they want to take away our social security, medicare, food stamps...

VICTORIA: Don't forget equal rights for women.

RICO: Affirmative action, everything! Don't turn your backs on us, please! Listen to us! Listen! *(They all come to.)*

JED: Attention! Attention, everybody! I have an announcement to make. First of all, I want to thank each and everyone of you for giving me another chance to prove to the entire world that Americans of different races, religions, and creeds can work together. That was very "white" of you! *(Everybody laughs.)*

ALL: All right! Let's hear it! Orale, etc.

JED: My friends, you all know of my deep involvement with the Screen Actor's Guild, and although some have said I might

---

[5]In a TV commercial, all the actors froze to listen to what E. F. Hutton had to say.

make a fine governor of this golden state, I have decided to take on an even more difficult directorial responsibility because, I, for one, believe that this country has suffered long enough!

ALL: You can count on us! We're with you!

RICO: What in the devil is he talking about?

JED: Spread the word, tell everyone. We'll be needing script writers, P.R. people, makeup artists, producers, everything that it takes to make a fantasy like "Rancho Hollywood" come true. My friends, I have decided to run for President of the United States of America! *(Silence. Everyone, except for JED, looks at the audience. Slow fade.)*

TELLING TALES
Migdalia Cruz

Winner of many writing awards, including a National Endowment for the Arts, Migdalia Cruz has had her plays widely presented throughout the United States and in Canada and England. A member of the New Dramatists, she was runner-up with her play, *The Have-littles,* for the Susan Smith Blackburn Prize.

Cruz, who calls herself a Nuyorican (a New Yorker of Puerto Rican heritage), grew up in a poverty-stricken area of the Bronx. Much of her writing is based on her own experiences and the people she has known. She says: "I write about people I know — as a married adult living in a house (for the first time in my life) in exurban Connecticut. Or sometimes, I write about the ones I feel I should know — as a Nuyorican living in the violent twentieth century. But always, I write about the people I knew — as a child in the South Bronx."[6]

Telling Tales is made up of a series of eleven monologs, obviously being delivered from a distance of years.

YELLOW EYES: FEMALE OR MALE MONOLOG

This monolog is about a child's memories of a grandfather and grandmother. For the most part, however, they are not fond memories. Rather, they show keen observation and memory.

The monolog could be presented either by a male or female performer.

1. How old do you think the narrator was when observing the events described here? What is the narrator's present age?

2. Why do you suppose the playwright refers to her great-grandmother only as "she."

3. What feelings do you have when reading this? Why?

4. Do you like this monolog? Why? Why not? Is there anything about it that bothers you? Explain. Why do you suppose Cruz would have written this?

---

[6]"Biography" of "Migdalia Cruz," in Kathy A. Perkins and Roberta Uno, eds. *Contemporary Plays by Women of Color: An Anthology* (New York: Routledge, 1996), p. 106.

5. Why do you suppose the children ate the "chocolate"? Why do you think no one prevented this sort of thing from happening?

6. The monolog could be staged in many ways — with the actor moving from one place to another, sitting on a high stool, and so on. What do you think would be an effective way for you to stage and present it?

I'm sitting in front of my great-grandfather. He is telling me a story about how he fell in love with my great-grandmother, but I can't hear him. He has beautiful yellow eyes and I'm hypnotized by them.

I just sit staring at him. I can see every line of his skull. Every vein. His skin is like coffee with milk, like my father's coffee with milk. He doesn't get out of bed anymore. He sits up though and we dress him. He's wearing a brownish-green sweater, a cardigan. His dirty undershirt shows beneath it. It is stained with cherry chewing tobacco. His words smell like mucus and tobacco. People think mucus doesn't smell. But I think it smells. It smells yellow. His pants are brown; they are too short and cuffed. One cuff is torn and hanging off his thin, long legs. He has the longest legs I've ever seen. He's the tallest man I've ever known. He has scars on his arms and his legs from chains. He is strong.

He used to hold me over his head with his feet. Like a circus act. Like a balancing act. We could be famous I always thought. He's so strong and I'm so graceful.

He has on the socks I bought him for Christmas. My ma said to buy him socks because old people's feet get very cold.

He was one hundred six when he died and she was ninety-nine. She was also nuts. She'd wake up a different person every day. We always had to guess three or four times before we hit on the right name to call her. She thought she lived in a great manor in the country and my great-grandfather was her valet instead of her husband. My mother was the poor woman who came in once a week to do laundry. She pitied all of us and gave us chocolates because "Poor people like chocolates. It takes their minds off their little problems...." They weren't really chocolates though – she used to cut out cubes from bars of soap and pretend they were chocolates. She'd watch you too. She'd watch you put 'em in your mouth and wait till your mouth foamed up before she'd turn away. "Good chocolates, huh? You people always enjoy my chocolates. You're like dogs for them. Hungry for them. I never liked sweets myself. They weaken your heart. People fall in love when they eat too much candy. Always with the wrong person. That's why so many children have children. They don't know. Their minds are in the sweets, covered with sugar. No sense."

PAPO CHIBIRICO: FEMALE MONOLOG

This is a poignant remembrance of someone who was kind to a younger child, who saw nothing extraordinary about him for a long time.

1. Why do you suppose Papo did so many nice things for the narrator of the monolog?

2. Why do you suppose people laughed at midget wrestling? What would make it funny? Do you think it is? Why? Why not?

3. Why did Papo become angry with the narrator? What emotions do you think she felt at these times? What emotions do you think she felt when she discovered Papo would never grow taller? When he became angry at her for helping him out of dumpsters?

4. What emotions do you feel when reading this monolog?

5. Why do you think Papo continued to show off on his bike even after the others stopped watching? Why was it important to him that they watch, particularly considering that people always watched him wrestle on television?

6. Why do you suppose Cruz ends the piece by saying Papo was a dwarf, after calling him a midget throughout the monolog?

Papo Chibirico was fifteen when I was seven. He was my first love. He bought me coloring books and candy and took me to the zoo. Anthony Vargas tried to give me coloring books too, but I punched him in the nose and made him bleed. Papo thought it was a good idea. "Don't let the boys bully you," he always said.

Every summer we formed softball teams. Once we were playing and I walked backwards to make a catch. I didn't know I was on a hill and fell off into a pile of beer bottles. Papo carried me the fifteen blocks home with one hand holding my left knee together. He pulled the glass out of the wound and went with my mom and me to the hospital. He was mature for a kid. That's what I thought.

When I turned eleven, I went to P.R. for the summer. I returned a foot and a half taller and five shades darker. Papo was six inches shorter than me then. How could he be six inches shorter, if he was eight years older? Papo changed that summer too, he got more muscles and was training to become a wrestler. My dad and I watched his first televised fight on channel forty-seven. That's when I found out he was a midget – because he was a midget wrestler.

Papo fought the Jamaican Kid. The strength was in their arms really. Their little legs just kicked the air. With their arms they pinned each other to the floor. My dad laughed and I wondered what was so funny. He explained to me that it was supposed to be funny – that's why you watch midget wrestling, to laugh. The Jamaican Kid won.

The next day I saw Papo. He was still friendly to me even though he was a TV star. All the kids on the block wanted to talk to him. But he talked just to me. The big kids were always challenging him to a fight. He would say "No," but they would push him and hit him until there was nothing left to say. Sometimes three or four would gang up on him and hold him up in the air. His useless legs would swing wildly at his attackers always missing their mark. "Some tough guy!" Then they'd throw him into a dumpster. I used to watch and cry because I didn't know what else to do. All I could do was wait for them to leave and help Papo out of the garbage. He always got mad at me then. "Don't you know you could get hurt?! Stay away from me, will you! I don't need your help!" But he always needed my help.

He got to be a really good wrestler. The kind the crowd stands up for. He got tougher too. Carried a knife and stabbed somebody, so I couldn't see him anymore. He'd look at me from across the street when I was sitting on the fire escape doing my homework. He waved and I waved back, but he always turned away before he saw me wave. I guess he was afraid I wouldn't.

When he got a little money saved, he got a special bicycle on which he could reach the pedals. He spent hours on that bike, circling the neighborhood. I watched him go by and go by and go by again. He looked normal on that bike – happy. He walked with a limp now. The Jamaican Kid went crazy one night and bit a chunk out of his calf. He got an infection from it. The Jamaican Kid never even apologized. I know because I asked. That's the last thing we ever talked about.

It was one of those real hot August nights, when everybody's on the street because nobody can sleep. Some guys are playing the congas in the playground, small children are playing tag, mothers are gossiping and the men are playing dominoes. Papo comes by on his bike. It's a pretty one – black with a red seat and Papo's in red and black too. He looks sharp. His face is pretty. He's the only one on the block with green eyes. Everybody wanted those eyes. Everybody says hello. He starts showing off, making the bike jump and taking turns real fast and real low. People applaud. He does this over and over. People finally stop watching but he keeps saying "Look at me, look at me!" Now people are embarrassed to look. Papo goes by one more time....

I don't know where the car came from. It was a new car, I think. Shiny. Maybe just freshly waxed. People always wax their cars in the summer. He wouldn't have lived long anyway – that's what people said. "God bless him. Midgets don't live very long."

But he wasn't a midget, he was a dwarf.

PARCHEESI: FEMALE MONOLOG

This monolog is about another of the narrator's friends, yet someone who seems to be a different sort of person than is the narrator.

1. What reason could Cruz have for describing the stage and auditorium before beginning with the more personal reminiscences?

2. Why do you suppose the narrator and Sharon were close friends? Why do you suppose the two girls became so close?

3. What does Cruz mean by saying that "she was always there in the back of my head — like a soft spot that babies have"?

4. Near the end of the monolog, Cruz writes that the narrator "wanted a history, and I wanted a past." What does she mean by this?

5. Do you like this monolog? Why? Why not? Is the ending effective? Why? Why not?

The stage of a school auditorium. The walls are mint green. The stage is just a platform. No walls. The floor of the stage is brown. It's two-thirty in the afternoon. Assembly time. All the children are saying the Pledge of Allegiance, except the Jehovah's Witnesses. The principal is seated in the front row. She's seven and a half feet tall with long, blonde hair and long, white teeth. Her bangs touch her eyebrows. Her ears touch her chin. Whenever there's an announcement made, she yells at the child to speak up. "How can you say something on a stage that no one can hear?!" I hated that stage.

I was My Fair Lady on that stage. Eliza Doolittle. I had a voice then. My friend Sharon Gray always forgot her lines and the principal would yell at her. "How can we enjoy the show if we can't hear you? Only stupid people forget their lines."

Sharon was very pretty...she's a cop now. I used to hate cops but I could never hate Sharon. She was my dumbest best friend. She didn't know how to read in the fifth grade and I taught her.

On my eleventh birthday, she came to my house with a Parcheesi game. I said "Oh, I have one just like that." I felt bad because as soon as I said it I knew she was embarrassed, so then I knew she had brought it for me. She was going to take it back, but I told her I lost all the pieces out of my other game and so it was a good thing she had bought this new set. It was prettier than the one I had. She bought it at John's Bargain Store. That was our favorite store because everything was either fifty-nine cents or eighty-eight cents. I couldn't believe she had bought me anything...it was a lot of money to spend on a friend.

We sat right in front of the television and watched Captain Jack's Popeye cartoons first – "Ahoy, ye maties!" – "Ahoy, Captain Jack." And then we played Parcheesi. She ate me first and went twenty spaces. I hate when someone eats me first because then I'm bound to lose. The first eater always wins in Parcheesi. She ate me second and third too. But then she stopped eating me even though she could. I guess because it was my birthday. I ended up winning.

Sharon had the blackest skin I've ever seen except in *National Geographic*. It was polished wood. My mother used to say she must use lemon Pledge on her face because it was so shiny. And she smelled like lemons too, because of our business. We sold coconut ices and lemonade. My dad showed us how to make the ices so we gave him part of our profits – that was Sharon's idea. Sharon made the lemonade because she was an expert. Her mother made lemonade for her to take to school on Pot Luck Lunch Day and all the kids loved it. It had rosehips in it. But we didn't know what they were then – we thought it was a drug because it tasted so good.

In sixth grade, we got separated by Mrs. Newman because she said Sharon wasn't smart enough to be in the same class with me. I was in six-one and they put her in six-twelve. That wasn't too bad though because we had up to six-twenty-six. The kids in six-twenty-six were called the F-Troop. They weren't bad but they were stupid. The kids in six-twelve weren't real stupid, they just smoked too much. The kids in six-fifteen were the school terrors. They started a war against all the other classes. Sharon got stabbed in the stomach after she stood up for me when some girls from six-fifteen tried to steal my bus pass. The next day they were waiting for her in the yard and worked her over. Sharon said if there'd only been three she could have handled it, but there were five.

I used to wonder what happened to Sharon until I met her on the bus. She saw me first and came over and hugged me. She remembered me. I was so glad to see her because I almost never stop thinking about her. She's always there in the back of my head – like a soft spot that babies have that if struck kills them instantly. Dogs have a spot like that too. It's on their sides. Sharon had a dog. His name was Don. Junie, her little brother named him – he just couldn't say dog, it came out like don. It was a big poodle with all its hair – not a clipped, ugly, French one. We took Don everywhere with us. He would come into the bathroom and watched everything you did in there.

He was curious and I don't blame him. I always liked watching dogs pee in the street. So shameless. I wanted a life like that. Sharon wanted order. She wanted money. She wanted to have a history and I wanted to have a past.

So now she can blow your head off with a three fifty-seven magnum and I can tell you about it.

RATS: FEMALE MONOLOG

This monolog differs from the others in that the author begins by talking about rats but then goes on to several other subjects before coming back to the rats. It seems to be more like a stream-of-consciousness writing, that is, saying things, one after another, as they occur to the narrator. In each of the other monologs, the audience learns a few things about the narrator. In this one, the audience can learn a lot more about her feelings.

1. How does the mood of this monolog differ from that of the others?

2. This monolog also is different in that it begins in the present and then goes into memories of the past. Can you think of a reason Cruz may have written it in this way?

3. Do you agree with the narrator or the scientist about the rats? Why? Why not? What do you think might account for the differences in which the two think about the rats?

4. Do you feel this is an appropriate subject for a monolog? Why? Why not? Would you want to present it to an audience? What sort of audience do you think would appreciate it? Explain.

5. Why do you suppose the woman at the party was so patronizing of the narrator's coming from the Bronx? Do you think it logical that the woman thought the narrator was from England? Why? Why not?

6. How do you think the narrator would feel at being asked if anyone still lived in the place where she grew up? What does this say about the personality of the other woman?

7. Why do you think in this monolog Cruz again referred to the woman who became a police officer?

8. Do you think the analogy of comparing people in barrios to rats in a plastic bag is truthful or realistic? Why? Why not?

9. In this monolog, Cruz jumps quickly from one subject to another? Why do you think she did this? Do you like this style of writing?

10. Do you think the ending of this monolog is effective? Why? Why not?

He says violence isn't the answer. They're just looking for a warm place to live out the winter, and in the spring they'll be gone. But I hear them. In the walls. In the drawers. Every day I check the flour for them. They get everywhere. He says we shouldn't kill them. That won't keep them from coming back. He's a scientist, so he knows. He also says how can you kill anything that's so cute.

"But they ate all my sweet corn and my marigolds and my squash seeds," I say. "We can buy more," he says. I say, "Why should we have to?" I say, "They're aliens, invaders. Get the hell out of my seeds and grains." I'm not a monster. I'm willing to give them my thyme. It's all dried up now anyway, but there's plenty of it. And it's right there in the front yard. Right where they can get their grimy little teeth on it. But no. They gotta come inside my house.

I never liked mice. The ones in my parents' apartment were gray – baby rats, really. Nobody cared about the souls of those guys. They were dirty, ugly and smelled like urine, other animals' urine – not even their own urine, you know what I mean? City mice are nobody's friends. You kill city mice. You don't gently catch them in Hav-A-Heart traps and release them into some pretty country field. There are no fields so if you let 'em go they will (a) come back or (b) bite you and give you rabies. So you have no choice. You use those lovely, back-breaking snap traps. By doing this, you prevent disease, death, desolation. You keep little rats from becoming big rats that will eat small children.

My father caught rats at work. They had contests to see who could catch the biggest one. The danger, of course, was that the rat might break out of the plastic bag it was caught in and rush the crowd of laughing men, throwing down their dollar bills in drunken bets. The rats usually lost.

There was this one guy – Paco Loco – my dad says Dominicans will do anything for money – who was offered twenty dollars to catch a rat with his bare hands and strangle it. Paco went after a big one, but he slipped when he got right up to it and had cornered it. As he grabbed for it, the rat jumped smack into his face, bit him and kept running past the other men who all ran screaming out the door. My dad was the only one who stayed. He says the rat stopped and looked at him. He said it looked scared. Imagine that. Even with blood hanging off his teeth, he was still scared of people. Then he kept right on going, under the steel machinery, disappearing into the wall. My dad went over to Paco and helped him up. Paco was crying. The rat got his left eye. I mean, it was completely gone. It was just a hole.

They stopped playing with the rats after that.

I thought I left those things behind me. In the Bronx. But they followed me here. To white suburbia. I'm the only Puerto Rican in New Canaan, Connecticut. I figure as long as I don't open my mouth I'm safe. I was at a party once and some WASPy lady in tennis whites asked if I was from England. England?! Can you imagine?! She said she thought I was from England because I had an accent. She looked real surprised when I told her I was from the South Bronx. "South what?" But once she got used to the idea, it seemed quite wonderful and she grabbed my elbow and brought me around to all of her friends. "Have you met this wonderful creature, yet? She's from the Bronx – the South Bronx!" "Amazing! Is anybody still living there?" No – nobody important...just people. My mother, my father, my sisters. The priest who gave me first communion. My friend Sharon whose little brother Junie died of sickle cell anemia when we were twelve and he was ten. She's a cop now. I bet she's a good cop. Forty-fourth precinct. Otherwise known as Fort Apache. It's funny...when I lived there it seemed more like Fort Navajo or Fort Chippewa. My people are a peaceful people. It's when they herd us into *barrios* that we turn – like a rat in a plastic bag. When you're fighting for your life, you get ugly. You get bitter. Or if you're like my mother, you spend a lot of time in church lighting candles. And you bring your children with you so they forget for a time that they've been forsaken.

153

The church is beautiful. It smells wonderful. It smells purple, like a purple, powerful drug. I loved the church. When I was sixteen I decided to become a part of the church. You know, settle down, get married to the Son of God. But it didn't work out too well. I liked to read too much. And I liked to write. Mother Superiors don't like that kind of stuff. After three weeks, four days, nine hours, I left. I think my mom was disappointed. Back to the Bronx. Wasn't any one of us going to get out? The Bronx – where people talk with such intriguing accents.

He doesn't understand why they upset me so much. With their cute little noses and big, brown eyes. They look just like his eyes. Just like mine. But they squeak. I don't squeak, do I? Maybe I do. Maybe I shouldn't be afraid of them, but I am. The scuttling sounds behind the wall remind me. I wonder if what they say is true – that you have the memories of all your ancestors inside your head. I wonder if my children will jump when they hear mice in the walls. I wonder if they'll remember too and get up in the middle of the night to check on people who aren't there anymore....

Maybe he's right. Maybe it's time to put away the knife.

African-American Theatre

African-American Theatre

Blacks were forced to sing and dance on slave ships bound for America, and in early theatrical presentations by whites, they most often were presented as stereotypes. By the 1850s, two black men, both named Brown but not related, had begun writing plays. In the same period Ira Aldridge became a internationally known Shakespearean actor. By 1897, Bob Cole had organized the first black stock company in New York.

African Americans were responsible, in large part, for the development of the American musical, which grew out of African-American minstrelsy. The first musical to depart from the format of a loosely structured revue was *Shuffle Along*, presented in 1921. During the Harlem Renaissance, many African-American theatres and companies were established, and writers began creating new forms of drama by, for, and about African-American life.

Alice Childress's *Gold Through the Trees* (1952) became the first play by a black woman to be produced off-Broadway. The play that changed the scope of black theatre in America, however, was Lorraine Hansberry's *A Raisin in the Sun* largely because people of all ethnic backgrounds could identify with the statements it makes on defining and achieving success.

The civil rights movement had a great effect on African-American theatre. Also in the 1960s and 70s there was a move away from Broadway and toward regional, nonprofit theatres, many of which worked with black writers such as George C. Wolfe, who became a successful Broadway director, and August Wilson. Off-Broadway had notable successes with shows by and/or about blacks throughout the 1980s and 1990s.

BLUE BLOOD
and
BLUE-EYED BLACK BOY

Georgia Douglas Johnson

A poet and a playwright, Georgia Douglas Johnson (1886-1996) also was important for hosting in her home in Washington, D.C., a literary salon that was attended by many black artists, intellectuals and writers. Johnson often wrote folk drama. One of her most notable is *Plumes,* which has been compared to John Millington Synge's Irish folk drama *Riders to the Sea,* which many consider to be the perfect one-act.

Favored by many Harlem Renaissance writers, folk plays, in their depiction of common people, portrayed believable characters that sharply differed from the comic, bumbling figures so often created by white dramatists.

Although Johnson wrote about thirty plays, only a few survive. Perhaps because she was biracial — her father was English and her mother African American — a number of her plays dealt with the theme of miscegenation or inbreeding between people of different races. Two of these plays are *Blue Blood* and *Blue-Eyed Black Boy.* Both are very short. The complete scripts of each follow.

Blue Blood is Johnson's only tragicomedy, and is a true mixture of comic and tragic elements. The situation itself is certainly tragic — white men taking advantage of black women. Unfortunately, this was not at all uncommon during the time of slavery and in the latter nineteenth and early twentieth centuries.

The play takes place in Georgia just after the Civil War. The action occurs in the combined kitchen and dining room of a frame cottage. One door leads into the back yard, another into a hall. There is a curtained back window and steps Stage Right that lead upstairs.

SCENE 1: ONE FEMALE AND ONE MALE

Randolph Strong, 20s

Mrs. Bush, 40s

As the action begins, Randolph Strong enters carrying a "large bunch of white roses and a package. He places the package, unnoticed, on the table — still holding the roses."

1. Do you think the situation is realistic? Is it logical that Randolph would bring roses for May? Why? Why not?

2. Do you think the dialog is true-to-life? Do you find it believable? Explain.

3. Why does Mrs. Bush think May and Randolph would make a perfect match? Why does she want so much for them to marry?

4. What sort of person is Randolph? Do you like him? Why? Why not? Do you think you would like Mrs. Bush? Explain.

RANDOLPH STRONG: How is my dear Mother Bush?

MRS. BUSH: Feeling like a sixteen-year-old! That's right, you come right on back here with me. *(Notices roses.)* Oh! what pretty roses! Snow white!

RANDOLPH STRONG: Like um? Thought you would.... May likes this kind!

MRS. BUSH: She sho'ly do. Pore chile! She's turning her back on the best fellow in this town, when she turned you down. I knows a good man when I see one.

RANDOLPH STRONG: You are always kind to me, Mother Bush. I feel like the lost sheep tonight, the one hundredth one, out in the cold, separated by iron bars from the ninety and nine! Bah! what am I doing? The milk's spilt! *(Arranging flowers)* Put these in here?

MRS. BUSH: Sure! My, but they look grand. There ain't many young doctors so handy-like!

RANDOLPH STRONG: *(Half to himself)* The first time I saw her she wore a white rose in her hair....

MRS. BUSH: Jest listen! May's plum blind! Oh! if she'd a only listened to me, she'd be marrying you tonight, instead of that stuck-up John Temple. I never did believe in two "lights" marrying, nohow, it's onlucky. They're jest exactly the same color...hair...and eyes alike too. Now you...you is just right for my May. "Dark should marry light." You'd be a perfect match.

RANDOLPH STRONG: *(Groans.)* Hold, hold, for goodness sake! Why didn't you lend that little blind girl of yours your two good eyes?

MRS. BUSH: Humph! She wouldn't hear me. *(Goes up to him, speaking confidentially.)* 'Tween you and me, I shorely do wish she'd a said "yes" when you popped the question las' Christmas. I hates to see her tying up with this highfalutin' nothing. She'll re'lize some day that money ain't everything, and that a poor man's love is a whole sight better than a stiff-neck, good-looking dude.

RANDOLPH STRONG: It can't be helped now, Mother Bush. If she's happy, that's the main thing!

MRS. BUSH: But is she going to be happy...that's jest it!

RANDOLPH STRONG: Let us hope so! And yet, sometimes I think –
do you know, Mother Bush, *(Lowering his voice)* sometimes I
think May cares for me.

MRS. BUSH: *(Confidently)* **Do you know, honey, somehow, sometimes I do too!**

RANDOLPH STRONG: *(Excitedly)* **You do too! Oh, if I could fully
believe that – even now – at the last minute –** *(Snaps his
finger.)* **Oh, what's the use?** *(Constrainedly)* **Is everything ready?**

MRS. BUSH: You bet! I'm all dressed under this apron. *(Swings it
back and discloses a brilliant and much decorated gown. Then
with a start)* **Lord save us! That Lyddie Smith ain't brought that
my'nase dressing yet. Vowed she'd have it here by eight sharp,
if she was alive. What time you got?**

RANDOLPH STRONG: *(Looking at his watch)* **Eight-thirty.**

MRS. BUSH: Eight-thirty? Good gracious!

RANDOLPH STRONG: I'll run over and get it for you.

**MRS. BUSH: Oh, yes, honey! Do hurry. Oh, what a son-in-law you
would'a made!**

RANDOLPH STRONG: Good joke...but I can't laugh! *(He goes. MRS.
BUSH busies herself with the table arrangements and finally
notices a package that had been left by RANDOLPH STRONG; she
opens it and discloses a beautiful vase.)*

SCENE 2: THREE FEMALES

Mrs. Bush, 40s

May, 20s

Mrs. Temple, 40s

The following is a continuation of the first scene. The only break in the action is when Randolph leaves and Mrs. Bush picks up a card that was with the flowers. The card, of course, came from Randolph.

1. Point out any humor you see in this scene. What makes it humorous?

2. This scene also has elements of the tragic. Point out these elements and explain what makes them tragic.

3. How does Mrs. Bush feel about Mrs. Temple? Why do you suppose she feels this way?

4. Considering the time period, do you think it logical that May and John have the same father? How do the two women feel about McCallister's being the father of their children? Why do you suppose they feel this way?

5. What sort of person is May? Why do you suppose she turned Randolph down in favor of John? Which of the two men do you think she should choose to marry? Why?

6. What can you tell about May's feelings from the way she reacts to the flowers and the vase that Randolph brought? Is it logical she behaves this way? Explain.

7. What personality traits of Mrs. Temple's can you discover in this scene? Explain how you know this.

8. Obviously, there is tension and conflict in the relationship between Mrs. Bush and Mrs. Temple. How is this apparent? Why do you think it exists?

9. Why do you suppose the two mothers value "blue blood" so much? Is this logical? Why? Why not?

10: Explain what part coincidence plays in this scene. Do you think the playwright handles it well?

11. Have things changed for African-American women since the time the play was written? If so, in what way? Is further change needed? Explain.

MRS. BUSH: *(Reading [from the card])* **For May and her husband, with best wishes for your happiness, Randolph.** *(She sets it aside without saying a word — only wiping her eyes — thinks a while; shakes her head; picks up the vase again and calls toward the stairway:)* **May! May! run down here a minute. I've got something to show you.** *(MRS. BUSH polishes the vase with her apron and holds her head to one side looking at it admiringly. Enter MAY in negligee. MRS. BUSH — with vase held behind her:)* **Not dressed yet?... Gracious! There...look...Randolph brought it!**

MAY BUSH: Oh!...did he? *(Reads card.)* **Randolph is a dear!** *(Fondles vase and looks sad.)*

MRS. BUSH: He brought these roses, too...said you liked this kind. *(MAY BUSH takes roses and buries her face in them, then thoughtfully changes them into RANDOLPH's vase; looks at it with head to one side, breaks off one rose, fondles it, places it in her hair.)*

MRS. BUSH: May — May — are you happy?

MAY BUSH: Why — why — *(Dashing something like a tear from her eye)* **of course I am.**

MRS. BUSH: Maybe you is...May...but, somehow, I don't feel satisfied.

MAY BUSH: *(Kisses her mother.)* **Oh, Ma, everything is all right! Just wait until you see me dressed.** *(Noise at door)* **Oh, somebody's coming in here!** *(MAY retreats partly up the stairway. Enter MRS. TEMPLE, talking. Voices and commotion heard as if coming from the front of the house, where heated argument is going on at front door, MRS. TEMPLE's muffled voice being heard. Hall kitchen door opens suddenly. Enter MRS. TEMPLE, excitedly.)*

MRS. TEMPLE: Heavens! They tried to keep me from coming out here! The very idea of her talking that way to me — the groom's own mother! Who is that little upstart that let me in at the front door? I told her I was coming right out here in the kitchen, for even though we have not called on each other in the past, moving around — as you know — in somewhat different social circles, and, of course, not being thrown very closely together, yet now, at this particular time, Mrs. Bush, since our two children are determined to marry, I feel that my place tonight is right back here with you! *(Glancing upward,*

MRS. TEMPLE discovers MAY upon the stairway.) **Why, May, are you not dressed yet! You'll have to do better than that when you are Mrs. John Temple!**

MRS. BUSH: Don't you worry 'bout May; she'll be ready. Where's John? Is he here?

MRS. TEMPLE: Sure – he brought me in his car, but the fellows captured him and said they were going to keep him out driving until the last minute. *(Again glancing upward toward MAY)* **Better hurry, May; you mustn't keep John waiting.**

MAY BUSH: *(Slowly walking upstairs)* **Oh, John will get used to waiting on me.** *(Exit MAY)*

MRS. TEMPLE: *(To MRS. BUSH)* **What's this...chicken salad? Is it finished?**

MRS. BUSH: No, it ain't. The my'nase ain't come yet. I sent Randolph for it. I jest got tired waiting on Lyddie Smith to fetch it.

MRS. TEMPLE: My gracious...give me the things and I'll make the dressing for you in a jiffy. *(MRS. TEMPLE removes her white gloves and gets ready for her new role in the kitchen. Without waiting for MRS. BUSH's consent, she rapidly walks over to wooden peg on wall, takes down extra gingham apron and removes her hat and lightweight coat, hanging both upon the peg.)*

MRS. BUSH: *(Remonstratingly)* **I'm 'fraid you'll git yo'self spoiled doing kitchen work. Sich folks as you'd better go 'long in the parlor.**

MRS. TEMPLE: Oh, no indeed. This is my son's wedding and I'm here to do a mother's part. Besides – he is a Temple and everything must be right.

MRS. BUSH: *(Takes materials for making the mayonnaise from kitchen safe and reluctantly places them before MRS. TEMPLE.)* **You needn't worry 'bout this wedding bein' right. It's my daughter's wedding – and I'll see to that!**

MRS. TEMPLE: *(Breaking and stirring eggs for the dressing)* **You'll have to admit that the girls will envy May marrying my boy John.**

MRS. BUSH: *(Stopping her work suddenly, and with arms akimbo)* **Envy MAY! Envy MAY! They'd better envy JOHN! You don't**

know who May is; she's got blue blood in her veins.

MRS. TEMPLE: *(Laughing sarcastically)* **You amuse me. I'll admit May's sweet and pretty, but she is no match for John.**

MRS. BUSH: *(Irately)* **She's not, eh? If I told you something about my May – who she is – you'd be struck dumb.**

MRS. TEMPLE: *(Nervously stirring the mayonnaise, replies in a falsetto or raised tone, denoting sarcasm)* **Remarkable...but I am curious!**

MRS. BUSH: *(Proudly)* **I bet you is – you'd fall flat if I told you who she is.**

MRS. TEMPLE: *(Suspending the operation of the mayonnaise and curiously assuming a soft, confidential tone)* **Pray, Mrs. Bush. Tell me then. Who is May?**

MRS. BUSH: Who is May? Huh! *(Proudly tossing her head)* **Who is May?** *(Lowering her voice, confidentially)* **Why...do you know Cap'n WINFIELD McCALLISTER, the biggest banker in this town, and who's got money 'vested in banks all over Georgia? That 'ristocrat uv 'ristocrats...that Peachtree Street blue blood – CAP'N McCALLISTER – don't you know him?**

MRS. TEMPLE: *(Starts at the mention of the name but recovers herself in moment)* **Y-e-s, I've heard of him.**

MRS. BUSH: *(Like a shot out of a gun)* **Well, I'd have you to know – he's May's daddy!**

MRS. TEMPLE: *(Agitatedly)* **W-h-y...I...I...can't believe it!**

MRS. BUSH: *(Dauntingly)* **Believe it or not, it's the bounden truth, so help me God! Ain't you never seed him strut? Well, look at May. Walks just like him – throws her head like him – an' she's got eyes, nose and mouth jest like him. She's his living image.**

MRS. TEMPLE: *(Almost collapsing, speaking softly and excitedly)* **You terrify me. Mrs. Bush...Captain McCallister can't be May's father!**

MRS. BUSH: Can't be May's father! Well, I reckon I ought to know who May's father is! Whut do you know 'bout it anyhow? Whut do you know 'bout Cap'n McCallister?

MRS. TEMPLE: Do you mean to tell –

MRS. BUSH: *(Interrupting)* **I mean jest whut I said. I'm telling you that my daughter – May Bush – has got the bluest blood in America in her veins. Jest put that in your pipe and smoke it!**

(MRS. BUSH here proudly flaunts herself around the kitchen, talking half at MRS. TEMPLE and half to herself.) **Huh! Talkin' 'bout May not bein' a match fur John. I should say they don't come no finer than May, anywhere.**

MRS. TEMPLE: *(Again collecting herself and speaking in a soft, strained, pleading voice)* **Mrs. Bush, Mrs. Bush, I have something to say to you and it must be said right now! Oh, where can I begin? Let me think –**

MRS. BUSH: **This ain't no time to think, I'm going to act!** *(Takes mayonnaise from MRS. TEMPLE's apathetic hands.)* **My chile's gotter get married and get married right. I...**

MRS. TEMPLE: *(Breaking in)* **Please, please, be still a minute for heaven's sake! You'll drive me mad!**

MRS. BUSH: **Drive you mad! The devil I will.** *(Abruptly runs and stands in a belligerent attitude in front of MRS. TEMPLE.)* **Say, look here, Miss High-and-Mighty, what's you up to? Git out of here, you ain't going to start no trouble here.** *(Tries to force MRS. TEMPLE toward the door.)*

MRS. TEMPLE: *(Breaking down in tears and reaching for MRS. BUSH's hands)* **Please, please, Mrs. Bush, you don't understand, and how can I tell you – what a day!**

MRS. BUSH: *(Standing squarely in front of MRS. TEMPLE)* **Look here, is you crazy? Or just a fool?**

MRS. TEMPLE: **Neither, Mrs. Bush, I'm just a brokenhearted mother and you must help me, help me, for May's sake, if not for mine!**

MRS. BUSH: **For May's sake! 'Splain yourself! This is a pretty come off. For May's sake.** *(Sarcastically)*

MRS. TEMPLE: **It's a long story, but I'll tell you in a few words. Oh, oh, how I've tried to forget it!**

MRS. BUSH: **Forget what! Look here, what time is it?** *(MRS. TEMPLE looks at her watch.)*

MRS. TEMPLE: **A quarter to nine.**

MRS. BUSH: *(Excitedly)* **Lord, woman, we ain't got no time fur story telling. I've got to hustle!**

MRS. TEMPLE: *(Hysterically)* **You must hear me, you must, you must!**

MRS. BUSH: Well, of all things, what *is* the matter with you?

MRS. TEMPLE: Be quiet, just one minute, and let me tell you.

MRS. BUSH: You'd better hurry up.

MRS. TEMPLE: Once...I taught a country school in Georgia. I was engaged to Paul Temple...I was only nineteen. I had worked hard to make enough to pay for my wedding things...it was going to be in the early fall – our wedding. I put my money in the bank. One day, in that bank, I met a man. He helped me. And then I see he wanted his pay for it. He kept on – kept writing to me. He didn't sign his letters, though. I wouldn't answer. I tried to keep away. One night he came to the place where I boarded. The woman where I boarded – she helped him – he bribed her. He came into my room –

MRS. BUSH: The dirty devil!

MRS. TEMPLE: *(Continuing her story)* I cried out. There wasn't any one there that cared enough to help me, and you know yourself, Mrs. Bush, what little chance there is for women like us, in the South, to get justice or redress when these things happen!

MRS. BUSH: Sure, honey, I do know!

MRS. TEMPLE: Mother knew – there wasn't any use trying to punish him. She said I'd be the one...that would suffer.

MRS. BUSH: You done right...and what your ma told you is the God's truth.

MRS. TEMPLE: I told Paul Temple – the one I was engaged to – the whole story, only I didn't tell him who. I knew he would have tried to kill him, and then they'd have killed him.

MRS. BUSH: *(Interrupting)* That wuz good sense.

MRS. TEMPLE: He understood the whole thing – and he married me. He knew why I wouldn't tell him the man's name – not even when – when that man's son was born to me.

MRS. BUSH: You don't mean John?

MRS. TEMPLE: Yes...John. And his father....

MRS. BUSH: Oh no...no...

MRS. TEMPLE: Yes. *(With a groan)* Winfield McCallister...is John's father, too.

SCENE 3: THREE FEMALES AND ONE MALE

Mrs. Bush, 40s

Mrs. Temple, 40s

Randolph, 20s

May, 20s

This scene comes directly after the last.

1. Why do you suppose Mrs. Bush wants to tell Randolph what happened? Why does Mrs. Temple agree?

2. Do you think the ending of this scene is believable, or is it too melodramatic to believe? Explain.

3. What emotions do you think each of the characters is feeling in this scene? How would you portray these emotions for Mrs. Bush? Mrs. Temple? Randolph? May?

4. Would you like to play one of these roles? Why? Why not?

MRS. BUSH: (*Clasping her hands excitedly*) **My God! My God!** (*Whimpering, between sobs*) **Whut kin we do?** **Just think of my poor, dear chile, May, upstairs there – all dressed up jest lak a bride – 'spectin' to git married – and all them people from everywhere – in the parlor – waiting for the seymoaney! Oh, whut kin we tell her...whut kin we tell them?**

MRS. TEMPLE: (*Looking at watch. Gets up, walks up and down excitedly.*) **Yes...we've got to think and act quickly! We can't tell the world why the children didn't marry...and cause a scandal.... I'd be ruined!**

MRS. BUSH: (*Getting irate*) **So far as you is consarned...I ain't bothered, 'bout you being ruined. May'll be ruined if we don't tell. Why – folks'll all be saying John jilted her, and you can bet your sweet life I won't stand fur that. No siree! I don't keer who it hurts...I'm not agoin' see May suffer...not ef I kin help it!**

MRS. TEMPLE: (*Bursting into tears*) **Oh! Oh! We must do something!** (*Enter RANDOLPH STRONG, breathlessly, with mayonnaise dressing from Lyddie Smith's – placing large glass jar of mayonnaise on kitchen table.*)

RANDOLPH STRONG: Good evening, Mrs. Temple. I'm a little late, Mrs. Bush, but here's what you sent me for. (*He notices MRS. TEMPLE in tears.*) **My, my, why, what's wrong?**

MRS. BUSH: Randolph, my dear boy....

RANDOLPH STRONG: What's the matter? What's happened awhile ago?

MRS. BUSH: (*Slowly and feelingly*) **Sump'n...sump'n turrible!**

RANDOLPH STRONG: Has anything happened to May?

MRS. BUSH: Not only to her – to all of us!

RANDOLPH STRONG: All! Heavens!

MRS. BUSH: Listen, Randolph, and help us, for God's sake! May and John can't get married!

RANDOLPH STRONG: (*Turning to MRS. TEMPLE*) **Can't get married! Why?**

MRS. TEMPLE: It's a long story. I've told – I've explained everything to Mrs. Bush. She – she understands.

RANDOLPH STRONG: You can trust me. I'm like one of the family.

You both know that I have always cared for May.

MRS. BUSH: *(To MRS. TEMPLE)* **Kin I tell him?** *(MRS. TEMPLE silently and tearfully nods her assent.)* **May mus' know it too – right away. Let's call her down. May! May! Oh, May! My dear chile, come down here a minute – quick – right away! My dear chile...my poor chile!**

MRS. TEMPLE: **What a day! What a day!**

MAY'S VOICE: **Coming, Ma!** *(Enter MAY BUSH, coming downstairs in her wedding gown.)* **Am I late?** *(Noting RANDOLPH)* **The roses are beautiful. See.** *(Points to one in her hair.)*

MRS. BUSH: **Randolph...Randolph remembered the kind you like, honey.**

MAY BUSH: *(To RANDOLPH)* **Just like you!**

RANDOLPH STRONG: **How sweet of you to wear one!**

MAY BUSH: *(Proudly walking across room toward MRS. BUSH)* **Look, Ma?**

MRS. BUSH: *(Tenderly kissing her daughter several times)* **Beautiful, my darlin',** *(Adding softly)* **poor chile!**

MAY BUSH: *(Walking toward and kissing MRS. TEMPLE)* **How do you like me – my other mama?**

MRS. TEMPLE: **Charming – God protect you, my dear!**

MAY BUSH: *(Noticing the sad expression on the faces of both mothers)* **My, you all look so sad; why so doleful? What is the matter with them, Randolph?**

RANDOLPH STRONG: **Why...I'm wounded, but smiling. The ladies...**

MRS. BUSH: *(Impatiently interrupting)* **Oh, children – don't waste this precious time. We've called you together to tell you sump'n...** *(Stuttering)* **we've got sump'n to tell you, and we got to tell you right now!**

(MRS. BUSH draws MAY aside toward MRS. TEMPLE, hastily and cautiously locking kitchen hall door.)

MRS. BUSH: *(Continuing)* **Listen, May. Come here, come here, Randolph, for I feel that both of you are my children. May, you got to be strong – for if ever you needed wits, now's the time to use 'em. May God forgive me – and Mrs. Temple there, both of us – I just got to tell you 'bout it quick – for all them folks are in the parlor and if we don't do something quick, right now,**

this whole town will be rippin' us to pieces – all of us, you and me – Mrs. Temple – and – and – the las' one of us! There ain't time to tell you the whole story – but – May – my poor chile – I know you kin trus' your own, dear ma that far?

MAY BUSH: *(Excitedly)* Yes, Ma, yes, but what is it?

MRS. BUSH: May, you and John can't marry – you jest can't marry!

MAY BUSH: *(Aghast)* Can't marry! Can't marry!

MRS. BUSH: No, never!

MAY BUSH: But why – why!

MRS. BUSH: Your father, and John's father – is – is –

MAY BUSH: You don't mean...

MRS. TEMPLE: Yes, May. John's father is your father.

MAY BUSH: *(Wrings her hands.)* Oh, I'd rather die – I'd rather die than face – this....

MRS. BUSH: *(Crooning)* I know, honey...I know...God forgive me...God forgive that man. Oh, no...I don't want Him to forgive him.

SCENE 4: THREE FEMALES AND ONE MALE

May, 20s

Randolph, 20s

Mrs. Bush, 40s

Mrs. Temple, 40s

This scene directly follows the preceding, and is the last one in the play.

1. Do you think the play's outcome is believable? Logical? Explain.

2. Why do you think May agreed to go along with marrying Randolph?

3. What does May mean when she says, "I've kept out of their clutches"?

4. Do you think it's a good idea for the women not to want to tell John why May is eloping with Randolph? Why? Why not?

MAY BUSH: Oh why, why did this have to happen to me – oh! I wish I were dead!

RANDOLPH STRONG: May – don't say that. You mustn't say that.

MAY BUSH: I do. Oh, God – I've kept out of their clutches myself, but now it's through you, Ma, that they've got me anyway. Oh, what's the use...

RANDOLPH STRONG: May!

MAY BUSH: The whole world will be pointing at me...

MRS. BUSH: Ah, honey, honey, I'll be loving you...

MAY BUSH: I wish I could die right now.

RANDOLPH STRONG: Will you listen to me now, May?

MAY BUSH: Those people in there – they'll be laughing... *(Knocking is heard.)*

MRS. TEMPLE: It's John. We can't let him come in here now. He mustn't know....

MRS. BUSH: No. We can't let him know or he'll kill his own father....

MRS. TEMPLE: What are you going to do, May?

MRS. BUSH: Yes, May – what are you going to do?

RANDOLPH STRONG: We are going to run away and get married, aren't we, May? Say yes, May – say yes!

MAY BUSH: John... *(The knocking is heard again.)*

MRS. BUSH: Keep it from him. It's the black women that have got to protect their men from the white men by not telling on 'em.

MRS. TEMPLE: God knows that's the truth.

RANDOLPH STRONG: May! Come with me *now!*

MAY BUSH: Randolph – do you want me?

RANDOLPH STRONG: I want you like I've always wanted you.

MAY BUSH: *(Shyly)* But – I don't love you.

RANDOLPH STRONG: You think you don't....

MAY BUSH: Do you want me now?

RANDOLPH STRONG: I want you now.

MAY BUSH: Ma, oh, Ma!

MRS. BUSH: *(In tears)* Quick, darlin' – tell him.

MAY BUSH: My coat.

MRS. BUSH: I'll get your coat, honey.

MRS. TEMPLE: Here, May, take *my* coat!

MRS. BUSH: What we going to tell John – and all the people?

MAY BUSH: Tell 'em – Oh, God, we can't tell 'em the – truth!

RANDOLPH STRONG: Mother Bush – just tell them the bride was stolen by Randolph Strong! *(RANDOLPH STRONG puts the coat around her and they go out of the door, leaving the others staring at them.)*

(Curtain)

BLUE-EYED BLACK BOY

Although *Blue-Eyed Black Boy* is based in the same sort of background or problem as the one in *Blue Blood*, it is intended to be taken much more seriously. Even more than the basic idea, there are many other similarities between the two plays. There are even a young girl wanting to get married and a young medical doctor who is to be her groom.

The action occurs in the kitchen of Mrs. Waters' cottage. The room contains a stove, an ironing board, a table with a lighted oil lamp sitting on it, and two chairs. A door, which stands slightly ajar, leads to the living room. A window opens onto a side street.

SCENE 1: TWO FEMALES

Pauline Waters, 40s

Rebecca, 20s

This scene begins the play. At the opening Mrs. Waters is sitting in a large rocker with her left foot bandaged and resting on a low stool.

1. What is the significance of Mrs. Waters' and Rebecca's conversation about people looking up to the family and about their "walking straight"?

2. Do you think the characters are realistic? Explain. Are they likeable? What are Mrs. Waters' and Rebecca's outstanding traits?

3. Why does Tom have blue eyes while no one else in the family does?

4. What do you think is the playwright's purpose in writing this scene? What does she want to communicate to the audience here?

MRS. WATERS: *(Calling to the other room)* **Rebecca, come on, your iron is hot now, I know.**

REBECCA: *(Answers from front room.)* **I'm coming now, Ma.** *(She enters holding a lacy garment in her hands.)* **I had to tack these bows on, how you like it now?**

MRS. WATER: *(Scanning the long nightdress set off with little pink bows that REBECCA is holding up for inspection)* **Ugh-hu, it shure is pretty, I don't believe anybody ever had as fine a wedding gown in this whole town.**

REBECCA: Humph! *(She shrugs her shoulders proudly as she tastes the iron to see if it is hot and then takes it over to the board and begins to press the gown.)* **That's to be expected sent it everybody in the Baptist Church looks up to us, don't they?**

MRS. WATERS: Sure they do. I ain't carried myself straight all these years for nothing. Your father was sure one proud man – he is put on a pinnacle.

REBECCA: Well, I sure have tried to walk straight all my life.

MRS. WATER: Yes, and I'm shore proud – now here you is getting ready to marry a young doctor – My! My! [...] Ouch, I wish he would come on over here to change the dressing on my foot – hope I ain't going to have the lockjaw.

REBECCA: You won't – Tom knows his business. *(She tosses her head proudly. She looks over to the stove and goes on.)* **Wish Jack would come on home and eat his supper so's I could clean up the dishes.**

MRS. WATERS: What time is it?

REBECCA: *(Goes to the middle door and peeps in the next room.)* **The clock in position to exactly five minutes after seven. He oughter been here a whole hour ago.**

MRS. WATERS: I wonder what's keeping him?

REBECCA: Well there's one thing sure and certain, he's not running after girls.

MRS. WATERS: No – he shore don't – just give him a book and he's happy – says he's going to quit running that crane – and learn engineering soons you get married. He's been mighty tied down since your father died – taking care of us.

REBECCA: Everybody says he's the smartest and finest looking black boy in the whole town.

MRS. WATERS: Yes, he is good looking if he is mine – some of 'em lay it to his eyes. *(She looks far off thoughtfully.)*

REBECCA: Yes, they do set him off – It's funny he's the only one in our family's got blue eyes though. Pa's was black and yours and mine are black too – It certainly is strange – I wish I'd had 'em.

MRS. WATERS: Oh, you be satisfied – you're pretty enough. Hush, there's the doctor's buggy stopping now – Go let him in. *(REBECCA goes to the door while MRS. WATERS bends over grunting and touching her foot.)*

SCENE 2: THREE FEMALES AND ONE MALE

Pauline Waters, 40s

Rebecca, 20s

Dr. Thomas Grey, 20s-30s

Hester Grant, 40s

This scene occurs directly after the preceding. After Rebecca answers the door, Dr. Grey enters with his bag.

1. In what way is this play similar to *Blue Blood*? How is it different? Which do you like better? Why?

2. Why do you suppose the playwright chose to write about such similar situations in the two plays and yet to write about them in such a different way?

3. Can you see any reason for Mrs. Waters' having an injured foot? Do you think this adds anything important to the plot? Why? Why not?

4. Do you think the idea of people planning to lynch Jack is realistic? Explain.

5. What does Mrs. Waters mean when she says she knows what to do to save her son and that she doesn't care what it will cost her?

6. What is the significance of the ring Mrs. Waters gets from the box that was in the trunk?

DR. GREY: Well, how's my patient feeling – better, I know.

MRS. WATERS: Now don't you be kidding me doctor – my foot's been paining me terrible – I'm scared to death I'm going to have the lockjaw. For God's sake, don't let me – *(REBECCA places chair for him near her mother.)*

DR. GREY: *(Unwinds the bandage, looks at foot and opens his bag.)* Fine, it's doing fine – you'll have to keep off of it for a week more and then you'll be all right.

MRS. WATERS: Can't walk on it for a week?

DR. GREY: Not unless you want to die of blood poisoning – lockjaw, I mean! *(He touches the foot with iodine and puts on new bandage.)* That was an old rusty nail you stuck in your foot – a pretty close call. *(He looks lovingly at REBECCA.)*

MRS. WATERS: Well I'm tickled to have such a good doctor for my new son.

DR. GREY: You bet. *(Then thoughtfully)* I saw some mighty rough-looking hoodlums gathering on the streets as I came in – looks like there might have been trouble somewhere.

REBECCA: Oh, they're always having a squabble on the streets – you get used to 'em and you will too after awhile –

MRS. WATERS: Yes, there's always something stirring everyday – I just go on and on and don't pay 'em no mine myself.

DR. GREY: *(Patting the foot tenderly)* Now that's all right. You keep off of it – hear me. Or I won't vouch for the outcome.

MRS. WATERS: It's so sore – I can't stand up even if I was a kind to – See who's that at the back door, Rebecca. *(She peeps out.)*

REBECCA: *(Goes to the door and cracks it.)* Who's there?

HESTER: Me – me, it's Hester – Hester Grant. Lemme in. *(REBECCA opens the door and HESTER comes panting in. She looks around as if hating to speak before the others, then blurts out:)* Pauline – it's Jack – your son Jack has been rested – rested and put in jail.

MRS. WATERS: Rested?

REBECCA: Good Lord.

DR. GREY: What for?

HESTER: *(Moving about restlessly)* They say he done brushed against

179

a white woman on the street. They had er argument and she
hollowed out he's attacked her – a crew of white men come up
and started beating on him and the policeman, when he was
coming home from work – dragged him to the jail house.

MRS. WATERS: My God. My God – it ain't so – he ain't brushed up
against no lady, my boy ain't. He's, he's a gentleman, that what
he is.

HESTER: *(Still moving about restlessly, she hadn't thought – she had
some thing else to say.)* **And, and Pauline – that ain't the worst –
that ain't the worst, they, they say there's gointer be a lynching
tonight! – They gointer break open the jail and string him up!**
(She finished desperately.)

MRS. WATERS: String him up – my son – they can't do that – not to
my son, not him!

DR. GREY: *(Excitedly)* I'll drive over and see the judge – he'll do
something to stop it.

HESTER: *(Sarcastically)* Him – not him – he's a lyncher his own self
– Don't put no trust in him – Ain't he done let 'em lynch six
niggers in the last year jes gone – him! *(She scoffed again.)*

REBECCA: *(Wringing her hands)* We got to do something – *(Goes up
to TOM.)* Do you know anybody else, anybody at all who could
save him?

MRS. WATERS: Wait, wait – I know what'll do – I don't care what it
costs. *(To REBECCA)* Fly in yonder *(Pointing to the next room)*
and get me that little tin box out of the left hand side of the
tray in my trunk – hurry – fly. *(REBECCA hurries out, while DR.
GREY and HESTER look on in wonderment.)* Lynch my son – my
son. *(She yells out to REBECCA in next room.)* Got it – you got it?

REBECCA: *(From next room)* Yes, Ma – I got it. *(She hurries in with a
small tin box in her hand and hands it to her mother.)*

MRS. WATERS: *(Feverishly tossing the odd bits of jewelry in the box,
finally coming up with a small ring. She turns to DR. GREY.)* Here,
Tom, take this, run, jump in your horse and buggy and fly over
to Governor Tinkhem's house and don't let nobody – nobody
stop you. Just give him the ring and say, Pauline sent this, she
says they going to lynch her son born twenty-one years ago,

mind you say twenty-one years ago – then say – listen close – look in his eyes – and you'll save him.

DR. GREY: *(Listens in amazement while grasping the small ring in his hand and hastens towards the door, saying)* **Don't worry, I'll put it in his hand and tell him what you said – just as quick as my horse can make it.** *(When he leaves the room, REBECCA and HESTER look at PAULINE with open mouths in astonishment.)*

HESTER: *(Starting as if from a dream)* **Well, well, well, I don't git what you mean, but I reckon you knows what you is doing.** *(She and REBECCA watch DR. GREY from the front window as he drove away.)*

MRS. WATERS: I sholy do!

REBECCA: *(Comes over and throws her arms around her mother's neck.)* **Mother, what does it all mean? Can you really save him?**

MRS. WATERS: *(Confidently)* **Wait and see – I'll tell you more about it after awhile. Don't ask me now.**

SCENE 3: THREE FEMALES AND ONE MALE

Pauline Waters, 40s

Rebecca, 20s

Dr. Thomas Grey, 20s-30s

Hester Grant, 40s

This scene follows the preceding, and is the last scene in the play.

1. If you were playing one of the women, how would you go about trying to keep the sense of tension high in this scene?

2. Do you think this scene is a good one? Why? Why not?

3. Do you think this play is still effective, or do you think it loses some of its value in the present time? Explain.

4. In your opinion, is this a good play? Explain.

HESTER: *(Going over to the window)* **I hope he'll get over to the Governor's in time.** *(Looking out)* **Ump! There goes a bunch of men with guns now and here comes another all slouched over and pushing on the same way.**

REBECCA: *(Joining her at the window with bated breath)* **And look! Look! Here comes wagons full.** *(The rumble of wagon wheels is heard.)* **See 'em, Hester, all piled in with their guns too –**

MRS. WATERS: *(Her lips moving in prayer, her head turned deliberately away from the window sighing deeply now and then.)*

HESTER: Do, Lord! Do, Lord! Help us this night.

REBECCA: *(With trembling voice)* **Hussies. Look at them men on horse!** *(Horses' hooves are heard in the street outside. REBECCA crying lightly)*

HESTER: Jesus! Jesus! Please come down and help us this night.

REBECCA: *(Running over to her mother and flinging her arms about her neck)* **Oh, Mother, Mother, what will we do – do you hear 'em – do you hear all them men on horses and wagons going up to the jail? Poor brother – poor boy.**

MRS. WATERS: Trust in God, daughter – I've got faith in him, faith in – in the Governor – he won't fail – *(She continues to move her lips in prayer. REBECCA rushes back to the window as new sounds of wagon wheels are heard.)*

HESTER: *(At window)* **Still coming!**

REBECCA: Why don't Tom come back, why don't he hurry?

HESTER: Hush, chile! He ain't had time yet.

MRS. WATERS: *(Breaks out in audible prayer.)* **Lord Jesus, I know I sinned against your holy law, but you did forgive me and let me hold up my head again. Help me again, dear Jesus – help me to save my innocent child – him who never done no wrong – Save him, Lord – Let his father –** *(She stops and looks around at the two women, then cautious)* **you understand all, I mean sweet Jesus – come down and rise with this wild mob tonight – pour your love into their wicked hearts – Lord, Lord, hear my prayer.**

HESTER: *(At window)* **Do, Lord – hear.**

MRS. WATERS: *(Restlessly looking toward the others)* **Any sign of Tom yet –**

REBECCA: No, Ma – I don't see him no where yet.

HESTER: Give him time –

MRS. WATERS: Time! Time! It'll be too late reckly – too late – *(She sobs. Her head lifted, listening)* **What that?**

MRS. WATERS: The sound of many feet, I hear.

HESTER: *(Peers out and listens.)* **What?**

MRS. WATERS: The sound of many feet, I hear.

REBECCA: *(Looks out interestingly.)* I see 'em – wait, wait – Ma! Ma! *(Hysterically)* It's the state troops – the Guards – It's the Guards, Ma – they're coming – Look, Miss Hester!

HESTER: They sure is Jesus – Sure as I'm born – them military – they come – come to save, save him.

REBECCA: And yonders Tom at the gate – he's coming.

DR. GREY: *(Rushes in, as the others look at him in amazement.)* **He saved Miss Waters, saved! Did the Governor send the troops?**

(Curtain)

Jewish-American Theatre

Jewish-American Theatre

Jewish religious leaders viewed theatre as immoral in that it defied the biblical injunction against men dressing as women. Yet plays began to be inserted as questions and responses in the worship service, from which evolved religious plays, which gradually moved outside the synagogue.

In 1918 in Moscow, Nahum Zemach founded a professional Hebrew theatre. Called Habimah (The Stage), it became one of three studios associated with the Moscow Art Theatre under Stanislavski. Among its early productions were S. Anski's *The Dybbuk*; David Pinski's *The Eternal Jew*, based on a Talmudic legend, and H. Leivick's *The Golem*, all of which were heavily moralistic and didactic.

Yiddish theatre, on the other hand, appealed to the common person through popular art, including song and dance. This form of theatre began in 1876 in Romania where Avrom Goldfaden founded the first Yiddish theatre company. Its premiere production, a two-act musical, was so successful that Goldfaden began writing other plays, little more than scenarios. The style included horseplay, burlesque, caricatures, and buffoonery, interspersed with lilting tunes.

The producer of the first Yiddish play in America was Boris Thomashefsky. By 1917, there were four Yiddish theatres in Manhattan, four in Philadelphia, two in Brooklyn, and others in the East and Midwest. The most prolific writers were Moyshe Hurwitz and Joseph Lateiner.

In the 1890s Jacob Gordin introduced realism into Yiddish theatre. Opposed to improvisation, he wrote complete scripts adapting many of the great European plays. A recurring theme in his work was the breakdown of the Jewish family due to stress caused by relocating to new surroundings.

Instrumental in establishing Yiddish theatre in New York was Maurice Schwartz, who recruited well-known actors for his company and presented classics along with the lighter Yiddish fare. Then during the Depression, a new sort of Jewish theatre emerged. The best-known group was Artef, a Yiddish acronym for Workers' Theater Group.

Jewish theatre of today is a combination of styles, including revivals of Jewish plays, new settings for examination of family values, nostalgia, the recasting of early Yiddish plays, and plays about the Holocaust.

THE CHOPIN PLAYOFFS
Israel Horovitz

The Chopin Playoffs is the third play in a trilogy about growing up Jewish. The plays, each self-contained, begin in 1941 and end in 1947. They are based in part on a collection of stories by Morley Torgov called *A Good Place to Be From* and on the author's own remembrances, despite the fact that Torgov's work is set in Canada, while the playwright Israel Horovitz grew up in Massachusetts.

Horovitz, who has had more than fifty plays produced, is the winner of numerous awards including two Obies for best plays off-Broadway and an Emmy.

The play takes place largely in the Yanover home, the Rosen home, and in the area of the park. Horovitz states: "A stern note on casting this play: It is my intention that the Rosen parents and the Yanover parents be cast with youthful, attractive actors. Stereotypes are to be avoided, entirely, as are Yiddish or Eastern European accents — or stereotypically 'Jewish' intonation."

SCENE 1: ONE MALE AND ONE FEMALE

Fern, 16

Stanley, 16

The play opens with "an old Jew" named Jacob Ardenshensky (the same actor plays both Mr. Wong and Uncle Goldberg) welcoming the audience and introducing the play. He sets the scene by discussing the time period: "The year is 1947, and the last of Canada's soldiers have returned home from Occupied Germany." He mentions that "Soo" is the nickname for Sault Sainte Marie, Ontario, where the action occurs. He introduces the characters and discusses the feud between the Yanovers (Irving's parents) and the Rosen's (Stanley's parents). He says that the play will be about a piano competition between the two boys, both high school seniors. He then asks Esther Yanover and Pearl Rosen to talk about the upcoming competition, which they do. There is the sound of a prizefight bell and we go into the following scene.

Keep in mind that the two boys are similar, that each wants to outdo the other, that they both play the piano well, that they both like Fern, and that they each have a weird sense of humor.

1. What sort of person is Stanley? Explain. What do you think is his most outstanding trait? Justify your choice.

2. Do you like this scene? Why? Why not? Do you think the characters are realistic?

3. Why is Fern so insistent in telling Stanley how he should dress?

4. What type of person is Fern? Do you like her? Why? Why not?

5. The play is a comedy. Point out instances in the script that prove this, and explain how they prove it.

FERN: This phone call had better be important, Stanley Rosen! My father is going to kill me.

STANLEY: You hear the rain, Fern?

FERN: It's raining? That's why you called, for the umpteenth time?

STANLEY: Listen. Isn't it beautiful?

FERN: Naturally, I perm my hair and what does it do?

STANLEY: When Chopin wrote the "Raindrop Prelude," he imagined that he drowned in a lake and drops of water were falling on his naked, dead chest. And when he told George Sand the story...about imagining himself drowned and the water on his chest, George Sand laughed at him and said, "It's raining out. You're just hearing rain hitting the roof!" [...]

FERN: *(Laughs.)* God, Stanley, you believe any cock-and-bull story anybody throws at you. As long as it's anything about Chopin, you believe it. You are so *gullible*.

STANLEY: Why do you say that, Fern?

FERN: Because it's true! Last year, you told me this completely nuts story that "I'm Always Chasing Rainbows" is based on something Chopin wrote called "The Waltz of the Little Dog"...

STANLEY: But it's true! "Waltz in D Flat"...Opus 64, Number 1. I learned it when I was twelve...

FERN: Oh, God, Stanley, *really*.... I've listened to Chopin's "Waltz in D Flat" and it sounds absolutely nothing like "I'm Always Chasing Rainbows"....

STANLEY: Okay, fine. I'd better get dressed, Fern.... What are you wearing tonight? I want to make sure we...you know...match.

FERN: Blue, definitely blue.

STANLEY: Great. I'll go blue too...

FERN: Stanley, not *dark* blue, okay? At least, not your sport coat...at least, not dark blue on your *shoulders*, okay?

STANLEY: How come?

FERN: Ask me no questions and I'll tell you no lies, Stanley.... See you at quarter to eight, sharp.

STANLEY: See you, Fern.

SCENE 2: TWO MALES AND ONE FEMALE

Fern, 16

Irving, 16

Stanley, 16

Esther Yanover is commenting about an article in the news-paper that mentions a husband and wife who both are M.D.s. Irving says he has no interest in medical school. He says that previously she's mentioned articles about twin brothers who are lawyers and that his father stacked accounting journals on his bed. Moses, Irving's father, then reads an article in the *Jewish Forward* about a music contest for which a full university scholarship is the prize. It says the man sponsoring the contest, Cyrus Drinkwater, used to live in the "Soo."

Irving asks to borrow the car, and Esther says she knows Stanley has borrowed the Rosen's car. Couldn't they double date? Irving replies that he has a really "big big *big* date."

Irving arrives at the Fipps's home where the dog tries to bite him. He calls to Mr. and Mrs. Fipps and tells them he came to pick up Fern. They tell him that she has gone with Stanley to a dance at the Y. Angry, Irving goes there and stares at Fern and Stanley. Finally, the two boys get into an argument which ends with each giving the other a bloody nose.

Stanley asks Fern to "kiss me and my blood." Irving staggers outside to a bench where Ardenshensky is sitting. The old man asks him why he's not out on a date.

The next scene occurs at "probably imagined" school lockers.

1. Do you think Fern is sincere in saying she was confused and wants to go out with Irving? Explain.

2. Why does Irving ask her about Stanley's dancing ability and then if there's anything "horrible" about him?

3. Do you think Irving is being immodest, or is he really stating what he believes is fact? Why?

4. What makes this scene funny?

5. What sort of relationship do the two boys have with each other?

FERN: I'm really sorry about the confusion on Saturday night....

IRVING: Oh, hey, don't even think about it.

FERN: I'm sorry, Irving. I really am. I really thought it was for next week that we'd agreed.

IRVING: Hey, really, don't worry.

FERN: I don't want to miss out.

IRVING: *(Amazed)* In what sense?

FERN: I want to make sure that we get to go out next Saturday night. I don't want to miss out.

IRVING: *(Smiles as little as he can.)* Oh...well...sure, we can do that. I'll have to break a *thing*...but...sure we can. *(New attitude here)* So...Fern...how's Rosen? Good dancer? *(They stop a moment.)*

FRAN: Stanley Rosen? Good dancer? Yes. Stanley's a *good* dancer, but not a great dancer....

IRVING: Oh, sure, I understand. It must have been a little, I dunno...embarrassing for you, dancing with him all last night....

FERN: One makes do, Irving.

IRVING: Oh, yes, Fern, one does.... *(Pauses; smiles and then looks at FERN seriously.)* Uh, Fern, is there anything about Rosen that you think is, I dunno, particularly *horrible?* From your particular point of view, I mean....

FERN: From my particular point of view? He fights. That's horrible. I hate that.

IRVING: Mmmm, yuh.... Anything else?

FERN: *(Pauses; confidentially)* Horrible? No.... Oh, well, he has a little dandruff. I wouldn't call it *horrible*, but it's a definite imperfection....

IRVING: Dandruff, huh? Poor Rosen, huh? Poor guy.

FERN: Isn't it wonderful news about the contest? About the scholarship and all. It's such a fabulous chance for us...for you, I mean...with your talent. Do you think you could win it?

IRVING: The contest? Me? Win it? Positive. Sure, I can win it. I'm the best musician around, right?

FERN: You shouldn't be immodest, Irving. It's immature. It's also *unattractive.*

IRVING: I'm just looking at the facts coldly, Fern, as though I weren't me...immodesty is, well, different. My view is cold, clinical, flatly realistic.... I'm simply the best musician in the "Soo"...

FERN: What about Stanley? *(STANLEY walks behind IRVING, faces FERN obliquely, puts fingers behind IRVING's head, discreetly, forming horns of a beast.)*

IRVING: Rosen? What about him?

FERN: *(Nervously)* Well, he, uh, he, uh...Stanley plays, uh, pretty well too...*He's with us!* Hello, Stanley. *(IRVING spins about; faces STANLEY.)*

IRVING: Rosen.

STANLEY: *(Nods.)* Yanover. Fern.

FERN: *(Trying to ease the unbearable tension)* Are you trying out for the contest, too, Stanley?

STANLEY: Does a bear pee in the woods?

FERN: That is so completely *uncouth*, Stanley Rosen.

IRVING: *(Happily)* Very little couth, Rosen.... It's true.... *(Looks at watch.)*

STANLEY: Right, Yanover, you oughta know....

IRVING: I oughta know what, exactly, Rosen? It's a little difficult to follow the twistings and turnings of your unique mind....

STANLEY: Fat lip is what springs to my unique mind, Yanover....

FERN: Is that a threat of violence, Stanley Rosen? Because, if it is, I'm going straight home.

IRVING: No, you stay, Fern. *I'll* go! I've got to practice. There's no magic to perfection. It's all in the honing of genius.... *(Smiles. To FERN)* I'll call you, usual time, Fern.... *(Starts off; stops.)* Oh, yuh.... Playing *pretty* well is not playing very well, Fern. *(To STANLEY)* Fern said you play pretty well, Rosen, but Irving Yanover plays very, very well. This is a hard, cold fact of life. I'll call you, Fern. It's always a pleasure, Rosen.... *(IRVING looks at STANLEY's shoulder and then looks up at the sky, then back at STANLEY again.)* Bizarre, huh, snowing at this time of year. Ah, well, that's Canada....

STANLEY: What's this, Yanover?

FERN: It's not snowing, Irving....

IRVING: Then what the hell's on Rosen's shoulder?

FERN: Irving Yanover! That is *so* cruel! *(IRVING reaches across and brushes dandruff from STANLEY's shoulder. STANLEY punches IRVING, who staggers backward and then rushes at STANLEY. FERN is horrified.)* **Stop! Stop it, you two, stop!**

SCENE 3: ONE MALE AND ONE FEMALE

Fern, 16

Stanley, 16

The two boys get into another fight. The scene shifts to where they're both playing the same Chopin piece at different pianos. It's late at night and both sets of parents want the boys to stop practicing.

The lights come up on the Rosen home. Stanley has just picked up Uncle Goldberg at the train station and is now in a hurry to leave. Goldberg keeps talking about how nice it was for Stanley to do this, though Goldberg is rich and could have hired a cab. Goldberg keeps talking while Stanley runs back and forth taking luggage to the bedroom.

The scene switches to the "soda shoppe."

1. Why does Stanley keep staring at Fern? Is this a deliberate thing, or is he lost in thought? Explain.

2. Both Stanley and Irving do dumb things. Can you find instances of that sort of thing in this scene? Explain.

3. Why does Stanley say that a wonderful thing about Fern is the way she eats her French fries? Does he really admire her for this? Explain.

FERN: Happy birthday to you.

    Happy birthday to you.

    Happy birthday, dear Stanley,

    Happy birthday to you.

    (FERN waits for a response.) **The song is over, Stanley. Stanley!**

STANLEY: Huh?!

FERN: You just keep staring at me, Stanley. It's unnerving. Happy birthday.

STANLEY: *(Leans in toward FERN and whispers to her.)* I've never had a nicer birthday, Fern, I swear to you...

FERN: Oh, Stanley, that's really nice of you to say that...

STANLEY: Oh, no, no, it's true. Every year – all of them before this – me and my parents, Chinese food, aunts and uncles... *(Even more quietly)* To be with you, on my own with you, in this restaurant, not eating, but instead watching you eat your French fries and cheeseburger...watching the red and green lights bounce from your hair...

FERN: *(Suddenly worried)* My hair? *(She whips around.)* Is my hair too close to the lights?

STANLEY: *(Trying to recapture the quiet tones of thirty seconds before)* No, no, Fern. The light from the light...the beams of light...red and green.

FERN: Oh, you mean the light from the lights, not the lights themselves.... I'm sorry, Irving.... I interrupted you....

STANLEY: Stanley.

FERN: I said "Stanley"....

STANLEY: You said "Irving."

FERN: That's ridiculous. I said "Stanley." Why would I say "Irving"?

STANLEY: I don't know why you would say "Irving," but "Irving" is clearly what you said.

FERN: Let's not argue, Stanley. It's your birthday.

STANLEY: I'm sorry, I'm sorry.... The pressure of the playoffs only eight weeks away...

FERN: What was that about the light on my hair? *(Smiles.)* The green and blue light?

STANLEY: Red and green.

FERN: Yes. *(She dips her potatoes into a circle of catsup on her plate and eats them.)*

STANLEY: May I tell you something wonderful about you, Fern?

FERN: Well, my, Stanley, sure...

STANLEY: All my life my parents have made me go out on dates with, well, a certain kind of girl...

FERN: Rosie Berkowitz?

STANLEY: How did you know that?

FERN: Rosie is my ultimate best friend, Stanley, so be careful....

STANLEY: Rosie Berkowitz is your *ultimate* best friend?

FERN: One of them. I happen to feel very sorry for her.

STANLEY: Because she's fat?

FERN: She's hefty, she's not fat.

STANLEY: *Hefty?* Like a Rocky Mountain is hefty! You wouldn't say "hefty" if you ever had to dance with Rosie Berkowitz.

FERN: I've danced with Rosie many times. Insensitive boys often leave her on the bench, so I've danced with her.

STANLEY: There. See? That's another wonderful thing about you, Fern.

FERN: What was the first wonderful thing?

STANLEY: Hmmm?

FERN: The first wonderful thing about me? You never told me what it was.

STANLEY: Oh. The way you dip your French fries into the catsup one at a time, instead of making a big glob that you shove into your mouth and glob down, like a dinosaur....

FERN: Rosie does that?

STANLEY: Sure. Why do ya think she's so fat? Rosie Berkowitz would never make a circle like you do with catsup. She just pours the whole bottle out on her plate and jams the old fries right in, fistfuls at a time. It's really revolting. *(We hear Chopin being played.)*

FERN: Well. *(Smiles.)* **Enough about Rosie, Stanley.** *(Looks into his eyes.)* **This is your birthday.**

SCENE 4: ONE MALE AND ONE FEMALE

Irving, 16

Fern, 16

Goldberg and Ardenshensky have an argument about who is older — an unusual moment since the same person plays both characters. The lights come up on Irving and Fern walking home from school.

1. Why does Irving say Fern is his "Goldberg Variation"? Do you think this is funny? Why? Why not?

2. Why do you think Fern brings up Rosie Berkowitz?

3. Obviously, Irving is acting conceited or superior? Why do you think he's doing that? Why is he so patronizing about Debussy?

IRVING: My life is music, Fern, and that's what you are to me: I am
Johann Sebastian Bach and you are my "Goldberg Variation"....

FERN: You mean music to your ears? That kind of thing?

IRVING: Roughly.

FERN: Let me just recap this. It's a little confusing. I am to you what
"The Goldberg Variations" were to Bach, right? *(Giggles.)* I got
a little confused, because Stanley's got an uncle named
Goldberg....

IRVING: So what?

FERN: It's just a little confusing, that's all! No big deal, okay? *(There
is a pause.)*

IRVING: Fern, I would like to tell you something I have never dared
tell another human being in the whole world.

FERN: Be careful, Irving, because Rosie Berkowitz – fat or not –
happens to be one of my very best friends....

IRVING: What are you *talking* about?

FERN: What are *you* talking about?

IRVING: My career.

FERN: Your career?

IRVING: My career. I hope I can trust you, Fern.

FERN: Of course you can trust me, Irving.

IRVING: I feel I can. I do.... Fern?

FERN: What?

IRVING: I feel that I might be another Horowitz....

FERN: In what sense, Irving? You mean as good?

IRVING: Of *course* I mean "as good!" You don't think I mean I think
I'm gonna wake up one morning and actually *be* Vladimir
Horowitz, do you?

FERN: Is that what you think I thought you thought? Because, if it
is, Irving Yanover, you are being *sooo insulting* –

IRVING: No, Fern.... Of *course* not! *(Pause/sigh)* Sometimes my
genius frightens me, Fern.

FERN: You must never be frightened, Irving...at least not of something like genius.

IRVING: I know you're right! *(Pauses.)* I knew I could trust you.
(Pauses.) I've chosen my piece for the playoffs, Fern.... Chopin.

"**Waltz in C-Sharp Minor, Opus 64, Number 2.**"

FERN: That's nice. I'm playing Debussy *[Title of Piece].*

IRVING: Oh, that's great....

FERN: Let me play my piece for you, Irving? Not the whole thing. Just a little....

IRVING: Oh, sure. I'd love it.

FERN: *(Taking a recorder from book bag)* I wish I could play like you...you really hate the recorder, don't you?

IRVING: The soprano recorder is a fine instrument, Fern... ancient...primitive, almost *tribal.*

FERN: Listen. *(FERN squeaks out a high-pitched half minute of Debussy. When she is finished, she smiles at IRVING. N.B.: Music can be on sound tape.)* Did I make a fool of myself? Just tell me if I did, Irving, please?

IRVING: Not at all. Not in the least. You are a fine and sensitive player and...

FERN: I can tell you loathed it.

IRVING: It's not you. It's him.

FERN: Who? *(Looks about for STANLEY; panicked.)*

IRVING: Debussy. It's Debussy I hate....

FERN: Irving Yanover! How can you possibly hate Debussy?

IRVING: Well, Fern, it's true. I just don't happen to like Debussy at all. He's sugary, syrupy. He's a minor, minor figure, in my humble opinion....

FERN: Calling your opinion "humble" is like calling Lake Michigan "damp," Irving Yanover! Debussy is a major figure and I happen to like him *enormously!* He happens to be my first choice!

IRVING: *(Deeply ashamed)* Oh, God, Fern, I'm really sorry. Of course, you're right. You should play Debussy. He was a man and he lived and he wrote music the very best he could and he died and you should play his music and I'm really ashamed of myself for having said that....

FERN: *(After a pause; quietly)* I understand, Irving. You needn't feel ashamed.

IRVING: Fern, I have spent many days of my life around many, many girls...

FERN: Rosie Berkowitz?

IRVING: Why do you keep bringing up Rosie Berkowitz?

FERN: She happens to be a friend.

IRVING: She's nice, Rosie Berkowitz. A nice girl. Sort of a tub, but very nice. Her cousin Arnold used to play first string on the James Street Aces with a friend of mine.

SCENE 5: ONE FEMALE AND TWO MALES

Fern, 16

Irving, 16

Stanley, 16

Stanley runs in and says he's been waiting two hours at Capy's Grille where Fern was supposed to meet him. Fern says she was confused; she thought she'd made a date with Irving. The two boys start to argue and insult each other. Fern tries to get them to stop. When they won't, she starts to leave. Stanley pleads with her to stay. The boys again start to argue but say they're not when Fern again wants them to stop.

1. Obviously, it's funny, but is it logical that Fern cannot tell the boys apart? Explain.

2. Do you think their insults are funny? Why? Why not?

3. Why do you think Fern becomes so emotional in talking about the phone?

4. Do you like this scene? Would you like to play one of these roles? Why? Why not?

5. What do you think of Stanley's suggestion about the winner of the contest winning Fern? Is it logical that she go along with this?

FERN: *(Starts to sob. Her shoulders shake. She moans, rasps, shouts.)* **Will you two *stop*...will you two please stop...will you two please please *please stopppp? Will you? Will yoooo?***

IRVING: We're not fighting, Fern...

STANLEY: Not at all...

FERN: That's not it! *(Moans; sobs.)* **Oh, Goddd...**

IRVING: We're really not fighting, Fern. Look at us...

STANLEY: There's no reason to cry...

IRVING: I apologize, Fern, I really do.... Don't cry.

FERN: *(Crying openly)* **I'm not crying....**

IRVING: We really weren't going to fight...not in front of you.

STANLEY: Honest to God...not in front of you....

FERN: *(Sobs.)* **That's not it.... That's not why I'm upset....**

STANLEY: What's it, then?

IRVING: Why are you upset?

FERN: Because...I can't...tell you apart!

IRVING: You can't tell who apart?

FERN: You and Irving.

IRVING: I am Irving.

FERN: *(Sobs.)* ***You seeee?*** *(STANLEY and IRVING stare at each other a moment.)*

STANLEY: You can't tell me apart from Irving Yanover?

FERN: No, I can't. I really can't. You both play piano, you both crack jokes, you're both depressed all the time, you're both Jewish, you're both skinny, you're both conceited...

IRVING: Rosen has dandruff.

FERN: Oh, my God! That was really *cruel!*

STANLEY: I'll kill you for that!

IRVING: Rosen is round-shouldered.

FERN: So are you. You're much more round-shouldered than he is.

IRVING: I am not!

STANLEY: You are, Yanover!

FERN: You are so!

STANLEY: Practically a hunchback....

IRVING: An hunchback....

STANLEY: How about *an* hit in the head, Yanover?

FERN: *No fighting!*

IRVING: Irving started it. I didn't. Don't blame me.

STANLEY: Don't blame me, either, Fern. Blame Rosen!

FERN: *Oh, my God*...I really can't tell you apart. It's true! *It's trooooo*.... *(She sobs.)* Every night, before I go to sleep, the phone rings and it's one of you...as soon as I hang it up, I know the other one will get mad at me...because the other one has been calling and calling, waiting for the line to stop being busy.... *(Pauses.)* Just the same, just exactly the same.... *(She sobs, again.)* You dance the same, you kiss the same, you both like to hold the same hand, you like the same books, the same movies, the same records, you're both terrible athletes, A-plus students, neither of you smokes, nor drinks, both of you crack bad jokes endlessly and you both talk about Chopin all the time and you both...upset me *so much!* Ooooo! *(She sobs, again.)*

STANLEY: Fern Fipps, this is really insulting. It's not insulting for Yanover to be mistaken for me, but I am...insulted deeply. Deeply!

FERN: I knew I made the date with you, Stanley, but I got confused and thought you, Irving, were Stanley...that's why I was late, Stanley.

IRVING: And our date was tomorrow, Fern.... I was supposed to practice in music hall today, so I can cream Rosen come the playoffs.

STANLEY: Come the playoffs, dear boy, the cream will be Rosen. The *creamed* will be Yanover. *(STANLEY threatens to hit IRVING.)*

FERN: NO FIGHTING! YOU PROMISED! YOU PROMISED ME, BOTH OF YOU! *(STANLEY and IRVING face each other, fists ready.)*

IRVING and STANLEY: We're not fighting!

FERN: I can't stand it! *I'm going to end up hating both of you!*

STANLEY: This is your [...] fault, Yanover!

FERN: ...I like being with both of you, but I can't be with both of you...and I can't choose one over the other because I can't tell you apart....

STANLEY: *Loookkk*, I have a simple solution, Fern....

FERN: *(Sobs again.)* What is it?

STANLEY: How about the concert? Maybe the better man should

win you in the playoffs, Fern. Let the winner really *win.*

IRVING: Aren't you kinda' making a mistake there, Rosen?

STANLEY: I hardly think so, Yanover....

IRVING: Oh, really?

STANLEY: Oh, really....

FERN: Oh, that's such a good idea, Irving.

STANLEY: Stanley...

FERN: *(To IRVING)* Stanley, I mean....

STANLEY: Me, Fern, me....

FERN: Ooooo, my God! The playoffs aren't until the end of June. It's only May tenth! How will I ever *live* till the end of June?

IRVING: Until then, you go out with only me, and after that the winner...Irving.

FERN: Until then I'll go out with you, Irving, one week, and you, Stanley, the next week, and then you, Irving, one week, and so on. *(Seriously)* Please say yes. *Please!*

STANLEY: Yes, I say yes....

IRVING: I really hate this. I want you to know that I really and truly hate this.... Yes, okay, yes.

FERN: *(Thrilled)* I...am...sooo...*relieved!*

SCENE 6: TWO FEMALES AND THREE MALES

Pearl, 40ish

Esther, 40ish

Barney, 40ish

Moses, 40ish

Mr. Wong (Ardenshensky, Goldberg), any age from 50s on

The scene switches to the Ritz Cafe where Mr. and Mrs. Rosen and Mrs. and Mrs. Yanover sit at a table discussing how well they get along. They wish their sons could do the same. They then start arguing about silly things, such as how a sentence one of them said could be improved. They talk about Rosie Berkowitz — how brilliant — but how fat — she is and that she's seeing a non-Jewish boy. Moses says this sort of thing happens, and the kids will outgrow it. Esther says they do *not* happen.

The mention of Truman refers to a meeting of the U. S. president with the Canadian prime minister.

1. Why do you think the competition is so important to the Yanovers and Rosens?

2. Why do you think Pearl says the two families are not close friends?

3. Do you think this sort of argument really could happen? Explain.

4. What makes this scene funny? Why? Which lines do you think are the funniest? Why? The most absurd? Why?

5. Considering the era, why do you think Rosen would have used the name Royal a few years earlier?

PEARL: [...] So? How's your Irving?

ESTHER: Exhausted. He practices day and night....

PEARL: Our Stanley, too...day and night.

BARNEY: We're sleepless.

MOSES: I wish Harry Truman never set foot in Canada. Competition is a waste of time, if you ask me....

PEARL: *That* you can say again, Mosie.

ESTHER: In what sense?

PEARL: Hmmm?

ESTHER: In what sense do you mean he should say that again, Pearl?

BARNEY: What Pearl means is that our Stanley is...well...unbeatable.

MOSES: What?

ESTHER: Oh, really? Mosie happened to mean that our Irving is wasting his time because he needn't practice to beat Stanley. He can beat your Stanley without practice. Isn't that what you meant, Mosie?

BARNEY: I don't think that's what your Mosie meant, Essie....

ESTHER: I think a wife knows what a husband means...

MOSES: Just a minute! I don't like what I'm hearing here!

PEARL: And neither do I!

ESTHER: I'll tell you what I think: I think that if the children want to compete, let them. If Mackenzie King and Harry Truman are both in favor of competition, then I'm in favor of competition, too.

PEARL: I agree....

ESTHER: As for us, we are all adults and we are very close friends....

PEARL: Don't be ridiculous!

ESTHER: In what sense am I being ridiculous, Mrs. Rosen?

PEARL: We're not close friends. We're neighbors and we're Jews. When you're a Jew in a town like Sault Sainte Marie, you take what other Jews are in the neighborhood. You're in the neighborhood, we're in the neighborhood...no more, no less....

ESTHER: That is possibly the most insulting thing I have ever heard in my life, Mrs. Rosen. (*All stop eating except for PEARL.*)

MOSES: I have a feeling, Essie, that what you have heard, so far, is nothing! compared to what's coming when my temper goes. And my temper is going, Mr. Rosen...Mrs. Rosen.... I warn you both!

BARNEY: You see, Pearl? I told you it would come to this!

ESTHER: You told her what would come to this, Mr. Rosen? That you could meet with the poor schlepp Yanovers at Ritz Cafe and make insulting remarks? Hmmm? I have a piece of bad news for you, Mr. Rosen...(or is it still Royal?)...my Irving Yanover could beat your Stanley in a Chopin playoff with one hand tied behind his back....

PEARL: I've heard him play, your Irving, and that's precisely the way it sounds....

ESTHER: I will not have my son slurred like this, Mrs. Royal-Rosen.

PEARL: This is not a slur. This is a fact of life. It so happens that Chopin has some heart and some soul...when your Irving played at shul last year, it was completely mechanical like a wind-up toy...no heart, no soul.

MOSES: I have heard enough.... Esther, hand me my coat.

BARNEY: Oh, sure, run. A typical Yanover move: there's trouble; run. Run, go, run, run...

MOSES: You want heart and soul? Good, great! Here from the bottom of my heart is sole.... *(MOSES picks up BARNEY'S fish and places it in BARNEY'S hand.)* **Here. Hand this to your wife. Wong! Our coats!**

BARNEY: I am... *(Pounds fist on the table)* ...**pounding**... *(Pounds table again)*...**pounding the table, Yanover**... *(Pounds table again)*...**so that I don't**... *(Pounds table again)*...**pound**... *(Pounds table again)* ...**you**... *(Pounds table again. Mr. Wong enters with coats.)*

MR. WONG: Excuse me, is everything all right here?

MOSES: Does everything LOOK all right? Give me my coat! Thank you!

BARNEY: "*My* coat" is right! It happens to be my coat, Yanover!

PEARL: Tell them, Barney! They should hear it clearly!	MOSES: What cost? I paid you cash money.	ESTHER: This is Mosie's coat?

BARNEY: There was another coat: a tweed, bluish gray mackinaw!... You borrowed it and I like that mackinaw, Yanover, I
do, I really do. I will have that mackinaw back, Yanover.

MOSES: You told me to *keep* that lousy mackinaw! You told me it
was a *gift!*

BARNEY: Like hell I did!

ESTHER: May I put in my two cents?

BARNEY: Oh, shut up!

MOSES: What?

ESTHER: I'll answer for myself, Mosie, thank you. *(To BARNEY)*
Until Mosie brings you your mackinaw, Mr. Big-Mouth-Tell
a-Lady-(a mother yet)-to-Shut-Up...if you are cold...then...wear
this! *(The war is on again. ESTHER mashes her egg foo yong on
BARNEY's shoulder. BARNEY takes the egg foo yong and mashes it
onto MOSES' shoulder. MOSES takes the egg foo yong and mashes
it onto PEARL's shoulder. All of this must be silent, wordless.
PEARL, ending the scene, takes the egg foo yong and mashes it
onto MR. WONG's shoulder.)*

MR. WONG: Get out! Get out of here! GET OUT!

SCENE 7: TWO MALES

Stanley, 16

Goldberg (Ardenshensky, Mr. Wong), any age from 50s on

The Rosens and Yanovers come home and scream at their sons to get up and practice. This shifts to a scene where Stanley and Fern are talking on the phone. Fern asks if Stanley heard what happened at the Ritz Cafe. He asks how she knows about it, and she says her parents were there and saw the fight. They agree to meet the following day.

This scene follows. The action occurs in the store owned by Stanley's father.

1. What is the significance of this scene? Why do you think Horovitz included it in the play?

2. Why do you think Stanley is surprised at Goldberg's reactions to what he says?

STANLEY: Uncle Goldberg, listen to me! I'm not crazy and you're not crazy, but they are crazy! Two weeks ago, they chastised me for being too competitive about the playoffs; now they are at me to practice more.... *(Imitates his father and mother.)* **Win, Stanley, win! Win, win, Stanley, win. You'd think it was the [...] Stanley Cup!**

GOLDBERG: It would kill you to win? You think your father doesn't deserve a victory from his son?

STANLEY: Et tu, Uncle Goldberg? Do you *really* know what's going on here?

GOLDBERG: The word is you're keeping time with a girl who isn't Jewish.

STANLEY: *(Shocked and amazed)* I shall just simply pretend I didn't hear what I just heard, Uncle Goldberg. That subject is a closed door. I will now tell you what's really going on with my parents –

GOLDBERG: "A closed door"?

STANLEY: Don't interrupt me!

GOLDBERG: Please, Stanley.... You're talking to a man my age with such disrespect?

STANLEY: Please, Uncle Goldberg. Last night, my father stood up in the middle of the Ritz Cafe in front of many, many people I know, and screamed at Mr. Yanover to return a mackinaw he borrowed...

GOLDBERG: *(Interrupting)* A borrowed mackinaw shouldn't be returned?...

STANLEY: Mr. Yanover borrowed the mackinaw nineteen years ago! I was going to tell you.

GOLDBERG: In the Talmud...

STANLEY: *Don't interrupt meee!* *(There is a small silence.)*

GOLDBERG: If you're not careful, you'll grow up and scream just like your father....

STANLEY: *(Softly)* That's just what I was thinking. I'll end up in the Ritz Cafe throwing egg foo yong at my closest friends.

GOLDBERG: He threw egg foo *yong*?

STANLEY: They ALL threw egg foo yong! Actually, Mr. Yanover

threw spicy sole.

GOLDBERG: I didn't know that.

STANLEY: Did you know that they've been banned from the Ritz Cafe for six months?

GOLDBERG: This I knew....

STANLEY: It's all because of the piano contest, Uncle Goldberg. My parents have *cracked* under the pressure, that's what!

GOLDBERG: I'm going to tell you something, Stanley...

STANLEY: It's getting late, Uncle Goldberg, I...

GOLDBERG: *(With authority)* Don't interrupt me!

STANLEY: Sorry.

GOLDBERG: When I was twelve years old, I was shipped across to this side, by boat, with an uncle. Ardenshensky was on the same boat. You know him?

STANLEY: The old, old guy?

GOLDBERG: He's not so old. Twelve, and my uncle leaves me with one of his wife's cousins, here in the Soo...a Mrs. Weinstein, who took me in mostly because my uncle gave her thirty dollars, and also because she needed somebody to sweep her shop for her. She sold chickens.... *(Pauses.)* I stayed here till I was twenty, and then I went to Montreal, and I made my fortune, but, all the time I was here in the Soo, I don't think ten people knew my name. I was just the skinny, sad nobody who swept up Mrs. Weinstein's chicken shop.... *(Pauses.)* Your mother's been writing to me for years about your piano playing. You want the truth? I came back here to see one of my relatives make a name for himself here...make a little bit of history for himself and for our family. *(Pauses.)* I have no sons, Stanley. I never married....

STANLEY: I'll do my best, Uncle, I... *(Sees FERN entering.)* Oh, my God, my God, it's way, way past three! *(FERN enters the store.)*

SCENE 8: ONE FEMALE AND ONE MALE

Fern, 16

Irving, 16

Stanley has forgotten his date with Fern. She enters the store and asks where he's been. Stanley introduces her to Goldberg, who asks if she's Jewish. The Yanovers enter. Moses is carrying the old mackinaw that he was accused of not returning. Obviously, they are not in the best of moods. Stanley introduces them to Goldberg. Fern introduces herself and says she's heard a lot of wonderful things about the Yanovers. Stanley's mother calls down on the intercom to see if there are any customers in the store. Stanley panics and says no and then tells everyone that wasn't his mother; his parents are on vacation. He shoves a suitcoat into Fern's hands and says she should take it and go home. She argues that it isn't her father's coat. He pleads with her to please go and shoves her out the door.

Esther tells Stanley he has a "lovely girlfriend." The store changes to a boxing ring where Stanley says Fern is Irving's girl-friend. Stanley and Irving each deny Fern is his girlfriend. Esther asks Irving to promise not to date her. He won't. Esther screams at him and ends up by saying she wanted more children; having only one is not normal.

The scene once more shifts to the Rosens' store where Pearl is asking Stanley why Fern was in the store if she's not his girlfriend. She asks him why he gave her Mr. Silversweig's suitcoat. He denies that he did even when she points out that the pants are still on the hanger.

Stanley and Irving meet and have a fight in slow motion. The lights shift to the park bench where Irving is moaning. Ardenshensky asks him what's wrong. He says it's his parents, and Ardenshensky asks if they're not well. Irving says they're not "kind" or "fair." Fern calls to Irving, and Ardenshensky leaves.

This scene goes directly into the next one. If you like, you can play them one right after the other with no break. Or you can play them as two different scenes.

1. How do Fern and Irving feel about each other in this scene? Explain.

2. Do you think this scene is funny? Why? Why not?

3. There is a difference in mood from that of the previous scenes. What is the difference, and what accounts for it?

4. There is some conflict here. What is causing it?

5. At what point does the mood of the scene change? What causes this change?

FERN: Do you know how truly insulting this whole thing has been for me?

IRVING: I have an idea....

FERN: You *don't*, Irving! You weren't there! Stanley Rosen actually said to me, "Get out of here before my parents see you!"...

IRVING: Oh, well, Rosen's an animal. We've established this as a fact of life....

FERN: It's all because I'm not Jewish, you know....

IRVING: Oh, God, well, why do you think that, Fern?

FERN: Oh, come on, Irving Yanover. You think I'm some kind of dumb dippy? I know about Jewish parents.

IRVING: How?

FERN: You forget who my ultimate best friend is.

IRVING: Rosie Berkowitz talks about it?

FERN: Constantly. I shouldn't be telling you this, but Rosie has a crush on Andrej Ilchak....

IRVING: Yuh, so? The Ilchaks are wonderful, wonderful people....

FERN: Yuh, but Andrei's Ukrainian, and Rosie's mother and father hate Ukrainians....

IRVING: My parents don't. I mean, you can't lump everybody together, you know. All Jews aren't exactly like the Berkowitzes....

FERN: Be careful what you say, Irving....

IRVING: I know she's your ultimate best friend....

FERN: That's not what I was going to say.

IRVING: What were you going to say?

FERN: Mrs. Berkowitz and your mother had a long conversation about me recently.... *(A beat)*

IRVING: Let's just drop the whole subject, Fern. You're not going out with my parents. You're going out with me....

FERN: I don't want to drop the whole subject! My parents don't have a prejudiced bone in their bodies....

IRVING: Oh, yuh, well, how come you never tell them it's me who's calling, hmmm?

FERN: I do so!

IRVING: Come on, will you? You think I'm a dope? You think I can't tell?

FERN: It's my father. He really hates Jews....

IRVING: He does? Oh, God, that's terrible.

FERN: How about *your* father?

IRVING: My father's no problem. It's my mother. You're not the first non-Jewish girl I've loved, you know....

FERN: I know. You told me....

IRVING: My mother tried to get me to promise that I wouldn't go out with you....

FERN: Did you?

IRVING: Promise? Uh-uh....

FERN: Did you stand up to her?

IRVING: Sort of. I stood up....

FERN: And?

IRVING: I, uh, ran out....

FERN: Oh, God, this is hard for me to admit out loud. You've got to take this in the right spirit, Irving....

IRVING: Of course I will....

FERN: My father said, "There's never been a Jew in our family, not since the beginning of time...."

IRVING: *(After a long, long, long pause; clench-jawed)* That is the worst thing I have ever heard in my entire life, and I have heard some horrible, horrible, *horrible* things....

FERN: Oh, yuh, well, how do you think I felt when Stanley Rosen shoved me out the door with a blue pin-stripe suitcoat, saying, "Get out of here before my parents see you!"?

IRVING: Oh, yuh, well, *Rosen*, sure, he's brain damaged....

FERN: Stanley Rosen is not brain damaged, Irving Yanover! He is my *friend!* It's not him, it's his *parents*, and my parents and *your* parents....

IRVING: I guess.

FERN: I *know*....

IRVING: You've talked to Rosen.

FERN: He feels awful....

IRVING: He smells pretty bad too....

FERN: What?

IRVING: Just kidding....

FERN: You're *always* kidding!

IRVING: Our parents are wrong. You are a wonderful, wonderful person, Fern, and I care for you....

FERN: You are, too, Irving, and I care for you, too....

IRVING: There is absolutely nothing wrong with our going out together!

FERN: Absolutely nothing....

IRVING: Our parents are acting unreasonably....

FERN: Totally.... All we're doing is *going out together, right?*

IRVING: And they're all acting completely insane! Imagine if we got married?

FERN: My father would kill me!

IRVING: My mother would kill *herself!*

FERN: Do you ever really think about us in the future together ...*married?*

IRVING: Us? I do, Fern. I think about it a lot....

FERN: I just got goose bumps.

IRVING: Me, too....

FERN: I want to be kissed.

IRVING: Yes.

FERN: No arms, no hands....

IRVING: What about lips?

FERN: Lips are fine.

IRVING: Fern. *Fernnn*...oh, Fern....

FERN: Irving. Irving...oh, *Irvinggg*.... *(IRVING and FERN kiss a long, passionate kiss — no hands, no arms, of course. We hear Chopin being played by a piano, on tape. And then a great symphony orchestra joins in. There are many stringed instruments, many human voices singing. The lights fade slowly to black. The music continues to play.)*

SCENE 9: ONE MALE AND ONE FEMALE

Stanley, 16

Fern, 16

The action, is continuous between the previous scene and this one.

1. Why do you think Horovitz wrote the scene so it seems that Fern is still kissing the same person?

2. Are you surprised by Fern's response after the countdown? Why? Why not?

3. Why do you think Fern is talking about marrying one of the two boys when she says she isn't in love?

4. Stanley and Irving are very similar. If you were playing Stanley, how might you try to distinguish him from Irving, while remaining true to what Horovitz wrote? What would you do if you were playing Irving to try to distinguish him from Stanley?

(The lights fade up again. IRVING is gone. STANLEY is in his place, precisely. At first, we do not realize that it is STANLEY that FERN is now kissing — no hands, no arms, only lips. They break from the kiss and the music stops. Now we know.)

STANLEY: Fern. *Fernnn*....oh, Fern....

FERN: Stanley, oh, Stanley, ohhh, oh, *Stanleyyy*....

STANLEY: You're wonderful to forgive me, Fern.

FERN: I know it's not you, personally, Stanley, I know it's your parents.

STANLEY: Sometimes I wonder if I were adopted.

FERN: You don't look like your parents?

STANLEY: Oh, no, I look exactly like them. It's just that we don't think the same.

FERN: Same exact thing as my parents. *(Hands suitcoat to STANLEY.)* Here's the suitcoat back.

STANLEY: Oh, see! You not only forgive me, you also return the goddamn suitcoat! *(STANLEY sighs three times.)* It's funny we've known each other since first grade. I mean, who would've ever guessed that you and I would end up...you know....

FERN: In love?

STANLEY: Are you?

FERN: Are *you* in love with *me?*

STANLEY: It's hard to be the one who answers first.

FERN: Let's answer at exactly the same time, Stanley. I'll count backwards from five.... Ask the question out loud...*now!*

FERN and STANLEY: *(Overlapping)* **Are you in love with me, (Fern?) (Stanley?)**

FERN: Five four...three two...one... *(In unison)*

STANLEY: Yes, oh, yes!　　　**FERN:** I just don't know, Stanley! *I just don't know!*

STANLEY: *(Truly upset)* **You just don't know?** My God. [...]

FERN: Well, I'm just being truthful....

STANLEY: Yuh, well, I never would have said what I said if I knew you were going to say what you said. I mean, I was pretty positive you loved me, ya know what I mean?

FERN: I *do* love you, Stanley!

STANLEY: You do?

FERN: Of course, I do....

STANLEY: Oh, God, that's *great!* I'm in love with you, too, Fern....

FERN: I didn't say I was *in love* with you, Stanley Rosen! I said I *love*
you.

STANLEY: What the hell is the difference?

FERN: Oh, God, Stanley, please, don't be upset! Please, don't spoil a
beautiful, beautiful evening.... *(Pauses.)* I know that I love you.
But I don't think I can technically be *in love* with two people at
the same time....

STANLEY: Oh, my *Goddd!*

FERN: Stanley Rosen, please, don't! We have a sacred pact.

STANLEY: I'm sorry, Fern. I apologize....

FERN: I know you do, Stan, and I accept.... What I mean, Stan, is
this: when people are *in love*, they marry, right?

STANLEY: They certainly should.

FERN: It shouldn't matter if one's Jewish and the other's
Presbyterian, right?

STANLEY: Not if they hide out in Saskatchewan for the rest of their
lives!

FERN: We're not marrying each other's *parents*, Stanley. We're
marrying each *other*....

STANLEY: *(Stunned; thrilled) Us?* Each *other?* Getting *married?* God,
Fern, I'm getting goose bumps! *(Moonstruck)* **Are you really
thinking about us getting married, Fern? You and me? Stanley
and Fern?**

FERN: You and me or Irving and me. It depends on how things, I
dunno...*progress.*

SCENE 10: TWO MALES

Stanley, 16
Barney, 40ish

Stanley becomes angry with Fern, and she accuses him of being jealous. The next scene takes place in Barney's store.

1. Do you think it logical that the Rosens and Yanovers are going out together again? Explain.

2. What is your reaction to Barney's admitting that he went out with Jeanie Shlopac?

3. What is your opinion of Barney's saying that people should always marry their own kind? Do you agree? Why? Why not?

4. What is Barney talking about when he mentions the six million babies? What do you think he is feeling when he talks about this?

5. Why, after being open with Stanley, does Barney then say in a quiet tone that he's "done with this conversation"?

BARNEY: I'm really glad you found Mr. Silversweig's suitcoat, Stanley. He was really furious.

STANLEY: Everything evens out, Poppy. I've got to use the car again tonight....

BARNEY: Out of the question. The Yanovers have driven two times straight. It's definitely our turn to drive tonight....

STANLEY: I thought you were fighting with the Yanovers....

BARNEY: We are.

STANLEY: And you're going out to dinner with them?

BARNEY: Of course. We always do.

STANLEY: I don't get it.

BARNEY: What's not to get? If Mosie Yanover shot me in the leg on Tuesday, I'd still have to eat supper with him on Wednesday.

STANLEY: *Why?*

BARNEY: Because we *always* eat supper with the Yanovers on Wednesday. We used to eat Thursdays, but it collided with the girls' mahjongg games.... *(Laughs.)* Friends fight sometimes, Stanley. It's a small town, Sault Sainte Marie. You see your friends a little too often....

STANLEY: Did you ever go out with a girl who wasn't Jewish, Poppy?

BARNEY: Where did *that* come from?

STANLEY: Did you?

BARNEY: I did, yes. Why? Did somebody say something to you?

STANLEY: No. Why?

BARNEY: I went out with a girl named Jeanie Shlopac...from my school. She was Russian Orthodox. Beautiful girl, good grades...very nice.

STANLEY: Did you ever think about marrying her, Poppy?

BARNEY: Jews marry Jews, Stanley....

STANLEY: Poppy, *please*. I need you to talk to me...

BARNEY: Not on this subject, Stanley....

STANLEY: Do you love Mama, Poppy?

BARNEY: What kind of a question is *that?*

STANLEY: I need to know.

BARNEY: *(After a long, long pause)* Yes, Stanley, I do. I love your mother very, very much. Your mother is my partner. She's my wife....

STANLEY: Did you love Jeanie Shlopac?

BARNEY: Honestly?

STANLEY: Please, Poppy....

BARNEY: If this ever gets back to me, Stanley Rosen, you will never borrow the car for the rest of your life. Even after I'm dead, you won't borrow the car....

STANLEY: You loved her?

BARNEY: *(He covers intercom mouthpiece, just in case.)* A lot.

STANLEY: So, why didn't you marry her?

BARNEY: Because, Stanley, people should marry their own....

STANLEY: Maybe things are changing, Poppy....

BARNEY: Sure. Things are worse then ever! *(Confronts his son, seriously.)* After what's just happened in the world, Stanley, it's more important than ever for Jews to marry Jews. Six million babies times six million babies times six million babies. It's going to take a long time to catch up for what's been lost....

STANLEY: Oh, God, Poppy, I know what you're saying. I really do. But people aren't *statistics*. People have *feelings*. Don't you ever regret not marrying Jeanie Shlopac? I know I never would have gotten born, I know what I'm asking. But answer me honestly, Poppy, *please?* Don't you ever regret it? Don't you?

BARNEY: *(Quietly)* I'm done with this conversation, Stanley. This is silliness. I'm done with this conversation... *(BARNEY turns his back on STANLEY. STANLEY pauses a moment and then runs from the store. There is a moment's pause. BARNEY bows his head, sadly.)*

SCENE 11: TWO MALES

Irving, 16

Stanley, 16

This scene comes directly after the preceding.

1. What differences can you see in Stanley and Irving's relationship in this scene from previous scenes? Do you think these feelings were always present, or are they new? Explain.

2. Beginning with the question about Plato, the scene for a time becomes almost a comedy routine. What do you think is the purpose of including this?

3. What is the point of the discussion about Gershwin and Levant (a well-known pianist)?

4. Do you like this scene? Why? Why not?

(STANLEY moves Downstage, talks as if on telephone.)

STANLEY: Yanover? I'm coming over. *(Lights fade up on an amazed IRVING YANOVER, in Yanover living room.)*

IRVING: Who's this?

STANLEY: Stanley Rosen. *(The fight bell sounds as STANLEY crosses into Yanover house.)* **She's nuts, you know. We don't look anything alike.**

IRVING: Of course she's nuts. Nuts is the human condition. Have you read Camus?

STANLEY: *(Lying through his teeth)* **Most of Camus. But it's been a long time.**

IRVING: Uh-hahhh! A blind spot in your intellectual growth, Rosen! Now that I know your weakness, I shall leap in and triumph....

STANLEY: I never saw two men look less alike!

IRVING: I agree. *(STANLEY crosses to table.)*

STANLEY: Do you think Fern's father is really a Nazi?

IRVING: Naw, I don't think he's so much a Nazi as he is a Nazi supporter.

STANLEY: Mmmm. *(Nods in agreement.)*

IRVING: It's exactly like you not being so much an athlete as an athletic supporter...

STANLEY: *(They both squeeze invisible horns and make "nahn-nah" sound.)* **Ho, ho! *That* was rich.** *(Pauses.)* **Could we leap over the small talk, up to some medium talk, Yanover?**

IRVING: Be my guest: leap.

STANLEY: How'd you get your parents around the idea of Fern Fipps being somebody you date?

IRVING: Parents, my dear Rosen, have a strong tendency to see life *as they want it to be*, rather than life as it most obviously is...until, of course, a Stanley Rosen comes along and takes the truth and tries *to rub it in my parents' eyes!*

STANLEY: A basic survival technique, my dear Yanover. Blind the enemy parent with the truth and your own parents will never see the *truth*....

IRVING: If I were you, I wouldn't go into philosophy for a living....

STANLEY: You know what Plato said?

IRVING: Remind me.

STANLEY: Plato said, "Never wear argyle socks with a glen-plaid suit."

IRVING: Plato was in the menswear business?

STANLEY: "Morris Plato's Togary."

IRVING: Is it true what my father said? That you wrote a song called "Prelude to the Sale of a Pair of Pants"? That's what your father told *my* father, anyway....

STANLEY: I did. I did that.

IRVING: I composed a tune called "Fanfare for Five Flannel Sheets and a Pillowcase."

STANLEY: You ever play four-handed Gershwin?

IRVING: Is that like doubles pinochle?

STANLEY: Aha! A major blind spot! Do you know Oscar Levant?

IRVING: Didn't he live over on Pim Street?

STANLEY: Get serious, Yanover! Oscar Levant is just about the greatest mind in the twentieth century, that's all.... He wrote a book called *A Smattering of Ignorance,* about how he and Gershwin fought all the time.

IRVING: They fought too, huh!

STANLEY: Oil and water.... I'll loan you the book. It's just probably the greatest book ever written in English, that's all.

IRVING: No kidding? *(STANLEY produces a dog-eared copy of a book by Levant.)*

STANLEY: *A Smattering of Ignorance.* Be my guest, Yanover. Just read the opening paragraph. *(STANLEY tosses book across store to IRVING, who catches it.)* My life was changed by Oscar Levant. There's more to life than Frédéric Chopin, m'boy. *(IRVING is reading; pretends to be engrossed totally.)*

IRVING: Shhh. I'm reading....

STANLEY: Some middlebrow would-be pseudointellectuals claim *Camus* has a brain, but history will prove that the great thinker of the twentieth century was, unquestionably, Oscar Levant....

IRVING: *(Looks up. Play-acts exasperation.)* If you think this is a good book, Rosen, you're out of your mind. This is a great book,

Rosen! A great book!

STANLEY: I gave this book to my father to read.

IRVING: What did he say?

STANLEY: Obvious line: "I used to think you were a lunatic. Now I'm *convinced!*"

IRVING: Lunacy is a son's birthright....

STANLEY: It's in the Talmud. Page eight....

IRVING: Page *nine.*

STANLEY: You know your Talmud....

IRVING: Back to front.... [...] Maybe I was Levant in an earlier life?

STANLEY: This is true, you were Levant and I was Gershwin. You see, my dear Yanover, the subtle difference between Levant and Gershwin is the subtle difference between talent and genius....

YANOVER: Really?

STANLEY: Really.

IRVING: You wanna try to back up your fancy talk with some fancy action?

STANLEY: Okay, palley-pal. You see these mitts? *(Makes two fists.)*

IRVING: Yuh, so?

STANLEY: Watch 'em and weep. *(STANLEY walks to IRVING's piano and plays Gershwin's "Rhapsody in Blue.")*

IRVING: That is just great, Rosen. Just *goddam great!*

SCENE 12: TWO FEMALES AND FOR MALES

Pearl, 40ish

Barney, 40ish

Stanley, 16

Irving, 16

Moses, 40ish

Esther, 40ish

Esther calls over the intercom to see what "Irving" is playing. Of course, Stanley is playing Gershwin. She then asks how he can continue to play and also answer the intercom. He says his arms are long but then admits that Stanley is playing the piano.

The action switches to a dining table where the two boys have finished eating a meal with Irving's parents. This is the first time Stanley has been at their home in six years. They talk about a long fistfight the two boys had when Stanley last was here, and then the talk turns to the upcoming competition. Esther asks if Stanley is still dating Fern. "In what sense?" Stanley asks, and Irving chokes. Then he tells Stanley to go home.

The next scene occurs in the park where Fern tells Irving she has been accepted by a school to study to be an elementary school teacher. When Irving tells her that's great news, she cries. She says the two boys are doing what they want, but her father, without asking what she wants, insists she become a teacher. Irving says it's her life; she should do what she wants, which is to be an engineer. He says she's better at math than anyone in the whole school. They kiss, and Fern tells him, "It's an awful thing to say out loud, but when we kiss like this, Irving, I really hope it's you who wins the playoffs tomorrow night."

Following is a scene between Fern and Stanley. He's standing on a gutter pipe outside her window asking for a kiss — "not for luck" but rather "for inspiration." She tells him he's "so romantic." He wants to kiss her, but the phone rings. The gutter pipe buckles and Stanley falls. We hear a dog growling.

Now we're at Irving's house where Esther asks why he's been in the bathroom so long. He says he's soaking his hands in tea to strengthen the skin. She asks if they're stained. He tells her they aren't, and then she smells bleach. Moses enters and demands Irving open the door. Irving sticks his hands onstage and asks if they're still brown. Moses tells him they are "dark brown." He pulls his hands back and says he'll put them back into the bleach. Irving sticks his hands back onstage. "Now, *this* you wouldn't call brown, would you?" Moses answers, "Brown. It's brown."

The lights come up on Stanley, who is holding his hands in front of him. He is in pain.

Similar to the scenes where Fern was kissing one of the two boys and then really was kissing the other, the following is composed of two parts showing parallels between the two boys and the two sets of parents. Then there is a third part that also could be a separate scene; yet it ties the other parts together.

1. Do you think it's true to life for parents to place so much pressure on their sons or daughters to succeed as the Rosens and Yanovers do? Explain.

2. Do you find these two scenes funny? Why? Why not?

3. Do you like Pearl? Esther? Why? Why not? Do you think they're good mothers? Why? Why not?

4. In what way is Moses's answer to the question about marrying outside one's religious faith different from Barney's answer? How is it similar? Which answer more matches your feelings?

5. Why is Esther so determined to have Irving win? Can you understand why she feels this way? Explain. Why do you suppose she wants Irving to be both a concert pianist and a lawyer?

6. Do you think it believable that both boys would harm their hands in some way? Why? Why not?

7. Are Fern's declarations believable? Explain.

PEARL: You broke your hand?

BARNEY: You broke your hand?

STANLEY: I broke my hand. I think so. It feels like it....

PEARL: How?

BARNEY: How?

STANLEY: Exercise. Exercise....

BARNEY: Exercise?

PEARL: Exercise?

STANLEY: Squeezing a rubber ball. I read that squeezing a rubber ball was the difference between good players and great players...so, I squeezed.

BARNEY: For how long, Stanley?

STANLEY: I had a little trouble sleeping, so I exercised a little extra ...about five and a half hours. *(Moans.)* It's really killing me....

PEARL: Between now and the contest tonight, young man...no more exercise and no more reading. Barney, get Epsom salts and he'll soak. *(BARNEY exits.)* Trust me. Don't I know?

STANLEY: *(Confidentially)* Mama, I know this sounds silly, but, you'll love me still if something goes wrong, if I don't, you know, win?

PEARL: Stanley David Rosen, what kind of a question is that?

STANLEY: What kind of an *answer* is that?

PEARL: Of *course* I'll love you! If you robbed a bank, I'd still love you....

STANLEY: Really?

PEARL: No ideas, you! Stanley, you have a talent and you have training. You will sit at the piano, you will relax, you will let your talent and your training control your playing, and you will win. This family has achieved something and the Yanovers must be stopped....

STANLEY: It's important to you that I win, isn't it?

PEARL: Very.

STANLEY: No matter what?

PEARL: No matter what. *(BARNEY reenters with Epsom salts.)*

BARNEY: An hour's soak in this stuff should do the trick....

STANLEY: Poppy, you want me to win, don't you?

BARNEY: Does a bear pee in the woods, Stanley?

STANLEY: *(Laughs. Groucho imitation)* **He soitenly does!**

BARNEY: I soitenly want you to win. Not for me, Stanley. For your mother.... *(They all laugh. PEARL looks up to heaven; talks to God.)*

PEARL: All night? You let him squeeze a rubber ball for five and a half hours? What's the matter with you?

(The lights cross-fade to IRVING with ESTHER and MOSES near the YANOVER piano, opposite side of stage. IRVING is trying to tie his necktie, but the pain is too intense.)

IRVING: Could you tie it for me, Papa? When I try to bend my fingers, the skin cracks. I can't make the knot....

MOSES: I'll tie the tie, but I can't play the piano....

IRVING: Can I ask you a question, Poppy? Fella to fella?

MOSES: If you're asking me if you have to win the contest, Irving, the answer is "No, you do not have to be a contest winner in this life."

IRVING: You don't think it's important to win?

MOSES: I think it's important to love life.

IRVING: I think you're right.

MOSES: There's no right or wrong about it. You're a wonderful son, Irving. I wish your hands weren't brown and cracked, but you're a wonderful son...nevertheless.... *(MOSES beams at his son.)*

IRVING: That wasn't my question, Poppy!

MOSES: What wasn't your question?

IRVING: The whole speech you made about contest winning. My question was different.

MOSES: What's your question?

IRVING: It's just between us, okay?

MOSES: Could there be any doubt?

IRVING: Poppy, what if, just before you and Mama were married – say, fifteen minutes before the wedding ceremony – you found out Mama wasn't Jewish. Would you have married her anyway?

MOSES: What a question!

IRVING: Would you have?

MOSES: Your mother, she could have turned purple fifteen minutes before the wedding and I would have married her....

IRVING: *(Relieved; big smile)* **I *knew* it!**

231

MOSES: But, that's not my whole answer, Irving.... *(IRVING looks at his father.)* It takes two people saying "I do" to make a marriage. You might want to ask your mother what she would have done fifteen minutes before the wedding if she found out I was really Michael Sean O'Yanover....

IRVING: I wouldn't dare ask her!

MOSES: What do you think she would have done?

IRVING: She would have walked away....

MOSES: That's one of the things I love most about your mother, Irving. She has rules.... *(Smiles.)* We're different, your mother and I. *(Pauses; smiles.)* It's important for Jews to marry Jews but, it's also important that the love be there in abundance.... *(Pauses.)* We happen to have a great abundance in this family.... *(Pauses.)* I saw her in Rosen's store, she seems like a nice girl.

IRVING: Thanks, Poppy. *(There is a pause as MOSES holds IRVING's face in his hands. ESTHER enters carrying long white gloves and cold cream.)*

ESTHER: Give me your hands. This will work....

IRVING: What are you doing?

ESTHER: Cold cream on your hands, first, and then my white cotton gloves...filled with cold cream. The cold cream will fill in the cracks from the tea....

IRVING: By tonight?

ESTHER: If God is kind... *(Looks up)* ...for a change! Mosie, start the car....

MOSES: *(Nods.)* I'll start the car. *(MOSES exits.)*

IRVING: I can't do this. I'd rather not compete!

ESTHER: You will compete and you will win....

IRVING: Do you really think winning is that important, Mama?

ESTHER: Winning, in general, no. Winning, specifically, tonight, absolutely *yes*....

IRVING: No matter what the prize turns out to be?

ESTHER: This is bigger than a prize, Irving....

IRVING: It certainly is, Mama....

ESTHER: Our next-door neighbor, when I was growing up, had a cousin who sang in the opera...a baritone. I can remember hearing the story over and over again when I was a girl. The singer came out on stage at the Metropolitan Opera House, in New York City, New York, and he had put his mother in a seat in the front row. When he came out on stage, just before be sang, he waved to his mother. Not a big wave. Just a wave. And then he sang. And all the people sitting around his mother kept asking her over and over again who she was, why did he wave? *(Pauses; smiles to IRVING.)* Ever since you started taking lessons, I've known what it was I wanted, Irving: to sit in the front row at Carnegie Hall in New York City, New York, and to have you come out on stage, sit at the piano, look at me, wave.... *(Smiles.)* Tonight is the first step on the road to Carnegie Hall, Irving. I know it is....

IRVING: I thought you were set on my going to law school.

ESTHER: Now there's something the matter with law school?

IRVING: Law schools don't prepare people for playing pianos at Carnegie Hall, Mama....

ESTHER: And lawyers can't also play pianos?

IRVING: I'll do my best tonight, Mama. I promise.

ESTHER: *(Holds IRVING's face a moment; then, simply)* You're Irving Yanover. *(Kisses him.)* Now.... *(Opens cold cream jar.)* cold cream on the hands and hands into the gloves.

IRVING: Mama, I absolutely won't wear gloves. I absolutely refuse....

(Mother stares at son. IRVING jams his hands into the gloves. STANLEY calls across to IRVING.)

(The lights cross-fade as IRVING moves to STANLEY and the park.)

STANLEY: Yanover.

IRVING: Rosen.

STANLEY: Cold night.

IRVING: Cold night.

IRVING: What's with your hand?

STANLEY: My hand? What's with your gloves?

IRVING: Gloves?

FERN: Nobody must ever know of our plan...of the way we worked it out. Whichever of you loses must never ever tell anyone ever.... *(STANLEY and IRVING nod. FERN smiles and then becomes stern.)* **Whichever of you who loses must accept the loss for what it is. You must promise to never call me again and if we meet in school or in the movies or on the street or something by accident, just nod.** *(IRVING and STANLEY nod.)* **I make my pledge now....** *(She looks at both of them.)* **I pledge to never talk to the loser again, except by accident....** *(She averts her eyes from them.)* **I pledge to love, honor and obey the winner.... I pledge to write a letter every day, without fail, at the very least for the next two years.... I pledge to marry and dedicate my life to the winner, the summer after next.** *(She looks at both solemnly. Her face is tear-stained as she weeps openly.)* **There is no way I can lose. I love both of you.** *(IRVING and STANLEY giggle. FERN pauses; then soberly)* **Do we all agree?**

IRVING: I...yes.

STANLEY: I...me, too.

FERN: There were times in the past few days when I've had great doubts do I want to be married to *anyone...ever?* But, standing here now, looking at both of you...knowing that promises and plans *must be kept*...knowing that my love for both of you is true...*really and truly true*...well.... *(She kisses STANLEY.)* **Good luck, Stanley.** *(She kisses IRVING.)* **Good luck, Irving.**

SCENE 13: TWO MALES

Stanley, 16

Irving, 16

An emcee announces how the competition will be judged. The Rosens, the Yanovers, and Goldberg are sitting facing the stage. The boys walk to the pianos and Irving waves to Esther. Pearl thinks he waved at her and asks why. They are about to argue when Fern enters. Then they do argue about whose girlfriend she is until she comes up to them. They ask about her family. Then they ask whose girlfriend she is. She tells them that she and the boys have made a sacred pledge. Pearl asks, "About going steady?" Ferns tells her it's "much, much bigger than that. It's about marriage."

The parents repeat the word marriage and slap their foreheads. The emcee asks if anyone knows where Mr. Drinkwater is. Goldberg says he's been detained. He "would like everybody to know that this whole thing is his fault and that he feels ashamed."

The contest is about to begin, with the boys playing the same Chopin piece simultaneously. As they play, Goldberg says he's made a "terrible, terrible mistake." What he means is that he really is Drinkwater, and it was his idea to sponsor the competition. Esther says it's all her fault and then shifts the blame to God. Fern says she has "made a terrible, terrible mistake" and doesn't want to get married. She asks God for a miracle.

For fifteen or twenty seconds more, the two boys continue playing "sweetly, perfectly;" and then Stanley switches from Chopin to Gershwin. Irving is startled and asks, "What the hell are you *doing?*" Stanley says he's making Irving the winner. "Like hell you are!" Irving replies and begins to hit "a series of clinkers that would curdle new milk on contact." Then each tries to "out-clinker" the other. As they continue, they argue over who's winning and who is going to marry Fern. Neither wants to.

Later, Fern, Stanley, and Irving sit in the park where Fern says she forgives them, if they forgive her for not being honest, in not wanting to get married. She says, "I love you both. I really do...." They say they love her too (of course, while insulting each other). In turn, the boys kiss Fern, who looks at them for a moment and leaves.

1. What is the overall mood of this scene? What emotions are the

boys feeling here?

2. Can you see any way in which the competition has changed Stanley and Irving? Explain.

3. What do you think the two of them will do with their lives? Why?

4. Do you like this scene? Why? Why not? How does it differ from the other scenes in the play?

STANLEY: So, Oscar?

IRVING: So, Gershwin?

STANLEY: I think we made trouble.

IRVING: I think we made trouble. Why'd you do it?

STANLEY: Blow the Drinkwater money?

IRVING: Yuh.

STANLEY: For you, boychik: I wanted you to win.... *(Pauses.)* You? What was in your sick mind?

IRVING: Same thing: abject generosity: I wanted you to win.

STANLEY: Uncle Goldberg wants to give us both equal amounts.

IRVING: I heard. Nice of him. How'd he make so much money?

STANLEY: Seltzer. Thirty-five years of selling seltzer, in Montreal.... Seltzer.... Drinkwater.... You get it?

IRVING: *(Play-acting)* Too deep for *meee*.... There's that much money in seltzer?

STANLEY: Apparently.

IRVING: Maybe I should go into seltzer.

STANLEY: Just don't go over your head....

IRVING: I always thought it was a tad strange that the Cyrus Drinkwater Prize was first announced in the *Jewish Forward*, in Hebrew.

STANLEY: That is probably because Uncle Goldberg does not, as they say, read a great English....

IRVING: So?

STANLEY: So?

IRVING: Would the co-loser of the Chopin playoffs like to sit?

STANLEY: He wouldn't mind. *(They sit.)* I heard you might study law.

IRVING: Why? Lawyers can't also play pianos?

STANLEY: Just in case, huh?

IRVING: Just in case. And you? I heard medicine.

STANLEY: I would prefer to lose a leg. *Buttt* just in case.

IRVING: We could live our whole lives doing things just in case, if we're not careful.

STANLEY: Precisely why we have to be careful, my dear Yanover.... Just in case!

IRVING: My father told me once that the way to choose a good

enemy is to pick a friend. He'll know exactly where to strike....

STANLEY: **My father said the same thing....** *(STANLEY and IRVING do secret handshake of cow being milked. Both say, "Moo.")* **How come your hands are brown, my boy?**

IRVING: **What's with the Ace bandage, Ace?**

STANLEY: **Long story.**

IRVING: **Long story.**

STANLEY: **Life, my dear Yanover, is full of mystery.... Look at the lights of our town...fireflies.... We shall name the streets between here and Algoma Steel: Lake Street, Churchill Avenue, Elizabeth...Pine.... I helped Uncle Goldberg relearn them.**

IRVING: **Make a right on Pine and a left on?**

STANLEY: **Wellington Street East.**

IRVING: *(W C. Fields voice)* **Ah, yes, Wellington was a great man and a good street to boot....**

STANLEY: **Pim, Pilgrim, East, Brock...**

IRVING: **...Spring, March, Elgin, Bruce....**

STANLEY: **...Dennis, Tancred, Gore, Andrew, Huron...**

IRVING: **And a left on Patrick to Algoma Steel.**

STANLEY: **It'll be a cold day in hell when we forget the names of these mighty streets!**

IRVING: **And I'll tell it to the world!** *(IRVING stands, moves to imagined cliff; yells out, singing to tune of "Sweet Sue.")* **Sweet Sooo....**

STANLEY: *(Does the same.)* **Sweet Sooo....**

IRVING: **It's a nice place to come from.**

STANLEY: **A** *nice* **place. Can you imagine what it's gonna be like for our parents after we leave?**

IRVING: **I can't imagine.**

STANLEY: **Try.** *(IRVING squeezes out a conjured look into the future, seeing his parents.)*

IRVING: **Not a pretty picture....**

STANLEY: *(Conjures up the same image.)* **Not a pretty picture.**

There are three more short scenes. The Yanovers and Rosens meet at the Ritz Cafe where Mr. Wong insists that they all hug each other. Once more, the two families are good friends.

Irving and Stanley meet, and the audience knows that once and for all they are leaving for the unknown.

In the final scene, a monolog, Ardenshensky tells what happened to the characters. "Fern became an engineer and designed many big bridges." Stanley moved back, married Rosie Berkowitz and opened a retail establishment. Irving became a lawyer in Toronto.

Asian-American Theatre

ASIAN-AMERICAN THEATRE

To a further degree than Europeans or Africans, the voices of Asian-Americans have been unheard, even though their cultures are rich in theatre. One of the reasons is that Asian theatre, similar to that of Native Americans, differs greatly from Western theatre.

For decades, Asians usually were denied entry into main-stream theatre — except as one-dimensional stereotypes. Up until the 1950s there were no plays about or by Asian Americans either on Broadway or in mainstream regional theatres. Even in the 1930s, when other ethnic minorities were given a voice by the Federal Theatre Project, there is just a single instance of Asian involvement, a written history of Chinese theatre in California.

Asian-American women began writing plays before men did. One of the earliest was Gladys Li (later she wrote under her own name of Ling-Ai Li). Most of the works, however, were never produced.

Instead there were productions like the 1902 musical *Chinese Honeymoon*, imported to Broadway from England with whites playing the roles of Asians. Occasionally, there were plays with Chinese servants. In the 1950s a few shows did have larger and more sympathetic roles for Asians. Examples are John Patrick's *The Teahouse of the August Moon* and Rogers and Hammerstein's *The King and I*. Often, however, the roles were played by non-Asian Americans, and though they were more three-dimensional than the usual stereotypes, they still presented Asians as exotic and foreign. Then in 1958 came Rogers and Hammerstein's *Flower Drum Song*, adapted from a novel by Chinese American writer C. Y. Lee.

The situation began to change for the better in the wake of the civil rights movement of the 1960s when young Asians of various national backgrounds joined together in forming nonprofit theatre groups.

In 1965, a number of actors of Chinese, Japanese and Korean heritage met in Los Angeles and established the East West Players. The company first dramatized the writings of such novelists as Yukio Mishima and also performed mainstream works. Then in 1973, a group including Frank Chin, Janis Chan and Jeffrey Chin founded the Asian-American Theatre Workshop in San Francisco. Here Frank Chin's *Chickencoop Chinaman* was developed to become the first major play by an Asian American.

Soon other plays, such as Genny Lim's *Paper Angels*, gained widespread recognition. Increasingly, playwrights such as David Henry Hwang, Velina Hasu Houston, Elizabeth Wong, and Phillip Gotanda are being produced for mainstream audiences. The most widely recognized is Hwang, whose *M. Butterfly* won a Tony for best play of 1988.

12-1-A
Wakako Yamauchi

Wakako Yamauchi, a Nisei (a second generation American), was born in 1924 and so writes from experience about one of the nations's most blatant racial disgraces — the relocation and internment of Japanese Americans during World War II.

Although there was no widespread physical cruelty nor severe disciplinary action, the camps were similar to Nazi concentration camps in at least two ways. The Nazis rounded up the Jews and stole their belongings. The United States government rounded up an entire group of American citizens (those of Japanese heritage) and stole their property and all their belongings except what they could carry with them and then placed them in camps from which some (younger men) could escape only by volunteering to serve in the American military.

After her release from the internment camp at the end of World War II, Yamauchi moved to Chicago. At first, she wrote only fiction until Mako, founder and artistic director of the East West Players encouraged her to adapt her short "And the Soul Shall Dance" into a play. The story had been published in *Aiiieeeee*, the literary anthology edited by Frank Chin. The play, with the same title, was produced in 1977. Yamauchi's second play was *12-1-A*, which is based on first-hand experience in being incarcerated during World War II. In fact, the Tanaka family of the play is imprisoned at Poston, Arizona, where the playwright herself was held.

One of the worst parts of the experience for the Tanakas and for real families was not knowing how long they would be held or indeed if they ever would be released from the camp. The play is divided into two acts, the first with three segments (scenes), the second with four. The time ranges from May of 1942 to July of 1943.

SCENE 1: THREE FEMALES AND TWO MALES

Mrs. Tanaka, 40

Michio (Mitch) Tanaka, 20

Koko Tanaka, 17

Harry Yamane, 25

Yo Yoshida, 25

Mrs. Tanaka, an Issei widow, her son, Michio (Mitch) and her daughter, Koko have just arrived at the detention center in Poston, Arizona.

1. Why do you suppose the United States government stripped Japanese Americans of their rights, their citizenship, and their dignity and treated them like prisoners?

2. What do you think would be your feelings if you were placed in a situation like this? What are the feelings of each of the characters in this scene?

3. Which role would you most want to play is this scene? Why?

4. What does Koko mean when she asks Yo if you ever get used to it?

(The tar-papered interior of a barracks faces Downstage. There are two workable glass-paned windows [sliding sideways] facing Upstage. Three army cots stand in an otherwise empty room. A naked light bulb hangs from the rafter. The barracks has a double door and a small wooden porch. 12-1-A is stenciled in white. The door faces Stage Right. In the background the silhouette of a guard tower looms ominously. A sentry is on duty at all times. This tower is barely visible in the first scene and grows more prominent as the play progresses. A wind blows. HARRY YAMANE, twenty-five, walks slowly and anxiously On-stage. He wears a battered felt hat and old-man clothes. He is somewhat stooped. HARRY has a twelve-year-old mentality and has spent many years working on his father's farm. He hums a tuneless rendition of "Yes Sir, That's My Baby" when he is anxious. He is lost and bewildered. He hums as he enters from Stage Left. HARRY takes out a scrap of paper, looks at the number on the barracks, shakes his head as though to clear it, and takes off his hat and spins it with his two hands. He hums louder. He sits on the porch for a while, his head down. He hears voices and steps Downstage, trying to be inconspicuous. MRS. TANAKA, forty, Issei widow in traveling clothes for middle-aged women of the period, carries a suitcase and a cardboard carton. MITCH, twenty, her Nisei son, in jeans and plaid shirt carries two duffel bags. KOKO, seventeen, her Nisei daughter, wearing a short dirndl skirt, white socks, and saddle shoes, carries two suitcases. They enter from Stage Left and walk in wordlessly — as though in a dream. MITCH leads the way. They open the barracks door, enter, and stare at each other in silence.)

MITCH: *(Tiredly)* **Did you see the baggage some people brought? They said only as much as the arms can carry.**

KOKO: *(Sitting on her suitcase)* **Some people must have arms like octopuses.** *(MITCH opens the windows.)* **Octopi? Octopedes?**

MITCH: What?

KOKO: That's obscure. Rarely used.

MITCH: What's wrong with you, Koko?

KOKO: It's an archaic form of the plural of octopus. *(Outside, HARRY moves Downstage and sits unseen by the family.)*

MITCH: Octopedes! Here we are in this goddamn place and you talking about fish! You act like nothing's happened.

KOKO: I'm trying to get my bearings!

MRS. TANAKA: Shhh! Don't fight. *(She opens her shopping bag and brings out a tube of salami and begins slicing. MITCH takes a bowling trophy from his suitcase and sets it on a rib of the barracks frame. He pulls out a letter-man's sweater and puts it on a wooden hanger and hangs it from the same frame rib.)*

KOKO: It's unreal. Rows and rows, miles and miles of barracks ...and people like us...zombies in the desert...with two duffel bags, suitcases...cartons. *(The light behind the Upstage window is yellowing.)*

MRS. TANAKA: *(Passing the salami as she scolds)* Not fighting like you. This is not time for fighting. Time for taking care of each other.

KOKO: I'm just trying to get my bearings.

MITCH: I'm sorry. *(Looks carefully at KOKO.)* What's the matter? You crying? *(The light grows murky and ominous. Wind sounds increase. Outside, HARRY looks at the sky and turns his hat anxiously.)*

KOKO: I'm not crying. The meat is...is spicy. *(HARRY acts like a cornered animal as the storm approaches. He finally hides behind the barracks. KOKO is attracted to the strange light. Her eyes turn to the window.)* Look at that yellow cloud. Like in Kansas maybe. Like in the movies.... *(MRS. TANAKA follows her gaze. The wind roars.)*

MRS. TANAKA: Michio!

MITCH: Holy Mack! It's a tornado!

(The three run around closing the door and windows. MRS. TANAKA rewraps her salami and puts it away. She finds handkerchiefs for KOKO and MITCH, who put them over their mouths. She pulls KOKO to the duffel bags and they huddle together. MITCH remembers his trophy and sweater and returns them to his suitcase. The wind howls, dust swirls, and the door flies open. The TANAKAS react to the wind, covering their noses and bunching up. YO YOSHIDA, twenty-five, a Nisei woman, staggers in. She is

dressed like a boy — in jeans and a work shirt. Her hair is tucked into a snow cap, and a red bandanna covers the lower half of her face. She carries a small sketch pad and pencil. She curses and mutters.)

YO: *(Startled to see MITCH)* **What are you doing here?** *(Sees MRS. TANAKA and KOKO.)* [...] **I'm in the wrong barracks. Where is this?**

MITCH: *(Dryly)* **Poston, Arizona.**

YO: **I know that. I mean what barracks? What block?**

MRS. TANAKA: **Twelve-one-A. What you looking for?**

YO: **Block eleven.**

MITCH: *(Pointing right)* **I think eleven is out that way. Eleven what?**

YO: **No number. I live in the spinsters' quarters there.** *(Dusts herself off.)* **Been sketching and got caught in the storm. You just get here?**

MITCH: **Yeah, just now. We're from Fallbrook. Where're you from?**

YO: **Originally? Terminal Island.**

MRS. TANAKA: **Ah, the fishing village.**

MITCH: **Does this kind of thing happen often?** *(Meaning the dust storm)*

YO: **Often enough. Mind if I stay awhile? I mean till the dust...**

MRS. TANAKA: **Please. Please sit down.** *(Offers the edge of a cot.)*

KOKO: **Do you ever get used to it?**

YO: **The dust?**

MITCH: **Dust...everything.**

YO: **Don't know. Just been here two weeks myself. Two weeks and three days. You do or you don't, I guess. What is, is.** *(Looks at the three cots.)* **Just the three of you here?**

MITCH: **Yep. Pop died long time ago.**

MRS. TANAKA: **Long time 'go. Maybe lucky he not here.**

YO: **You're lucky you don't have another family in here. They still might do it. Throw in another family.**

KOKO: **You mean strangers living together?**

YO: **Sure. Oh, say, I'm Yo. Yo Yoshida.**

MRS. TANAKA: **We're Tanaka. This is Michio and Koko. You here all by yourself, Yo-Chan?**

YO: **Yeah. My father's in another detention center. They took him**

early. They took all the fishermen who owned boats.

MRS. TANAKA: Yo-chan lonely without family, ne?

YO: Well there're ten, twelve of us girls – bachelor women – in the barracks. We're sort of kin, I guess. We have one thing in common: we're alone. *(Laughs.)* You know, they give us just this much room... *(Indicates the bed space)* ...like single people need less space than others. You should see us at night – all line up in a row on these narrow beds [...] like inmates in a prison. Orphans in an orphanage.

MITCH: *(Laughs.)* That's what you get for being a woman.

YO: Yeah, for being a woman. For being single. For being Japanese. I think someone up there dealt a stacked deck.

SCENE 2: THREE FEMALES AND THREE MALES

Yo, 25

Mrs. Tanaka, 4

Koko, 17

Mitch, 20

Ken [Kenji] Ichioka, 19

Harry Yamane, 25

This scene follows directly after Scene 1.

1. Why do some of the characters react strongly to Koko's wanting to play cards?

2. Why do you think the bowling trophy is so important to Mitch?

3. What does Koko mean when she says, "Do you think they'll do anything to us?" If you were playing this role, what feelings would you want to express here?

4. What does Yo mean by saying that no matter what the outcome of the war, the Japanese Americans will lose?

5. If you were directing this scene, what emotions would you want most to emphasize? Explain.

(KOKO opens her suitcase and brings out a deck of cards.)

KOKO: What do you want to play?

MITCH: *(Incredulously)* **You're not going to play cards, are you?** *(KOKO makes a table with the suitcase.)*

MRS. TANAKA: You people crazy!

KOKO: Maybe we *are* crazy. Maybe this is really a booby hatch and we're the lunatics.

YO: No, there're thousands of us. There can't be that many boobies. *(Takes the cards from KOKO. The noises outside grow louder.)*

MITCH: Hey! There *is* someone out there! *(KEN ICHIOKA, nineteen, bangs on the door.)*

KEN: Open up! Let us in! *(MITCH opens the door. KOKO, YO, and MRS. TANAKA protect themselves from the wind. KEN and HARRY stumble in. They have a difficult time closing the door. MITCH helps them. Brushing himself off)* **Boy! The dust out there... Thanks...** *(Peers around.)* **Ken. Not much better inside.** *(Looks at MITCH.)* **Hey! I know you!**

MITCH: You know me?

KEN: Sure! Fallbrook High! Class of '40. Mitch Tanaka, right? Varsity football?

MITCH: *(Eagerly)* **No kidding! You were on the team, too?**

KEN: No, no. I was a couple classes below.

KOKO: Hi, Ken.

KEN: Oh! Hi.

KOKO: Koko. Remember? Latin II, room twenty-three?

KEN: Oh, yeah, yeah. Mr. Nelson, right?

KOKO: Yes. Right.

YO: Looks like a class reunion. Hi. I'm Yo. Who's your friend? *(HARRY spins his hat.)*

KEN: *(Turns to HARRY.)* **I don't know. He was huddled against the door when I came by. I thought he lived here.**

MRS. TANAKA: No. We just came.

KEN: *(Loudly)* **What's your name, friend?** *(HARRY shrinks.)*

MITCH: *(Loudly)* **What's your name?**

KOKO: You're scaring him, Mitch.

HARRY: *(Turns his hat rapidly.)* **Ah...ah...Harry.**

MRS. TANAKA: Ah, Harry-san.

YO: *(Counts heads and shuffles the cards.)* **Good! Just enough. Five.**

KEN: No kidding! You really playing cards?

YO: Why not? What else is there to do?

KEN: Crazy.

MRS. TANAKA: That's what I said.

KEN: *(To YO)* **Are you related or something?**

MITCH: *(Overlaps with YO.)* **No!**

YO: No, sir! I'm just like you. I blew in with the wind. *(MITCH brings his trophy out of the suitcase. HARRY watches.)*

HARRY: Whazzat?

MITCH: *(Looks at KEN.)* **It's a bowling trophy.** *(Polishes it with his sleeve before setting it against the wall. HARRY picks up the trophy and examines it.)*

MITCH: *(To KEN)* **You bowl?**

HARRY: Naw...

MRS. TANAKA: Michio was champion bowler...outside...before.

KEN: Yeah?

MRS. TANAKA: Michio win fifty dollars with that. *(Indicates the trophy.)*

KOKO: For the team's most valuable bowler.

MITCH: We tore that championship right from Sweetwater's mouth. Man-o-man! They were already tasting it! *(Takes the trophy from HARRY and sets it back on the wall.)*

HARRY: Fifty dollars?

KEN: Fifty dollars, eh?

MITCH: Yep. It was a regional. You bowl?

KEN: No, not me. *(Looks at YO.)* **I don't even play cards.**

YO: No problem.

KOKO: We'll teach you.

YO: You'll be an expert by the time we get out of here. *(They look at each other and turn silent.)*

YO: Well, what'd you want to play? *(Looks from face to face.)*

HARRY: I don't wanta play.

KEN: *(Overlaps HARRY.)* **Not me.**

MITCH: *(To KEN)* **How long you figure we'll be here?**

KEN: *(Shrugs.)* **Probably till the end of the war.**

MRS. TANAKA: **Whaa...**

KOKO: *(Overlaps.)* **Do you think they'll do anything to us?**

YO: **They already have.**

KOKO: **I mean, you know...**

MRS. TANAKA: **Till end of war?**

KOKO: **Then what?**

KEN: **That'll probably depend on the outcome.**

MRS. TANAKA: **Outcome?**

YO: **In a war, Obasan, one country wins; the other loses.**

MRS. TANAKA: **What if Japan wins?** *(Fearfully)* **What happen if Japan lose?**

YO: **We all look the same to them. We lose both ways.**

SCENE 3: TWO FEMALES AND TWO MALES

Mrs. Tanaka, 40

Koko, 17

Mitch, 20

Mr. Endo, 45

The next scene occurs a few months later. The audience can see the silhouette of a guard tower. A hand-sewn curtain divides the sleeping and living areas. Inside are a table and crude bench. Another bench stands outside. It is midday. Koko is playing solitaire, and Mitch is at work. Somewhere a radio plays "Don't Sit Under the Apple Tree." Mitch is at work. Harry enters and leaves lumber he has stolen from the construction camp.

In preparing the scene, you can skip Mr. Endo's role.

1. What difference in attitude can you see here between the older and younger generations? How do their values differ?

2. Why does Koko say she won't need a coat? What is her attitude — obstinate, defeatist, realistic, apprehensive, or otherwise? What makes you think so?

3. What feelings do you think Mrs. Tanaka has for her daughter here? Point to the lines that show this.

4. Do you think it's fair for Mrs. Tanako to say people are talking about Koko? What is her attitude toward Yo and Harry?

5. Why do you think Koko doesn't want to get a job?

6. Do you think Mitch's attitude is realistic? Explain.

MRS. TANAKA: Most girls like you find jobs already.

KOKO: *(Continuing her solitaire)* I know.

MRS. TANAKA: *(Pretending to be involved in her sewing)* No use to stay home all the time. *(KOKO shuffles the cards.)* Ichioka-san says many jobs open in camp office now. Jobs in hospital, too. You work there...nurse's aide or something.

KOKO: *(Dryly)* And meet a nice young doctor maybe?

MRS. TANAKA: Nothing wrong with that.

KOKO: No. Not for you.

MRS. TANAKA: *(Hanging the curtain on the window)* I wish I didn't sell my sewing machine. Man only gave me five dollars for it.

KOKO: That's what I mean. What good is money here?

MRS. TANAKA: You need money here, too.

KOKO: For what?

MRS. TANAKA: *(Exasperated)* You tryna give me hard time, Koko? You know what I mean...cold cream, magazines... *(Inspired)* Lipstick?

KOKO: They're going to give us a clothing allowance. I'll use that for what I need.

MRS. TANAKA: That three dollars a month? You need that for shoes. Pretty soon it will be cold and you will need coat.

KOKO: No I won't.

MRS. TANAKA: You going stay naked in the barracks? You not going to come out of barracks? *(Reconsiders.)* Ne, Koko. Michio got nice job in motor pool. Twelve dollars a month. Pretty soon he's going to get raise.

> *(MR. ENDO, forty-five, enters from Stage Right with a tenugui [thin cotton towel] around his neck. He walks leisurely across, swabbing at his face.)*

KOKO: Ma, I told you I don't want to work here.

MRS. TANAKA: Who likes here? You think Mama put you here? *(KOKO is silent, still concentrating on her cards.)*

MRS. TANAKA: *(Muttering)* Hunh! She thinks Mama put her here. *(More reasonably)* Koko...Mama don't want you to be alone all time. Go out, have good time, make nice friends.

KOKO: I have friends.

MRS. TANAKA: Oh? Who your friends? You sit home all time, play cards all....

KOKO: *(Irritated)* I have friends. Yo says all you need is one....

MRS. TANAKA: "Yo says, Yo says." Yo-chan crazy girl! Don't you know that?

KOKO: Yo is not crazy!

MRS. TANAKA: People laughing at you. They say Koko got funny friends: one crazy girl and one funny man. They think maybe Koko's funny, too. *(Taps her head.)*

KOKO: So what? Who needs them? I don't care what they think.

MRS. TANAKA: *(Lowering her voice and giving KOKO a warning look toward the ICHIOKA barracks)* Koko, if you don't make nice friends, how you going to find good husband?

KOKO: Oh, please!

MRS. TANAKA: Never mind, "Oh, please." One day you going be all alone. Then you say...

KOKO: *(Under her breath)* Good God!

MRS. TANAKA: Koko's going be just like Mama. Alone. Going to work in restaurant every night; every night come home, soak feet, count tip money...

KOKO: Pa died! He couldn't help what happened to you!

MRS. TANAKA: All same. Same! This is first time I don't work ten hours a day. First vacation.

KOKO: Don't call this a vacation, Ma!

MRS. TANAKA: You know what I mean. This is first time I don't worry about shoes, clothes...if Koko...

KOKO: Oh, for crying out loud! *(Picks up her cards and storms out of the barracks.)*

MRS. TANAKA: *(Calling after her)* What'sa matter you! You listen to Mama! *(Sees KOKO's shoes.)* Put your shoes away! *(MRS. TANAKA picks up the shoes and sets them in the bedroom area.)* Lazy girl! *(MITCH enters from Stage Left. He glances at the sullen KOKO, who plays solitaire on the bench. He enters the barracks to hear MAMA fuming.)*

MITCH: Aw...simmer down, Ma. Don't get your blood pressure up. Leave her alone. *(He looks in his suitcase for his catcher's mitt.)*

257

MRS. TANAKA: Michio. Koko is going have hard time like that.

MITCH: She'll be all right.

MRS. TANAKA: What's going happen to her? Mama can't be all time with Koko, you know.

MITCH: Don't worry, Ma. Give her a chance to grow up. She's only seventeen. When we get out of here, well, things will...

MRS. TANAKA: How? How we getting out? We can't get out. We got no friends to help us and we got no money.

MITCH: *(Examining his mitt)* I don't know yet, but I'll find a way. We're not going to stay here forever. And don't worry. I'm going to take care of you and Koko.

SCENE 4: ONE MALE AND ONE FEMALE

Harry, 25

Koko, 17

Yo tells Koko she has quit her job, the third one she's had because she can't get along with "these people." Koko reminds her that "these are us." Yo says she just doesn't fit in. Koko and Yo accuse each other of being oddballs. Yo teases Koko about "having it bad" for Ken. Koko tells Yo she is her first real friend and that the two of them should make a pact.

Yo tells her that friends don't need pacts and then sings a funny song about friendship. Koko says she never takes anything seriously. Yo, in turn, accuses Koko of being edgy but then apologizes and says she's a cynic. "I want to laugh," Yo says. "I don't want to cry anymore."

"Was it a man?" Koko asks.

Yo answers, "Father, mother, sister, country...it doesn't matter."

Ken enters carrying three cups of punch he bought at the canteen. He asks Koko how she is. She says that all things considered, she's okay. Ken's mother criticizes him for wasting his money on the punch and says "Papa" is feeling bad again.

The following scene occurs in September, 1942. "The barracks is considerably more habitable. A tablecloth, pitcher, and glasses are on the table." It's another hot day. A radio somewhere else plays "I Got a Gal in Kalamazoo." Koko and Harry are playing cards. Harry holds his hat in his lap.

1. What is the playwright's reason, do you think, for including this scene?

2. Why do you think Koko says she sometimes thinks she won't get a job just because her mother wants her to get one? Is this a natural feeling? Explain.

3. Do you think Koko's description of the relocation center is a good one: "This place is like..like a vacuum...you're shut out from the outside and inside everyone pretends like nothing's wrong." Why do you think people would go on pretending nothing is wrong?

4. What is your reaction to the ending of this scene?

HARRY: *(Setting down his hand)* **Gin!**

KOKO: *(Checking his hand)* **No, Harry. Every trick has to have at least three cards. See, you have only two here.** *(Shows him her hand.)* **You have to have three cards of the same suit.**

HARRY: Oh, yeah. I forgot.

KOKO: We'll play something else. How about...

HARRY: I don' wanta play cards.

KOKO: Okay. Well...you want me to read to you?

HARRY: I can read. *(Spins his hat.)*

KOKO: You want to talk?

HARRY: Okay.

KOKO: Well...tell me about your mother.

HARRY: She's dead.

KOKO: Well, shall we talk about your father, then? What's your father like? Is he... *(HARRY moves from the table to the Upstage bench.)* **Is he tall? Is he short? Is he...**

HARRY: He's not very nice.

KOKO: How come? Does he hit you?

HARRY: He don' talk to me.

KOKO: No, that's not very nice.

HARRY: He always say, "Baka, baka..." Baka means stupid. Make me feel bad. He don' like me.

KOKO: Harry. He likes you. He's like my mom. She keeps nagging, "Find a job, go to work, find a nice man." Sometimes I think just because she tells me to, I won't. Funny, hunh? *(HARRY laughs.)*

KOKO: I don't know why I feel so...I don't know. Maybe it's the weather. It's so hot here. Maybe it's this place. Maybe it's the world...the war.

HARRY: Yeah...

KOKO: Maybe everyone feels like this. This place's like...like a vacuum...you're shut out from the outside and inside everyone pretends like nothing's wrong.

HARRY: Yeah.

KOKO: Like this is normal. But it's not normal. What are people really feeling?

HARRY: I don't know.

KOKO: Maybe we shouldn't worry about things we have no power to change. Maybe we should go to work every day, smile hello, say good-bye...spread small joys...inflict little hurts...skirt around this whole crazy situation. Maybe this is the way it's supposed to be.

HARRY: *(Depressed)* Yeah...

KOKO: *(Realizing she's depressing HARRY)* Yo's got another job. She's so strong...all alone here. I'd probably fall apart. But, of course, I have my mom and Mitch...

HARRY: Yeah...

KOKO: And Yo and Ken...

HARRY: And me, too.

KOKO: Harry?

HARRY: Hunh?

KOKO: Do you...do you think he likes me?

HARRY: Who?

KOKO: You know who. *(HARRY shrugs and turns inward.)* I suppose I'd know it if he did...wouldn't have to ask anyone.

SCENE 5: TWO FEMALES AND ONE MALE

Mitch, 20

Koko, 17

Mrs. Tanaka, 40

Ken brings candy bars he shares with Koko and Harry. Koko is really surprised; she hasn't had candy in a long time. She gives half the bar back to Ken and starts to put hers away to save it. Ken tells her that if she doesn't eat it, it will melt. Koko asks about his job. He says he just walks around out in the field. She asks if he's a reporter.

Mrs. Tanaka asks Mrs. Ichioka inside and gives her two of the eggs she's "appropriated" from the kitchen. She complains about Koko's playing cards with Harry. Koko answers that Harry has feelings, and he's not deaf.

1. Why do you think Mitch is so enthused about harvesting beets?

2. Why do Koko and Mrs. Tanaka not want Mitch to leave?

3. Do you think Mitch is right about being able to take care of himself? Explain.

(MITCH enters. He's in great spirits.)

MITCH: Hello-hello-hello! What're you doing? [...]

KOKO: Something good happen?

MRS. TANAKA: Michio! Look. *(Shows MITCH the eggs.)*

MITCH: That's nice. Guess what I heard today! They're recruiting volunteers to harvest sugar beets.

KOKO: Sugar beets? Here?

MITCH: Not here, silly. Outside! Yeah! Looks like our white citizens are all doing defense work and making a pile of money, so the farms are short of help. All you gotta do is get a clearance and you can get out of here! Ain't that something?

KOKO: *(Jumping up and down)* I can't believe it! Ma! We're getting out!

MRS. TANAKA: *(Almost screaming)* That's good!

MITCH: No-no. Just me. Just men. We go on a seasonal leave and we come back after the harvest.

MRS. TANAKA: That's no good, Michio. No good. We stay together. We are a family. We stay together.

MITCH: It's just for a short time, Ma.

KOKO: You mean you'd leave us? You'd leave us here? You'd go without us?

MRS. TANAKA: Michio is not going.

MITCH: It's a short-term leave. A month or two and I'll be back. It's a chance to make a little money, buy a few things... *(Gently)* What do you want, Koko?

KOKO: I don't want anything. I don't want you to go. You can't do that, Mitch.

MITCH: Aw...don't be like that.

MRS. TANAKA: *(Firmly)* No, you don't go, Michio. We stay together.

MITCH: *(Very patiently)* It's a chance to be free for a little while, Ma. I'll look around. Maybe I'll find a little place where we can settle. I'll make a little money. It'll be a start. Later we can get out of here – all of us together. Just think, Ma – free! *(HARRY spins his hat.)*

KOKO: What will happen to us while you're away? What if you don't come back?

MITCH: Don't be silly. What can happen?

KOKO: Don't leave us, Mitch. Don't go. Yo says blood is only thing you can count on. She really misses her dad.

MITCH: I know, Koko. But I can't stay here just because of that. We got to start doing something. We can't grow old here. You know that, don't you?

MRS. TANAKA: No good! Don't like! Ichioka-san says people spit on you!

MITCH: Don't worry, Ma. I can take care of myself. And I'll come back. By then, I'll have a plan. Everything will be all right.

MRS. TANAKA: Maybe just a rumor, Michio. Lots of talk 'round here, you know.

MITCH: It's not just a rumor! Guys are signing up already.

MRS. TANAKA: Don't make up mind yet. We talk some more.

KOKO: What if...

MITCH: "What if, what if..." What can happen? Don't you think I can take care of myself?

KOKO: Anything can happen! You can't tell. Did you think you'd be *here* last year? Oh, Mitch, don't go.

MITCH: I gotta, Koko.

MRS. TANAKA: You head of family, Michio. Don't forget that. You don't go and leave Koko and...

MITCH: Ma! I'm not leaving her. I'm not leaving you. If I'm the head of this family, I gotta get out and make plans for us. Don't you see? You gotta trust me. You gotta let me try it!

MRS. TANAKA: See, Koko? You going be all alone. You see what Mama was talking 'bout? You see? We going be all alone.

MITCH: Cripes! I come rushing home with the best news since they put us here...and...and...Jesus Christ!

MRS. TANAKA: We talk 'bout it. We talk first!

KOKO: Listen to Ma!

MITCH: I'm going back to work [...]

SCENE 6: TWO FEMALES AND ONE MALE

Mrs. Ichioka, 45

Mrs. Tanaka, 40

Harry, 25

Mrs. Tanaka nearly goes after Mitch but decides not to. Koko gently tells her, "That's okay, Mama." Then she says she'll start looking for a job.

Mitch returns and starts to go inside but changes his mind. Yo sees him and asks what's wrong. He tells her he finally found a way to do something and.... "The whole world's against me." Mrs. Tanaka invites Yo in to help eat the eggs. Yo pulls an egg from underneath her cap. Koko and Mrs. Tanaka laugh and then "a pall settles over the group."

Ever wisecracking, Yo asks, "What is this? The Last Supper?" Mrs. Tanaka tells her Mitch is going to pick sugar beets. Yo asks where she can sign up, and Mrs. Tanaka says it's only for men. "Who said it's a free country?" Yo responds.

It is November, 1942. Mrs. Tanaka and Mrs. Ichioka are outside folding clothes. Harry enters carrying a handmade chair covered in an army blanket. One leg is shorter than the others.

1. Do you agree with Mrs. Tanaka's attitude about the food poisoning? Explain.

2. What do you think of the two women's treatment of Harry in this scene?

MRS. TANAKA: Hallo, Harry-san. What you got there? *(HARRY sets the chair down and pulls off the blanket.)*

MRS ICHIOKA: Two hundred people in Fresno camp; one whole block sick.

MRS. TANAKA: How come? That's purty, Harry-san. *(HARRY beams.)*

MRS. ICHIOKA: Food poisoning. They going kill us all. Two hundred people at a time. Manzanar got big trouble, too. M.P. stealing food from Manzanar people. People saying...

MRS. TANAKA: Ichioka-san, don't listen to everything. Can't help those things. Don't listen. Too scary. *(To HARRY)* **You made it?**

HARRY: Yeah.

MRS. ICHIOKA: Tanaka-san, no good to hide head all the time.

MRS. TANAKA: *(To HARRY)* **That's nice. Your papa be proud, ne?** *(Starts to sit on HARRY's chair.)*

HARRY: *(Stops her midway.)* **No! It's for Koko.**

MRS. TANAKA: Koko?

MRS. ICHIOKA: You made chair for Koko-chan! *(Suspiciously)* **Very nice chair, Harry-san.**

HARRY: *(Troubled)* **Yeah.**

MRS. ICHIOKA: *(To TANAKA)* **Koko-chan is working now. Harry-san got lots of time now.** *(Exchanges significant nods with MRS. TANAKA.)*

MRS. TANAKA: Ah-ah...Harry-san. You know...ah...Koko is not good for you. Koko is not nice girlfriend for you.

HARRY: I don' care.

MRS. TANAKA: Koko's going hurt you, Harry-san.

HARRY: I don't care.

MRS. ICHIOKA: Better find 'nother girlfriend. Koko-chan is too smart for you.

HARRY: I don' care.

MRS. TANAKA: You going one day cry, Harry-san. Koko going make you cry.

HARRY: I don' care.

MRS. TANAKA: Ah...Harry-san.

SCENE 7: THREE FEMALES, TWO MALES

Mrs. Tanaka, 40

Mrs. Ichioka, 45

Koko, 17

Ken, 19

Harry, 26

Harry wipes off the chair and recovers it. Koko and Ken enter. Koko now wears a white uniform. She has a job as a nurse's aide. She says that all day she's been washing bedpans. Ken says his work gets him down too.

1. Why do you think Ken won't talk specifically about his job?

2. Do you think Ken or the two older women are right about the beatings? Why? Why not?

3. Why does Mrs. Ichioka mention Joe DiMaggio (a professional baseball player)? What is she implying here?

4. What does Mrs. Tanaka mean when she says, "We are only leaves in the wind"?

5. Why do you suppose Mrs. Ichioka speaks with such certainty when she says Japan will win the war? What are the feelings behind these words?

6. What emotions would you want the audience to feel after hearing the last line in this scene?

KOKO: What exactly do you do? I never knew what you did.

KEN: Ah...I just shuffle papers.

KOKO: What kind of papers?

KEN: Surveys. You know. Sociological surveys.

KOKO: Sociological?

KEN: Yeah. You hear from Mitch?

KOKO: Not very often. He says it's backbreaking work...you know, bending over, topping sugar beets...

MRS. TANAKA: *(To ICHIOKA)* Michio says Nebraska is too cold. He's too tired to write. Just only postcards.

MRS. ICHIOKA: That so?

KEN: *(Overlapping)* What else does he say?

KOKO: Not much else.

KEN: Well, say hello for me.

MRS. ICHIOKA: *(To TANAKA)* Big crowd at police station, people say.

MRS. TANAKA: Oh, yeah?

MRS. ICHIOKA: They put in jail two people who beat up informers.
(KEN listens from Stage Right.)

MRS. TANAKA: Informers?

MRS. ICHIOKA: Yeah. Informing on own people. Inu! Dogs! They deserve beating.

KEN: *(Moving in)* Now wait, Mom. Wait a minute. The informing hasn't been proven yet. And, even if they did inform, those two guys have no business beating on people. They're thugs! How would you like to be dragged out in the middle of the night and beaten? No one would be safe. It's lawless!

MRS. ICHIOKA: Law? Don't talk law. You going make lots of people mad, talking law here.

KEN: Mom...

MRS. ICHIOKA: Mo... *(Meaning "already")* ...enough! We already talk over and over. You never listen.

KEN: *(Patiently)* The law, Mom. You're innocent until proven guilty.

MRS. ICHIOKA: If there is law like that, then why you here? You been proven already? And Koko-chan and Harry-san, too?
(HARRY spins his hat.)

KEN: That's different, Mom. We're talking about people who beat up other people...

MRS. ICHIOKA: Nobody says Joe DiMaggio is guilty. He's enemy alien, too. How come you and Koko guilty? How come we guilty?

MRS. TANAKA: *(Very concerned)* That's all right, Ichioka-san. No use. We only leaves in the wind.

MRS. ICHIOKA: That's all right. Kenji will understand when Japan wins the war.

KEN: Mom, there's no way Japan can win this war.

MRS. ICHIOKA: Japan will win!

KEN: Already they're being slaughtered in Guadalcanal. What kind of resources do you think they have? Just look at it logically. You think planes and...you think the Sun God supplies the oil and ammunition and ships and...

KOKO: Just read the papers, Obasan.

MRS. ICHIOKA: Papers? You reading American papers! You better think these Japanese people as your brothers. When they die, you die, too! *(To TANAKA)* Young people, baka. Don't understand. Don't know Yamato Damashi, nah, Tanaka-san? *(To KEN)* Spirit of Japan can beat bigger, richer countries. Look Russia. Big Russia! Read your history book! Americans – heh – call Japanese "Little Yellow Men." They will show you. You watch!

MRS. TANAKA: *(Picking up her laundry)* Ichioka-san, come on. I will make tea for you. No use fighting with own son. Better, more better families stick together. No good to fight. *(She pulls MRS. ICHIOKA with her and the two enter the barracks and prepare the tea.)*

MRS. ICHIOKA: Young people empty head. Freedom only for white people. When they going learn that. Baka... *(HARRY grows uncomfortable and spins his hat.)*

MRS. TANAKA: Can't help. Young people learn from American books and we learn from Japanese books. Michio and me...we fight, too. Now Michio is far away. Now we don't fight no more.

SCENE 8: THREE FEMALES AND FOUR MALES

Sam, 19

Bill, 19

Ken, 19

Mrs. Ichioka, 45

Koko, 17

Mrs. Tanaka, 40

Harry, 26

This scene follows directly after the preceding. Sam and Bill (both minor characters) enter. Sam waves to Ken.

1. Why do you think Ken doesn't want to attend the protest rally?

2. What do you think Ken feels in talking about his father?

3. How do Ken and Koko's outlooks differ here? Can you see any way in which Koko has changed since the beginning of the play?

4. Why does Ken talk about being torn between two countries? How do you think he feels? Is it different from the way the two older women feel? From the way Koko feels?

5. What do Ken and Koko mean when they agree that they don't know how they feel?

SAM: Let's go to the police station!

KEN: What's going on?

BILL: Where you been, man?

SAM: They're tryna take the guys to Tucson!

KEN: The ones who were arrested?

SAM: Yeah! We gotta stop them! They'll never get a fair trial in Tucson!

BILL: Come on! It's a mass assembly – ho ho – against all those camp regulations! *(SAM cocks his ear and hears faint strains of Japanese martial music.)*

SAM: You hear that? That's the old "Gunkan Maachi." I hear they hooked up loudspeakers and they're playing all those old military songs. Boy! *(MRS. TANAKA and MRS. ICHIOKA come from the barracks and MR. ENDO appears from Stage Right. He carries an army blanket. BILL exits left.)*

MRS. ICHIOKA: *(Listening and smiling)* Ah...Japanese music. Let's go, Tanaka-san. Come on, let's go.

MRS. TANAKA: *(Looking at KOKO)* Too cold out there.

SAM: No worry, Obasan! They got bonfires and everything! *(MR. ENDO exits Upstage Left.)* You coming, Ken?

MRS. ICHIOKA: We just go hear music. Iko ya, Tanaka-san. *(Meaning "let's go.")*

KEN: Wait, Mom...

MRS. ICHIOKA: You come, too. Papa be all right.

HARRY: Koko, I made...

KOKO: Let's go, Ken. *(Everyone leaves but KEN, KOKO, and HARRY.)*

KEN: Wait. This is...this is mob action.

KOKO: Just see what's going on.

KEN: I can't take part in this sort of thing.

KOKO: We don't have to participate. Come on. My mom went. She's not going to get in trouble. She's a coward.

KEN: No telling what my mom will do.

KOKO: Well, we better go keep an eye on her then.

HARRY: Koko...

KEN: Until this war, she's always said, "Study hard; be a good citizen." She was the most American of us all. Now she's trying to erase everything she's taught me.

KOKO: She's hurt.

KEN: Well, who isn't? *(Moves away from KOKO.)* I wish my dad were well. He'd straighten her out. He's so sick, he doesn't care what happens. He used to be so strong. Now look. Doesn't care about anything. *(Looks away.)* When I was a kid, I wondered if I'd ever be the man he was. *(HARRY takes his chair and enters the barracks. He sits on it dejectedly.)*

KOKO: I used to feel like that, too. I wondered if I could get up in the morning and cook breakfast and make lunch for my kids and go off to work, hurry home at night and make dinner and go off to work again. I thought I'd have to do all those things. We never had a man around, you know.

KEN: Sounds like a dream: settling down with someone... marrying... *(MR. ENDO enters from Stage Left. He wears a pea coat.)*

MR. ENDO: Come on. Everybody. Station, station. *(Gestures Downstage Left and exits.)*

KEN: I wonder if it will ever happen. I mean to us.

KOKO: Of course it will. It always happens.

KEN: You grow up thinking life will continue forever, night following day, people marrying, having children...

KOKO: Night always follows day. People will always marry and have children.

KEN: But things are so changeable. Suddenly there's a war and all your values shift and change. You're torn between countries – between families... *(Shakes his head.)* Look at my dad...fallen so low.

KOKO: Those things happen, war or no war.

KEN: But there is a war. And things are not the same.

KOKO: I know that. I feel it, too.

KEN: We're in limbo, Koko. One day, this; another day, that. We can't make plans. We can't make promises.

KOKO: But people do.

KEN: You may be unable to keep those promises.

KOKO: You keep them as long as you're able. That's all.

KEN: What about "till death do us part"?

KOKO: Only as long as you're able. That's all you can do. That's what

Yo says.

KEN: I wish I could say what I feel...or be sure of what I feel. I don't even know that. I feel so...

KOKO: Me, too, Ken. Let's go inside.

SCENE 9: TWO FEMALES AND ONE MALE

Mrs. Tanaka, 40

Mitch, 20

Koko, 17

Yama enters and hands out flyers about a strike. He warns Ken about working for the administration, telling him that he might get hurt. He says, "Nights get plenty dark here. Plenty hotheads 'round, you know." He says it's people like Ken who "put us here in the first place." He calls Ken names and gives him a shove. They fight. Yama punches Ken in the belly and knocks him down. Both Koko and Mrs. Ichioka come in and attack Yama. He says Ken is an informer. Ken denies it. Mrs. Ichioka then asks Ken if he is an informer, and he tells her he writes reports about things that have already happened.

"Then, Kenji," she says, "you make report of man shot in back for getting too close to the fence? You write that, too, nah? Sick people dying, no medicine, son turn against mother — you write all that, nah?"

Ken and Mrs. Ichioka exit. Koko and Harry are left alone. He shows her the chair and tells her he made it for her. She "utters a small cry and runs to the bedroom area." Harry is puzzled, but then leaves.

It is now early December, 1942. Mitch has just come home, and his mother is giving a small party, with crackers, three apples and chips. She and Koko are trying on dresses Mitch brought them.

1. What do you think is the prevailing or overall mood of this scene? Explain.

2. Why does Mrs. Tanaka complain about what Mitch bought, about his spending his money, and so on?

3. What do you think of the government's deporting Japanese Americans to Japan? Do you think this was justified? Why? Why not?

MRS. TANAKA: *(Behind the curtain)* **That's pretty, Koko.**

MITCH: You like it?

KOKO: *(Behind the curtain)* **Oh, I like it. Ma likes hers, too, don't you, Ma?**

MRS. TANAKA: Yes, yes. You spent too much money. You shouldn't spend so much when you work so hard for it. *(KOKO comes out like a model, holding the skirt of a pinafore outward, humming "A Pretty Girl Is Like a Melody." MRS. TANAKA also parades in a drab new old-lady dress, a size too large, another gift from MITCH. MRS. TANAKA continuing, pinching in the excess of her dress)* **Michio, you think Mama's an old lady and Koko's still a little girl, ne?**

MITCH: There wasn't enough to save. I couldn't bring anything home, Ma.

MRS. TANAKA: That's all right.

KOKO: You're home...I mean, here with us. That's the main thing.

MITCH: We had to buy our own groceries and pay for that lousy cabin we slept in, too. There wasn't much left after that. *(MRS. TANAKA sneaks into the bedroom area to get a "Welcome Back, MITCH" poster while KOKO holds MITCH's attention.)*

KOKO: Did you...ah, look around? Was it a nice place to move to...?

MITCH: We worked six days a week. Didn't have much time after that. No, it's not a "nice" place to move to. It's cold there. *(KOKO stands by her mother by the sign and simultaneously they speak.)*

KOKO and MRS. TANAKA: Ta-daaa!

MITCH: *(Trying to look happy)* **That's nice. Real nice.** *(Moves Downstage.)* **Well, what's new here? Anything good happen?**

KOKO: Like what? *(KOKO and MRS. TANAKA start to decorate the bleak barracks walls with crepe paper streamers.)*

MITCH: Like I thought Ma would have found a nice doctor for you – ha ha – by now.

MRS. TANAKA: Not yet. But Koko got a nice job.

KOKO: If you call cleaning bedpans nice.

MITCH: Bedpans?

KOKO: *(Engrossed in decorating)* **We had a strike not long ago.**

MITCH: No kidding. What d'you strike for?

275

KOKO: Well, it started with two men being jailed for beating an informer and ended up a strike against general policy.

MRS. TANAKA: Everybody out in firebreak, day and night. Two weeks. Singing songs, making speeches...music going all the time...

MITCH: Did you get what you struck for?

KOKO: Not much change here. But the men who were arrested... they were scheduled to be tried in Tucson...you know they wouldn't have gotten a fair trial there...well, we stopped that.

MITCH: So they'll be tried here?

KOKO: No no.

MITCH: Well, where then?

KOKO: They disappeared. Talk is, they were sent to Tule Lake.

MITCH: Tule Lake! That's the camp up north where they send all the troublemakers.

KOKO: Yes, the dissidents, incorrigibles, recalcitrants, repatriates...

MITCH: [...] I hear it's a maximum security camp...tear gas, riot guns, curfew...the whole thing. Why the hell you let 'em do that?

KOKO: It's still better than being tried in Tucson. At least they'd be with their own. *(Helps MITCH unpack.)* They say it's a deportation center. It's from there and on to Japan. The last stop before Japan.

MRS. TANAKA: Last stop before Nihon.

MITCH: Must be a holy hellhole.

SCENE 10: FOUR FEMALES AND THREE MALES

Yo, 25

Mitch, 20

Koko, 17

Ken, 19

Harry, 25

Mrs. Tanaka, 40

Mrs. Ichioka, 45

Mitch says he is too tired and wants to call off the party. Mrs. Tanaka says she can't do that, and it's just a small party for his friends — Yo, Ken, Harry. Koko tells him the army is recruiting volunteers for a segregated unit of Nisei soldiers. Mitch says he doesn't believe that will happen. No one will volunteer. Koko tells him that men in Hawaii are already signing up. Mitch says that's different because with all the Japanese on the islands, "they didn't get rounded up." Mitch says he won't volunteer. Mrs. Tanaka is relieved at this. Yo arrives wearing high heels and a party dress.

1. What do you think each of the characters is feeling in this scene, taking into consideration their talking about the first day they met?

2. What do you think Ken means by saying everything's changed? Why do you think he leaves?

3. What does Yo mean by telling Mitch, "You've learned something"?

4. Why does Yo suddenly start talking about getting free, seeing that her father is released, and finding a vine-covered cottage? Do you think she really believes this? Is she deluding herself? Being cynical?

5. What is the mood at the end of the scene? What is the significance of the ending — whispering, "Hooray for freedom"?

KEN: So you made it back! Good to see you. How's everything?

MITCH: Yeah, yeah. Okay. I'm okay. Hi, Harry, how's the world treating you?

HARRY: *(Grinning broadly)* **Okay.** *(Shakes MITCH's hand.)*

MRS. TANAKA: Come sit down, everybody.

KOKO: This reminds me of the first day we met.

YO: *(Passing out the drinks)* **A toast!**

KOKO: Remember that terrible dust storm, Yo?

YO: Do I ever. I thought this was my barracks.

MITCH: Hell, she wanted to know what I was doing here.

YO: A toast to the return of the prodigal! *(They toast MITCH: "To Mitch!" "Bottoms up!" "To the future!")*

KOKO: *(To KEN)* **And you came in with Harry. Just like tonight.**

KEN: He was huddled by the door. I don't know how long he was there before I came along.

MRS. TANAKA: Yo-chan playing cards. I remember.

MITCH: *(Quietly)* **Seems a long time ago. And we're still in the same place. Nothing's changed.**

KOKO: But it has! Look, you went outside...and we're good friends now.

YO: Hear, hear! Our own Miss Goody Two Shoes!

KEN: *(Turning inward)* **Everything's changed.**

YO: Aw, come now. Stop this serious talk. This is a party! *(To MRS. TANAKA)* **Obasan, you should have planned a program.**

MRS. TANAKA: Program? But Ichioka-san's not here yet. *(YO pours another round for everyone. KEN drinks morosely.)*

YO: Well, let's rehearse then. Who wants to sing?

MITCH: Naw, we don't want to sing. I can't even carry a tune.

YO: *(Slightly drunk)* **Harry, you wantta start it?**

HARRY: *(Grinning foolishly)* **I know only one song.**

YO: Well, hit it, baby!

KOKO: Sing, Harry!

MRS. TANAKA: Ichioka-san's not here yet.

HARRY: *(Standing)* **Yes, sir, that's my baby/No, sir, don't mean maybe/Yes, sir, that's my baby now...**

MRS. TANAKA: Ichioka-san's...

YO: *(With HARRY)* **And by the way/And by the way...** *(Everyone joins in. MRS. TANAKA reluctantly keeps time on the table.)*

EVERYONE: When we reach that preacher/I will say/yes, sir, that's my baby/No, sir, don't mean maybe... *(There is a loud banging on the door. YO, still singing, opens it. MRS. ICHIOKA enters.)*

MRS. ICHIOKA: Too much noise! *(One by one, people stop singing. HARRY is the last to stop.)*

MRS. TANAKA: Sorry, sorry. Sit down, Ichioka-san. We expected you...

YO: *(Inebriated)* **Come in, come in. Bring Papa, Mama. Join the party.** *(Pushes MRS. ICHIOKA to a chair.)*

MRS. ICHIOKA: Can't sit down. Papa pretty sick, Kenji.

KEN: I'd better go. *(KEN gets up and leaves quickly with his mother. Everyone is surprised.)*

YO: *(To HARRY)* **'Smatter with him?**

HARRY: I don' know.

MRS. TANAKA: I'm going to bed. I think I'm a little bit drunk. *(Turns back.)* **Be quiet now.**

KOKO: 'Night, Ma. *(To YO)* **Ken's...something's wrong with him.**

YO: Aw...he's no fun. He's been like that ever since...ever since... what?

KOKO: He's changed. That's what he said. [...]

YO: Oh, hey, did you get your bowling done outside? Bet you just parked your butt right in that ol' bowling alley, hunh?

MITCH: *(Turning grim)* **No.**

KOKO: Didn't you bowl, Mitch?

MITCH: I said no!

YO: Temper, temper. *(To HARRY)* **'Smatter with him?**

HARRY: He's mad.

MITCH: [...] I'm mad. They wouldn't let us in the alleys, let alone bowl. Or the barber shops...or the restaurants. [...]

YO: Well, you see, you've learned something.

MITCH: Damned right, I learned. I learned good. You're going to learn, too. It's mean out there. A hanging party on every good ol' main street, USA.

YO: Come on, kid. You just had some bad luck. It's not like that in every town.

279

MITCH: Wantta bet?

YO: You can't start thinking like that, Mitch. We're going to get out pretty soon and... *(Pours another drink.)*

MITCH: Go easy on that stuff. That's gotta last me till the end of the war. Or forever. Whichever comes first.

YO: Don't worry. We're going to get out purty damn soon and...I'll tell you what. I'll buy you the next bottle. Okay? We're getting out purty soon now.

MITCH: Sez who?

YO: Sez me. I happen to know something.

MITCH: Yeah? What's 'at?

YO: We're all going to get out of here. All of us. We-are-getting-out-of-here. You hear 'at? All we do is...

MITCH: Yeah, hang yourself.

YO: No, no, no. We fill out a questionnaire and get a clearance 'n voilá! We're free!

KOKO: That's all? Fill out a questionnaire?

MITCH: *(Suspiciously)* What kind of questions?

YO: Easy ones. You know: Where're you born, what schools, what organizations...were you ever arrested and why?...those kinds.

MITCH: How come so easy? What's the catch?

YO: They wanna get rid of us. It's getting kind of embarrassing to 'em, you know, corbeas hab...due process and all that stuff. *(Takes a drink.)* Know where I'm going?

KOKO: Where?

YO: I'm agoin' to Montana. Missoula, Montana, look out!

MRS. TANAKA: *(Off-stage)* Shhh!

YO: I'm going get my daddy out of that prison. 'N I'm gonna find a vine-covered cottage an' get me a job 'n take care of my little ol' daddy. He's my family. All I got.

KOKO: That makes me sad. Mitch, can we go to Montana, too?

MITCH: We'll see if it's true first.

YO: Sure, it's true. You'll see.

KOKO: Let's go to Montana, Mitch.

MITCH: We'll see. We'll find a place.

YO: Know any Montana songs?

HARRY: Not me.

YO: Let's hear it for good ol' Montana! *(Sings to "Oh Susanna.")* **I'ma goin' to ol' Montana/Oh, my daddy for to see...**

KOKO: **Gonna find a...vine-covered cottage/For my daddy and for me...**

YO and KOKO: **Oh! Montana! Oh, don't you cry for me...** *(Dance together)* **Gonna find a...**

MRS. TANAKA: **Be quiet!**

YO: *(Whispering)* **Hooray for freedom!** *(HARRY spins his hat nervously. Fade out.)*

SCENE 11: THREE FEMALES AND ONE MALE

Mitch, 21

Koko, 18

Mrs. Tanaka 41

Mrs. Ichioka, 45

This scene comes right after the preceding.

1. What does Mrs. Ichioka mean in the speech that begins, "Tell him come live with us. Sell everything for five dollars..."?

2. What has happened to make the characters talk so much about where they are going to go?

3. What is the significance of the questionnaires?

4. Why do you think Ken looks bad?

5. What do you think of the question about being willing to serve in the military? Should that be included? Why? Why not?

6. Do you agree Mitch is right in saying he is not willing to serve in the military? Why? Why not?

7. Why does Mitch start quoting patriotic speeches and singing "The Battle Hymn of the Republic"?

8. Why does Mrs. Tanaka insist that the answers for all three of them be the same?

(Time: A February night, 1943. Inside 12-1-A. HARRY'S chair is in the corner. The bowling trophy remains visible. It is bitter cold. MITCH sits at the table in a bathrobe, pajama tops, shoes, and socks. MRS. TANAKA, in a robe, crochets a muffler. MITCH fills out a questionnaire, squinting over the forms in the weak overhead light. There is quarreling in the ICHIOKA barracks. MRS. TANAKA looks at MITCH.)

MRS. ICHIOKA: *(Off-stage)* **You writing again?** *(No response)* **More better you write to President Roosevelt. Give him report of camp.** *(KOKO enters. She wears a pea coat over her uniform. She shivers from the cold.)*

MITCH: Working overtime?

MRS. ICHIOKA: *(Off-stage)* **Tell him come live with us. Sell everything for five dollars a piece and come live with us.**

KOKO: *(Overlapping)* **There was an emergency. Are those the questionnaires?**

MR. ICHIOKA: *(Off-stage)* **Mo ii yo!** *("Enough!")*

MITCH: You ought to come home after eight hours.

KOKO: Can't. Patients get sick regardless of the time. Well, I guess the experience will come in handy outside. I could get a job in a hospital. I guess they'll be paying more than sixteen dollars.

MITCH: *(Reading the form)* **I should hope so. Ma, are we registered with the Japanese consul?**

MRS. TANAKA: I don't think so. No. Papa died before. *(Reminisces.)* **I told him every year, every year, "Register the kids; register the kids..." But he never did.**

MITCH: Lucky for us now.

KOKO: Have we decided where to go?

MITCH: Lot of guys at the motor pool are talking 'bout Chicago. You wantta go there?

KOKO: I want to go back home.

MITCH: Forget that. They won't let us back there. *(Reading the form)* **Was Pa ever in the Japanese army?** *(To KOKO)* **Plenty of bedpans in Chicago, Koko.**

KOKO: Funny.

MRS. TANAKA: Papa don't like army. That's why he came to America...

so he won't have to go to army. He was peaceful man. He was eighteen then. Younger than you, Michio.

KOKO: There's a lot of army people...suddenly you see so many soldiers around. They're stepping up the recruiting.

MITCH: *(Contemptuously)* Fat chance they got! You'd have to have rocks in your head to volunteer. No one I know is... They'd have to sneak out in the middle of the night... *(Still reading the questionnaire)* Look here. It says, "List all the addresses you have ever lived in for the period of as much as three months during the last twenty years." For crying out loud!

MRS. TANAKA: We moved lots...lots. Mama had to live near work. Ah...can't remember addresses.

MITCH: I'll just put down some that I remember.

KOKO: Do them right, Mitch. You're filling out ours, too, aren't you? They should be consistent. Otherwise, they might not release us. *(Removes her coat and quickly puts it back on after realizing the cold.)* Or, worse yet, they might let us out one at a time. *(MITCH stretches, yawns, and rubs his eyes.)*

MITCH: They'll be the same. They'll be perfect. We'll get out together or we won't go at all. Don't worry.

KOKO: Have we decided where to go?

MITCH: Let's get free first.

KOKO: We ought to go with friends. Yo or Ken. It'll be so lonely without friends. I wonder where the Ichiokas are planning to go.

MRS. TANAKA: I don't know.

KOKO: Since I started working nights, I hardly see Ken anymore. I wonder if he's all right.

MITCH: I saw him in the mess hall tonight. He looks bad. Maybe he's sick. God, I hope he's not cracking up. Those types sometimes do, you know.

MRS. TANAKA: Lots of fighting over there. *(Meaning the ICHIOKA barracks)*

KOKO: Poor Ken.

MRS. TANAKA: Maybe sometimes better to be like Harry-san. Don't care 'bout nothing.

KOKO: Oh, he cares, Ma. He cares about a lot of things. He's very sensitive. He feels a lot of pain.

MRS. TANAKA: Yo-chan still going Montana?

KOKO: That's what she says. Gosh, I'm going to miss her.

MRS. TANAKA: Can't go with everybody, Koko. When we make nice home, she will visit, ne? *(MITCH returns to the questionnaire and suddenly springs to life.)*

MITCH: Holy mack! It says here... Boy, what a nerve!

KOKO: What? What?

MITCH: It says here: "Are you willing to serve in the armed forces of the United States on combat duty wherever ordered?" That means... *(MITCH stops. No one speaks. He slams the paper on the table.)* So that's why they're here.

KOKO: Who?

MITCH: *(Grimly)* That's why they're here. The goddamn recruiters. It's a frame-up...it's a trap! They need cannon fodder! *(Slams his fist on the table.)* They got us again. They got us again! What does it take for us to wise up? *(He grows stony.)* Well, I'm not falling for it. No. I'll stay right here. I'll stay here till I rot. *(KOKO takes the paper and reads it.)*

KOKO: But, Mitch, if you don't say yes, they might put you in jail!

MRS. TANAKA: Jail!

MITCH: I don't care. If I say yes, they'll put me in the front line. They take away every right we have except the right to be shot at. No. I'll rot here first. I'll rot.

MRS. TANAKA: What it say, Michio? *(MITCH walks away from the table and pours himself a drink from the bottle and swallows it. He pours another and drinks.)*

KOKO: It says if he says yes to the question, he goes to combat. If he says no, he's a traitor, Ma. A traitor is...Ma, Mitch might have to go jail or they might...Mitch! You can't say no!

MITCH: Hell, I'm not scared of no firing squad. I'm not afraid to die...not for what I believe in. I believe in freedom...equal rights for all men! I'm the real patriot! *(Jumps on the table.)* Look at me, Koko...I'm the true patriot! I'm acting the grand tradition of Patrick Henry. Remember the guy? "Give me liberty or give me death!" *(Makes a trumpet with his hands.)* Ta-

da-da-dum-ta-da!

KOKO: Mitch, don't...

MRS. TANAKA: Come down, Michio. *(In his bathrobe, MITCH marches in place on the table.)*

MITCH: Mine eyes have seen the glory of the coming of the Lord/ He has trampled out the vintage where the grapes of wrath are stored... *(KOKO puts her hands on MITCH's legs.)*

KOKO: Stop...Shhh...Mitch. Make him stop, Mama.

MRS. TANAKA: Shhh! Ichioka-san's sick. Be quiet! Stop right now, Michio!

MITCH: Glory, glory hallelujah!/Glory, glory, hallelujah!/Glory, glory...

MRS. TANAKA: Michio! No more! Koko is crying now! *(MITCH jumps down.)*

MRS. TANAKA: *(Trying to calm herself)* **Calm down.**

MITCH: It's okay, Koko. I'm not going crazy. But I'm not going to say yes. You have to understand that. You'll have to shoot me on the spot before I say yes.

KOKO: But, Mitch, I don't want to say no. I don't want to go to prison. I want to stay right here. I want to stay here!

MITCH: You can answer yes. There's no reason for you to say no. Hell, they can't take women for combat duty. It's all right. You and Ma, you'll be free. You can make it together.

MRS. TANAKA: We stay together, Michio.

MITCH: I've made up my mind, Ma. You can't change it.

MRS. TANAKA: If we separate now, we maybe never see each other again. We stay together.

MITCH: I made up my mind.

MRS. TANAKA: Mama make up mind, too. *(More calmly)* **Now. All questions same for everybody?**

MITCH: The same for everybody. Everyone over seventeen.

MRS. TANAKA: We say no then. Koko and Mama, too.

KOKO: No!

MITCH: No? But Ma, it won't hurt to say yes. You'll be free.

MRS. TANAKA: We say no together.

MITCH: I'd rather do this alone, Ma. It might get pretty rough

and...I can do it alone better. You can't tell what will happen.

MRS. TANAKA: If they shoot, they shoot us together.

MITCH: I don't think they'll do that. They'll probably deport us. Send us to Tule Lake and then...

KOKO: Tule Lake!

MRS. TANAKA: Tule Lake, this camp, that camp, all the same. Camp is camp, ne, Koko?

KOKO: *(In protest)* We'll be leaving all our friends!

MRS. TANAKA: *(Firmly)* We stand by Michio, ne, Koko? Together. One family. We live together or die together. We be together.

SCENE 12: TWO FEMALES AND TWO MALES

Mrs, Tanaka, 41

Ken, 20

Mitch, 21

Koko, 18

Mrs. Tanaka and Koko decide to answer "no" to the questions about unqualified allegiance to the United States and to fore-swearing any allegiance to Japan. They will go together to Tule Lake. Ken comes from next door.

1. Why do you think there was so much public hysteria over seeing Japanese Americans?

2. Why do you think Ken feels as he does? Why does he want Mitch to change his mind?

3. Who do you think is right in the arguments Ken and Mitch make against each other's actions? Why?

4. Obviously, this scene has a powerful ending. How might you try to direct it to convey all the emotions here?

(The door opens and KEN enters.)

MRS. TANAKA: Oh, Papa can't sleep, ne? We make so much...

KEN: I think you're wrong, Mitch. I heard you and I...

MITCH: *(Surprised)* Wrong? Where am I wrong?

KEN: The questionnaire. I think...

MITCH: You want me to say yes [...]?

KEN: I don't "want" you to say anything...

MITCH: You want me to say yes, right?

KEN: No! I just say...

MITCH: Yeah! "My country, right or wrong," eh?

KEN: I didn't say that.

MITCH: *(Patiently)* Look, fella. You ain't never been outside. I ain't told you half what happened to me out there. They think I bombed Pearl Harbor, you know that? Me, Mitch Tanaka, all-American bowler! They think I'm going to blow up those bowling alleys, so they won't let me in. *(Gets excited.)* "Japs! Keep out!" Okay, top the sugar beets, but don't come in. I'm the Jap! And you want me to fight for this country? If I fight for freedom, I want that good stuff, too!

KEN: All right! You're entitled to your opinion, but... [...] But you shouldn't take everyone with you. You can't take Koko and your mother...

MITCH: Hey! They're going because they want to. They made up their own minds. They believe in me. That's more than I can say for...

KEN: Let Koko talk then. Let her say what she feels...

MITCH: She talked! She talked!

KEN: *(Stubbornly pursuing)* Koko, do you really want to go...

MITCH: Hey, wait a minute! Who the hell you think you are come busting in here like you owned the place...

MRS. TANAKA: Michio, likagen ni shinasai. *("That's enough now.")*

MITCH: Hey, Mr. USA. You sit up there in your cozy barracks writing your little reports...calling it your patriotic duty...while your Ma's eating her heart out and your Pa's dying.

MRS. TANAKA: *(Overlaps.)* Michio...

MITCH: *(Waving MAMA away)* Yeah, he's been lying on that straw

> **mattress from the day he got here and you say it's the water that makes him sick. His heart is breaking, man, don't you know? [...] When you going to be man enough to say, "Enough! Enough! I had enough!"?**

KOKO: *(Overlaps.)* **Mitch, don't.**

MRS. TANAKA: *(Overlaps.)* **Michio, yoshinasai.** *("Stop now.")*

MITCH: *(Pushing KEN)* **Look at you, Mr. Home of the Brave. Hiding behind Mama's skirts! Yeah, I heard about it...** *(MRS. TANAKA steps up to MITCH and slaps him.)*

MRS. TANAKA: Baka! *(Without further word, KEN stalks out, slamming the door behind him. KOKO looks at MRS. TANAKA, waits a moment, and follows KEN. KEN moves Downstage Left, stops and looks back toward KOKO. KOKO stops. KEN then moves toward his barracks, Upstage Left. The night is cold and dark. KOKO slowly returns to her barracks. Fade out.)*

SCENE 13: THREE FEMALES AND THREE MALES

Mrs. Tanaka, 41

Mitch, 21

Koko, 18

Sam, 20

Harry, 26

Yo, 26

This scene comes directly after the last one. It is now July of 1943. The barracks 12-1-A is empty and luggage is outside. Mrs. Tanaka, Koko, and Mitch are dressed for travel. Harry and Sam are present.

1. Do you think it is believable or logical that Mrs. Tanaka, Mitch, and Koko are going to let themselves be deported to Japan? What would you do in a situation like this? How do you think Koko feels, going to a country where she's never lived?

2. Do you like this scene? Why? Why not?

SAM: All this stuff goes, Mitch?

MITCH: Yeah. That stuff there. *(To MAMA)* Ma, I'm going ahead and see the baggage off. I'll be back.

MRS. TANAKA: All right. *(To KOKO)* Mama going say good-bye to Ichioka-san, Koko. *(YO enters from the right, just before MITCH leaves.)*

YO: You leaving now?

MITCH: Gotta see this luggage gets on. I'll be back. *(YO stops MRS. TANAKA as she goes toward the ICHIOKA barracks.)*

YO: Obasan, you look nice.

MRS. TANAKA: Thank you. Going now to say good-bye to Ichioka-san.

YO: What? She's not going, too? I thought she would be on the first boat to Japan.

MRS. TANAKA: *(Sadly)* She talk like that, ne? But she don't want to move. She says Tule Lake too mean. She says husband going die there. He is so sick.

YO: I'm going to miss you, Obasan. Maybe we'll see each other again. Never can tell.

MRS. TANAKA: Maybe in 'nother life. Tule Lake is long way away. *(Laughs weakly.)* Japan is far away, too.

YO: I'll miss you. *(MRS. TANAKA puts her hand on YO's head.)*

MRS. TANAKA: Be good girl now. *(Laughs softly and exits.)*

YO: Okay, Obasan. *(Enters the barracks.)* Well, kiddo, how you doing? *(KOKO simply smiles.)* I guess this is it. Don't think it ain't been charming... *(Sees KOKO holding back tears.)* Don't cry, Koko.

KOKO: I won't. It would be a good time to say good-bye right now.

YO: Now?

KOKO: Before we make fools of ourselves. So long, Yo. *(YO embraces KOKO for a moment. HARRY spins his hat.)* At least I know it can't get much worse. It can't, can it?

YO: Jesus, I hope not. Well...say good-bye to Mitch for me. I've loved you a lot, Koko. *(Leaves.)*

KOKO: I can't take the chair with me, Harry. I'll leave it for you. Funny how things turn out. Your present to me is now my present for you.

HARRY: Funny, hanh? *(Tries to smile.)*

KOKO: Harry?

HARRY: Hunh?

KOKO: You've been a good friend to me. I thank you for that. You'd better leave now, okay?

HARRY: Hunh?

KOKO: You'd better go.

HARRY: Not yet.

KOKO: We're not going to cry, are we?

HARRY: No.

KOKO: Ma says, "Time passes; tears dry..." But what happens to tears we can't let go?

HARRY: I don' know.

KOKO: I wonder if we'll remember today when we grow old? Will we remember how we met...how we said good-bye...and how we wouldn't let ourselves cry? Maybe those tears stay with us until we're old. And maybe one day, a little punch in a Dixie cup, half a candy bar, or maybe one of those orange sunsets will open up the memory. Maybe we will cry then.

SCENE 14: TWO FEMALES, THREE MALES

Koko, 18

Ken, 20

Mitch, 21

Mrs. Tanaka, 41

Harry, 26

    Koko walks outside, and Ken comes toward her. This is the final scene of the play.

1. Why do you think Ken feels he has to join the army?

2. Koko and Ken's attitudes and philosophies are in direct opposition? Which of the two do you agree with or support? Why?

3. Why do you think Ken waited so long to hint at how he feels about Koko? How does he feel?

4. Do you think the ending is effective? Logical? Why? Why not?

5. Do you like this play? Why? Why not?

KEN: *(Seriously)* **Hi, Koko.**

KOKO: Hi. *(Turns her back to him so he can't see her face.)*

KEN: I'm joining the army tomorrow.

KOKO: No!

KEN: I have to do it.

KOKO: Why didn't you tell me?

KEN: I've been thinking about it for a long time and...

KOKO: But your mother...your mother will die!

KEN: Shhh...She doesn't know yet. I'll tell her just before I leave.

KOKO: Ken, how can you do such a thing?

KEN: I can't help it.

KOKO: And your dad. He's so sick.

KEN: I know, I know. Christ, I know. But I just got to do this. I just got to.

KOKO: God forgive you, Ken.

KEN: Koko, don't blame me. I have to make a decision and this is what I choose...in spite of everything. If all that talk about freedom and democracy is a lie, then I have to try to change it. That's all. I have to try. Do you understand, Koko?

KOKO: No, I don't understand. Who knows what's right or what's wrong? Who cares? And what good does it do to care? I don't care about freedom or democracy or countries or nations anymore. I don't care who wins or who loses. I only care for myself.

KEN: I'm really sorry how things turned out.

KOKO: You got to care for yourself. Who else will do it for you?

KEN: I wanted to tell you...so often...how I felt about you...

KOKO: It's too late. I may never see you again. It's too late now.

KEN: I'm sorry. What can I say?

KOKO: You can say good-bye. That's all there's left to say. *(KOKO picks up her suitcase and starts to go. KEN takes it from her and leads her to the bench.)*

KEN: Koko, not like this. Don't say good-bye like this. Let me know you'll think of me now and then. Help me. Tell me something...anything...that will make me want to live through this. Tell me when the war is over, you'll...you'll...

KOKO: How can I say such things? How do we know what will

happen to us? You're going one way, and I'm going another.

KEN: But you can say, "I promise to think of you," can't you?

MITCH: *(Off-stage)* Ma! Koko! Let's go! Come on, let's go!

KEN: Koko, can you say that?

KOKO: Yes, I promise to think of you.

KEN: Will you write me?

KOKO: I will. As long as I am able. Will you write me?

KEN: As long as I am able. That's my promise.

KOKO: And let's promise to live a long, long time, so that one day we may meet again...okay?

KEN: That's our promise.

MITCH: *(Entering)* **Koko? Ma?** *(Sees KEN and KOKO.)* **What say? Take it easy, pal.** *(Shakes hands with KEN and turns to KOKO.)* **Get a move on, Koko.** *(Goes to the barracks door and sees HARRY.)* **So long, Harry. Don't take any wooden nickels.** *(Calls to the ICHIOKA barracks.)* **Come on, Ma! Bus leaves in ten minutes!** *(Nods to KEN and leaves. KEN touches KOKO on the shoulder as she follows MITCH out. MRS. TANAKA enters Upstage, looks at KEN and smiles.)*

MRS. TANAKA: **Ken-chan...** *(Takes a last look around and exits. KEN exits slowly. Inside the barracks, HARRY walks to the iron cots, goes to the wall, and touches the trophy. He picks up the cards and lets them flutter to the floor. He sings, softly at first, then loudly.)*

HARRY: **Yes, sir, that's my baby/No, sir, don't mean maybe/Yes, sir, that's my baby now.** *(The guard tower is strongly visible. Wind sounds grow and turn into the music of a flute playing "She's My Baby" in minor key.)*

TILL VOICES WAKE US

Louella Dizon

A native of the Philippines, Louella Dizon grew up in Michigan. As a senior at Princeton University, she wrote her first play, *The Color Yellow: Memoirs of an Asian American.* She wrote *Till Voices Wake Us* in 1991. The play was first produced at the Soho Repertory Theater in New York in 1994.

The action occurs in the Bay Ridge section of Brooklyn and in the towns of Lahug and Catmon on the island of Cebu in the Philippines beginning in 1979 and going "far back in time."

SCENE 1: THREE FEMALES

Rosie, about 12

Susie, about 12

Tessie, 42

This scene is the opening of the play. Although Rosie says in the first scene that she is twelve years old, except for the very brief birthday scene, she is much more mature than twelve in her outlook and attitude. She also comes across to the audience as more mature because of her use of poetic language, which includes well-chosen imagery and analogies. There are only a few times throughout the play when she actually appears to be so young. The first time is in the following scene where you may choose, in presenting this in class, to skip from "Me and Rosie/Susie havin' fun" to the end of the line "Bigger than the other one..." This, of course, eliminates the minor role of Susie.

1. Do you think the fairy-tale quality of the opening is effective?

2. Why do you suppose Dizon chose to begin the play with the two characters performing soliloquies or monologs?

3. Are you drawn in by what Rosie and Tessie say? Explain.

4. How would you stage the birthday part of this scene? Would you try to make the scene realistic? Why? Why not?

5. How might you make it easier for the audience to know when Rosie is talking to the audience and when she is involved in the scene?

6. Can you understand Tessie's ambivalent feelings about her mother's upcoming visit?

7. Do you think the ending of the scene is effective? Why? Why not?

(There are three important elements in the set: ROSIE's bedroom, a "living room" area with dining table, and an open space for dreams and other non-interior scenes.)

ROSIE: Once upon a time, I was a little girl with a secret and wonderful power. I could see things in a way no one else could see.

To me, the morning was a great snail, crawling along with a sky-blue shell, and one red eye as the sun. And dragging behind it was the rich, moist, velvet cloak of the night.

Wrapped in the covers of night, I would dream.

And I could remember all my dreams as if I were dreaming them for the first time.

TESSIE: You see, the Filipino woman – the Filipina – is descended from a long line of priestesses. They were known as the "catalonan" to the Tagalog; "baliana" to the Bicolano; "managanito" to the Pangasinan; and to the Bisaya, "babaylan." For their tribes, these women performed the most sacred rites. They could heal with herbs, speak with the gods, and exorcize devils. They found their darkest powers in dream-like trances.

ROSIE: In fact, once I knew that I could relive each dream, I realized I could put them away, like books, that could be pulled out and read over, like a map for another adventure.

And that's when I decided that I should play the heroine in these dreams.

And I wanted to shape these dreams.

And sometimes I wondered if God must have felt a little like me, amazed at my own creations.

TESSIE: To this day, there are still wise old women in the smaller towns who still act as links to the supernatural.

ROSIE: Dreams showed me everything I ever wanted to see. Until one day.

TESSIE: That was something I couldn't take with me when I left the Philippines: the links to the spiritual world through wise old women.

ROSIE: Birthdays to me are no big deal. But the birthday I remember best wasn't even my own.

TESSIE: The links to the past through my mother and grandmother.

ROSIE: It was at my friend Susie Locke's house. She turned twelve six months before me. It was at her party.

ROSIE and SUSIE: Me and Rosie/Susie havin' fun
    Chewin' on some bubble gum
    Pop goes the bubble gum
    Figger I could double one
    Pop goes another one
    Bigger than the other one...

SUSIE: Hey, let's go look at my presents.

ROSIE: Okay. *(SUSIE sings the bubble gum song again throughout ROSIE'S next speech.)*

SUSIE: Me and Rosie havin' fun
    Chewin' on some bubble gum
    Got it stickin' on m' thumb
    Blowin' on that bubble gum
    Pop goes the bubble gum
    Figger I could double one
    Pop goes another one
    Bigger than the other one...

ROSIE: We always shared presents. I would even know which ones she would share with me. We opened them all together: a doll, a Nancy Drew book, puffy stickers, earrings, bicycle handlebars...

SUSIE: Wait!

ROSIE: What is it?

SUSIE: It's from my dad.

ROSIE: It was a little girl, sitting with her hands folded. She was wearing lace petticoats and her curls were tied up in a big ribbon. She sat, with her solemn face, not with a big grin like you see on kids' pictures at the department store. A face with no expectations. Like the picture were a duty, not a gift. She looks just like you.

SUSIE: It's my grandmother.

ROSIE: I've never had anything like that.

TESSIE: Most of our pictures were lost in the war.

ROSIE: Not even ones when Mom and Dad were young.

TESSIE: Those were left back home. When we left our lives behind, we left almost everything behind.

ROSIE: When I looked up on the wall, I could see all the generations behind Susie. The families of Lockes, way beyond Susie's grandmother. That picture made Susie's past seem real and immediate. While mine seemed like a folktale, that was passed on from story to story.

TESSIE: When my sister Lorna called me, it was six o'clock in the morning. That means that in the Philippines it was seven o'clock at night. She said, "We have just come back from immigration. You will be seeing your mother in six months."

ROSIE: I looked at Susie's picture of her grandmother as a child. I wished I had something like that to help me claim my link in Time.

TESSIE: She said,"Your mother," as though I might have forgotten. She said, "Your mother," instead of "Ma," "Nanay," "*Our* mother." Still, I thought of saying "No" when Lorna asked me to buy the ticket.

ROSIE: Mom says that you can't tell how far you've climbed up a mountain until you see where you've come from.

TESSIE: It had been ten years since I had seen Ma.

ROSIE: Until you see the view from halfway up.

TESSIE: One part of me remembered wanting to be with my mother again. One part of me was ashamed and asked, "What would we finally talk about?"

ROSIE: I wished I could somehow know. I wished that I could somehow have that view.

TESSIE: And then I realized my daughter Rosie had never met her grandmother before.

ROSIE: I wished I could have a picture of my grandmother as a child.

Once upon a time...October, 1979...six months before my grandmother was to arrive. I made a wish because of someone else's birthday. The gods must have heard me, and made my wish come true.

SCENE 2: THREE FEMALES AND TWO MALES

Grandma, 65 or older

Tessie, 42

Rosie, 12

Ben, early 40s

Albert, 19

This scene comes directly after the preceding one. The time is six months later when Grandma arrives at Rosie's home. They recognize each other immediately, and Grandma raises her hand, palm down, in blessing "while Rosie slowly bows her head." The rest of the family rushes up and "engulfs Grandma, who must break the gaze." Rosie, however, remains where she is, looking at Grandma.

1. Why do you think Grandma says Lorna is prettier than Tessie? Do you think she should do this?

2. What do you think of the style of writing where some of the dialog is conversation, some is directed to the audience? Do you think this is a good way to have written this play? Why? Why not?

3. Why do you suppose Albert is so tactless as to say that he thought Paolo was dead?

4. Do you think not finishing the story about what Paolo meant is effective in creating suspense? Why? Why not? Why does Ben tell Albert, "That's enough"?

5. What is your opinion of Grandma's gift, a picture of a dead uncle whom Rosie never met?

GRANDMA: Ay, Tessie...your house is so beautiful!

TESSIE: Yes, well...

BEN: Tessie is our interior designer.

GRANDMA: Ay, Benito, her husband. A good man, but always a little quiet. When Tessie left us, she was very young. I didn't even know she knew how to keep a house. *(Sniffs the air.)* I smell adobo.[1] *(Sounds of approval from the family)* Lemonsita plants. *(More sounds of approval)* A little bit of sweat.

ALBERT: That might be me.

GRANDMA: My grandson, Alberto. When I saw him last, he was yet so small. Now my daughter's son is big and guapo. Handsome and smiling, as a son should be.

TESSIE: Ma...Ma, here take your coat off...come on, show us what you brought from home.

GRANDMA: *(As she rummages through her trunk)* Of course, our small gifts are nothing compared to what you have here. *(Pulls out a mestiza dress.)*

TESSIE: Oh, Ma, this is gorgeous.

ALBERT: That really is nice, Mom. So's this, Grandma! *(Holds up a batik shirt.)*

BEN: *(Walking over to TESSIE)* What do you think, Nanay? Isn't she the prettiest girl ever to come from Lahug?

GRANDMA: *(Thinking, quite seriously)* No...Lorna is prettier.

TESSIE: *(Ruefully)* Well, that's always been the case. *(She hugs her mother.)* Thank you, Ma.

GRANDMA: Rosie, come here and sit by me.

TESSIE: Rosie...Grandma wants to see you.

GRANDMA: *(Softly, to the others)* She's embarrassed.

ROSIE: *(Pointing to GRANDMA's trunk)* What's that?

GRANDMA: Oh these? These are YOUR presents! *(ROSIE remains in her place, watching silently.)* I have two things for you here, Rosie. Here, the first one *(She unwraps it)* – see? A necklace that is made of coral. And this one... *(ROSIE rushes over with a cry of surprise.)*

---

[1] A native dish of the Philippines. It is chicken or pork stew with garlic-flavored gravy, which also contains soy sauce, vinegar and bay leaves.

ROSIE *(Holding it with awe)* **A...picture!**

GRANDMA: It's your Uncle Paolo. My oldest son.

ALBERT: I thought he was dead.

BEN: Albert!

TESSIE: *(Rushing over to look)* **Let me see!**

GRANDMA: *(To ROSIE)* Yah, your Tita Lorna is the eldest now, and then your mother. But long time ago, before Lorna, I had a baby girl, who died very young. And before her...my first child. My son, Paolo.

ALBERT: When did he die?

GRANDMA: He died a long time ago, Albert. Shortly before your mother left the Philippines. I think it was...let me see...19...67. I remember the day he came to visit. My Paolo was always handsome, although before he died he had gotten so tired-looking, so old. But that day he came to visit, he looked like an angel. His eyes were so bright – probably because he had not slept – but they were shining as though he would deliver a great secret. We ate dinner together – the two of us only – and before he left, he leaned forward and said to me, "You know, Ma, I really love this place." I thought he meant the family house, because you know as a teacher, his apartment was not very big. But now I ask myself what he meant. *(Pause)*

ALBERT: How did he die?

BEN: Ahem, that's enough, Albert. This is a nice barong,[2] Nanay. Salamat po.[3]

TESSIE: *(Distracted)* **Paolo...** *(Abruptly)* **Why are you giving her this?** *(GRANDMA crosses to ROSIE, but does not touch her.)*

GRANDMA: Because I know of a little girl who is very bright and very talented, and I wanted her to have a remembrance of someone who was very dear to me and who would have liked her very much.

---

[2]A gossamer-thin shirt, usually with elaborate embroidery, it is tradtionally worn at formal occasions.

[3]A formal way of saying thank you.

SCENE 3: TWO FEMALES

Grandma, 65 or older

Rosie, 12

Rosie cries when Grandma says Paolo would have loved her very much. Ben tells Rosie that Grandma will think she isn't glad to see her if she cries. Tessie tells them she has prepared a big lunch, and everyone else goes into the kitchen. Tessie picks up Grandma's suitcase, the lights change and it is ten years ago. Grandma comes back from the kitchen.

The scene switches back to when Tessie and her family were moving to the United States. Grandma says everyone who is well educated then moves "to America or something" and leaves us here alone. Tessie promises both to send money and to come back to visit. The scene then returns to the present. Grandma says Tessie has never seen how nice the house back home is or the garden and greenhouse. Softly, Tessie answers, "I left so you could have a garden and greenhouse."

The mood switches when Grandma remarks about her beautiful grandchildren. Tessie tells Grandma she's hardly aged, while "I have become fat." Grandma responds, "You have become American."

Grandma asks why Tessie is just staring at her. Tessie says she hasn't seen her in ten years. She's only heard her voice on the phone. She rushes to Grandma and hugs her.

They have lunch, and the "family begins to disperse in slow motion" while Grandma talks to the audience about how different Brooklyn is from Cebu in the Philippines. Brooklyn is confusing and loud. The cars and the people are in a hurry; they become impatient with those who move more slowly. Tessie is going to work; Ben is on call at the hospital and so will probably sleep there. Albert leaves to go back to college. Rosie always has something planned — a piano lesson, the newspaper, orchestra practice, or a play.

In the Philippines, Grandma says, precise terms of time are not used. When a guest arrives it is always the right time, even if the visit has not been expected.

Rosie tells the audience that it is strange, but she has been dreaming of her mother's country. And suddenly the scene switches to the past. Paolo enters, followed by Tessie dressed as a much younger person. He asks where she came from, and she said she was walking from school and saw him leave the house. Tessie asks Paolo where he's going. He says it's to a meeting. He tells her the Filipinos have been running and hiding from the Japanese, and "our grandfathers" bowed to the Spaniards. He wants to know what it is to be free.

Rosie asks what Paolo was like. Grandma admits that Albert looks a lot like him, but Paolo had a quieter personality. Grandma asks Rosie to call her Lola; they are developing a close relationship.

Albert comes in and gives Rosie a big hug, and she asks him if he remembers the Philippines. The lights fade, and we hear the ebb and flow of breathing and the music of a Philippine native dance in which a prince courts a princess. As the lights come up again, the dance begins slowly onstage. It grows wilder and wilder until the princess kneels. Just as she grasps the veil to reveal her face, the music stops, and there is a blackout.

1. Why does Grandma want Rosie to tell her the dream? Why does Rosie not want to do it?

2. In what way is the relationship between Rosie and Grandma changing in this scene?

3. Why do you think — from the first time they saw each other — that Rosie and Grandma liked each other so much?

ROSIE: Hi...Lola.

GRANDMA: Oh, Rosie, you are home. You called me Lola. Salamat.

ROSIE: You're welcome. *(She runs upstairs.)* Albert?

GRANDMA: Oh, Alberto left.

ROSIE: *(Extremely disappointed)* He did! He wasn't awake when I left this morning, and now he's gone!

GRANDMA: He said he had to run errands.

ROSIE: *(Sullenly)* No, he didn't. He had to see his GIRLfriend!

GRANDMA: Hah?

ROSIE: Never mind. *(She sits at the dining table and props her face up on her hands.)*

GRANDMA: Here, Rosie. *(Pushing a foil-covered plate toward her)* Do you like fried bananas?

ROSIE: Thank you. *(She takes one. GRANDMA sits at the table, opposite ROSIE. ROSIE finishes a whole banana slice and starts on another before GRANDMA makes another effort.)*

GRANDMA: It was important that you see your brother?

ROSIE: Yeah. I had to talk to him about something I dreamed of last night.

GRANDMA: Ah, a dream! Paolo used to tell me all the time about his dreams. Would you like to tell me about your dream?

ROSIE: *(Wrinkling her forehead)* No...

GRANDMA: *(Trying again)* I remember a game Paolo used to play with me – like hide and seek. After I put him to bed, he would start dreaming, and no matter where I would go, even outside of the house, he would dream of finding me.

ROSIE: The next day, did you find out he was right?

GRANDMA: Well, he was right once.

ROSIE: Wow, really? *(Pause)* Actually, I do have strange dreams. *(Laughing)* Sometimes I dream about something, and it HAPPENS to me later! Or *(More quietly)* it's happened way before.

GRANDMA: *(Expressing obvious interest)* Ay, really?

ROSIE: *(Warming up)* Yes. Most of the time, I dream about strange places and people.... I hardly ever dream about people I know.

GRANDMA: No? What do you dream about?

ROSIE: Once I dreamed I was in a huge stone castle, with lots and lots of rooms. I liked exploring it so much, I memorized the road that got me there so I could dream about going back. And you know what? I did!

GRANDMA: How wonderful! What else?

ROSIE: If I can remember most of the dream, I write it down, and I use it to write my stories.

GRANDMA: Ay, yes. Your mother told me that you want to be a novelist and travel all over the world.

ROSIE: Sure. I used to tell all my stories to Albert and he loved them so much, he told me to write them down, so that other people could read them. I'm glad he told me that, too, because... *(She munches reflectively for a moment on her banana)* ...because I think he's busy with other things right now, and even when I'm talking to him, I don't think he always hears me. *(She is suddenly lost in thought for a moment. Still staring out into space)* Lola...

GRANDMA: Yes, Rosie, I'm listening.

ROSIE: *(Snaps out of it and looks at her.)* You are. Lola, what is your name?

GRANDMA: My name is Rosamunda..."Rose of the World."

ROSIE: *(With a big grin)* Like mine. *(She has finished eating.)* Have you been outside yet, Lola?

GRANDMA: No, not yet.

ROSIE: I can take you around, Lola. I can show you around the whole neighborhood! I know you might be cold because it's not as warm here as it is in the Philippines, but I know where we can get good hot chocolate.

GRANDMA: Ay, how very nice! Okay, Rosie. Okay, Rosamunda. *(ROSIE giggles and GRANDMA nods, smiling. Lights fade and music brings the scene into blackout.)*

SCENE 4: THREE FEMALES AND ONE MALE

Grandma, 65 or older

Tessie, 42

Rosie, 12

Ben, early 40s

We hear the music of a native song. As the lights come up, Rosie "is clowning through the verses in true burlesque fashion." At the end, she bows dramatically as the others applaud. Albert asks how she learned the song and she says Lola (Grandma) taught her. Grandma says she also taught Rosie other songs, which she learned quickly.

1. Which three or four exchanges of dialog are most important in this scene? Why?

2. How many things can you list that *are* bothering Tessie? Why is each of them bothering her?

3. Can you see any potential conflict beginning to develop in this scene? Can you see any hints of future difficulty? Explain.

ROSIE: Well, Lola has also learned a lot since she got here.

BEN: Like what, Nanay?

GRANDMA: Ah, I can use the microwave. I can program the VCR.

ROSIE: *(Amidst surprised laughter)* Even I didn't know that – she figured it out herself!

GRANDMA: I have also learned how to use the map of the subway alone. Except that my eyesight is very poor and I must look closely to read it.

TESSIE: Ma, I don't want you riding on the subway alone! Rosie, I don't want you two going around in the subway too much.

GRANDMA: *(Getting up and slowly crossing to the kitchen)* Ay, Teresita, there you go again. After I have already survived through fever, war, marriage, martial law...

TESSIE: I'm just telling you and Rosie, Ma, especially since Rosie is still young – what if something should happen. What do you need, Ma?

GRANDMA: I don't know... *(Shaking her head, laughing)* Crazy...I was going to the kitchen to wash the dishes from supper. I forgot we did that already.

TESSIE: Did you take your vitamin today?

BEN: *(Changes the mood to a brisk one.)* I think we're all tired.

TESSIE: In these situations, Ben suddenly becomes efficient.

BEN: Nanay, remember you're still suffering from jet lag. Albert, don't use the phone too long. Rosie, I hope you finished your homework. Good night.

THE REST OF THE FAMILY: *(Except TESSIE)* Good night. *(BEN sits down beside his wife. He strokes her cheek. No response. He pinches her cheek. Still no response. He puts his finger under her nose so she suddenly cannot breathe.)*

TESSIE: Ben, stop it! *(Slapping his hand away and getting up to straighten the living room)*

BEN: I'm only trying to distract you. What is bothering you, Tessie?

TESSIE: I don't know.

BEN: You know, Rosie and Nanay are getting along very well. In fact, the whole visit is going well. We are all glad to see Nanay.

TESSIE: What about that spell by the kitchen?

BEN: We all forget sometimes the reason why we walk into a room.

TESSIE: I still worry about leaving Rosie alone so much. And now there's Ma, and you know how old she is.

BEN: So, we're lucky they can keep each other company.

TESSIE: But what must she think — I don't even stay home with my own children.

BEN: Why would she think anything?

TESSIE: I didn't even know she knew that song!

BEN: That's okay — I didn't either.

TESSIE: I've never taught her little songs.

BEN: Is that what's bothering you?

TESSIE: *(To audience)* I know it's something that shouldn't bother me — it wouldn't bother him.... Dear sweet, sane Ben. A quiet rock next to my storm of a family. Imagine the dramatics — I had a politician for a father, a beauty queen for a sister. And then there was Paolo — well, I always loved Paolo, but he was always...tortured. He and Ma were closest. They had something even I couldn't be part of. Only Ma could have known everything about Paolo. Rosie is a lot like him. Maybe that's why —

BEN: What are you mumbling about, mahal? Are you still worried about Rosie and Nanay? So — you think Rosie has found a mother in Nanay and Nanay has found a daughter in Rosie, so you feel left out? You're jealous!

TESSIE: No, Ben, that's not it.

BEN: Jea-lous! Se-lo-sa! *(Starts to tickle her.)*

TESSIE: Stop it, Ben!

BEN: Ha, ha! Now no one wants you! Now I've got you all to myself!

TESSIE: Stop it! Crazy! *(She exits, running, shrieking with laughter in spite of herself, BEN in hot pursuit.)*

SCENE 5: ONE FEMALE AND ONE MALE

Tessie, 42

Ben, early 40s

Grandma and Rosie are sitting on Rosie's bed. They hear Ben and Tessie laughing. Grandma asks what is going on and Rosie assures her its just her mom and dad acting crazy. Grandma tells her she will one day be a writer. Rosie says what she writes is only half of what she sees in her head where so many dreams are stored away. Often, she dreams of the princess dancing but never has more than a glimpse of her face before she wakes. She wonders why the dream princess is so important to her. Grandma asks what she did see and Rosie tells her she saw her. That is why she recognized Grandma at the airport. Grandma says she recognized Rosie also. Rosie then asks Grandma about the dream game Paolo played with her, in which he could tell Grandma where she had gone while he slept.

While Rosie is sleeping, there are "wisps of voices and sounds of footsteps." Bodies "dart in and out," and there are "disturbing images: a woman cradling the body of her son, two men grappling; a woman priestess performing sacred rites for the gods."

"An eerie light grows in intensity to reveal Grandma kneeling in the living room with her rosary." As the lights and music increase in intensity, Grandma "looks up, surprised by the call of Rosie's dream."

She calls to Rosie. There is a sudden blackout; the music stops abruptly. Rosie turns on the light in her room and calls, "Lola."

The lights come up on Tessie who is putting on makeup for an evening out with Ben.

1. Why is Tessie remembering the shoes now? What do they symbolize for her?

2. Do you think Tessie is happier with her life now or back when she was a child? Explain.

3. Do you think Ben should have followed his dream of becoming a painter? Why? Why not?

4. What do you think Ben means when he says Tessie "knew what it is to want to be an artist"?

5. How would you block this scene? Why?

TESSIE: Before we moved to Cebu, we lived in Camotes, an island so small that even now it has no electricity. We didn't have indoor toilets. We didn't have running water in the house. We didn't have shoes – we had bakya – those sandals with two strips that run from your toes across the top of your foot. But we were happy with what we had. Then one day, one of the girls at school got a pair of shoes. She was the only little girl in town with shoes – and they were so pretty and clean and white. I thought I had never seen anything as beautiful as those new white shoes and I wanted a pair for myself. My father was going to Cebu in a few days, just in time for my birthday. And I told him, I wanted a pair of shoes like that little girl's. I told him what kind, what they look like, what color. And he traveled the two days there and the two days back from Cebu.

BEN: *(While shining his shoes)* I remember, the year I graduated high school and got my scholarship to the University of the Philippines, my father asked me what I wanted to do with myself. And I told him I wanted to be a painter. Of course, he laughed and told me how impractical that was.

TESSIE: When my father came back, he brought back a pair of shoes like the ones the little girl had. And they were too small! I cried and cried having those shoes in my hands and not being able to wear them. And he had to go back again the next time in order to get the right size.

BEN: "What about Uncle Ramon," I said, "what about Uncle Ramon, who writes songs?" "What about him?" he said, "do you want to be like Uncle Ramon and always need me to support you?" I was oldest, you know, so there was really no question about what I was going to do. I was going to be a professional, a doctor, so I could support my parents in their old age and provide for my family.

TESSIE: I laugh to myself now, thinking about those shoes. And sometimes, driving my Cadillac down the FDR Drive, I have to pinch myself. Who would've thought that poor little girl in Camotes would be here, living like this, talking like this? If you had told me that day that one day my shoe collection would fill its own closet, I wouldn't have believed it.

BEN: I even fell in love with someone at U.P., an artist, very pretty and very flighty – I almost lost my scholarship because of her. Then I met and fell in love with Tessie. A sharp woman always, in her studies and in business, and yet, she knew what it is to want to be an artist. *(As TESSIE joins him, "Stars and Stripes Forever" begins to play. She takes his arm.)* You look beautiful, mahal.

TESSIE: Thank you, Ben.

SCENE 6: TWO FEMALES AND THREE MALES

Grandma, 65 or older

Rosie, 12

Man 1, early 20s

Man 2, early 20s

Young Man, probably 20s

This scene follows immediately the preceding one. Rosie is sitting on her bed staring at the picture of Paolo. Grandma appears in the doorway. Music begins.

This scene can be very effective; however, the person playing Grandma should learn the right way to say the words in the Filipino language. This is the end of Act I.

1. Why are both characters afraid to experience the dream?

2. Why does Rosie ask Grandma to show her what she has dreamed?

3. Why do you suppose Dizon wrote the scene this way, with Rosie translating what Grandma says? What is this supposed to show? Why is it suddenly possible for Rosie to understand Grandma's language?

4. Why do you suppose the Spanish students are so prejudiced against the Filipinos?

5. Why does Grandma say the line, "Once upon a time"?

6. Do you think this is an effective way for the playwright to show glimpses of Filipino history? Why? Why not?

7. Do you think the scene has an effective ending? Why? Why not? How would you place the actors in this scene? Why?

ROSIE: *(Without turning around)* **I thought you were sleeping.**

GRANDMA: **I am afraid to sleep.**

ROSIE: **So am I.**

GRANDMA: **Last night —**

ROSIE: **You had a dream, too?**

GRANDMA: **It was the princess.**

ROSIE: **With the veil.**

GRANDMA: **You were there?**

ROSIE: **I saw you there, too.** *(She turns to face GRANDMA, who is now standing next to the bed.)* **It's you, isn't it? You're different, like me.**

GRANDMA: **It's not me. It is our family.**

ROSIE: **Mom?**

GRANDMA: **No.**

ROSIE: **Uncle Paolo?**

GRANDMA: **Paolo, yes.**

ROSIE: **Who else?**

GRANDMA: **My grandfather. He was the first to bring us all the gift.**

ROSIE: *(In awe, a whisper)* **The gift.** *(She is silent for a moment with the revelation. Then...)* **Come on, Lola, you have to show me more.** *(They both sit on the bed and clasp hands.)* **Show me what you've seen. Show me what you remember. Show me what you have dreamed about.**

GRANDMA: **Ay, Rosie...** *(The lights fade slowly)* **it is almost like sleep.**

ROSIE: **Sleep.**

GRANDMA: **You see, Rosie...**

> **Adona pay manga Filipino mo tuo nga ana-ay espirito, nag puyo sa ialum sa yuta, sa bato, sa landong sa dagko ng' kahuy. Ang akong apohan nga lalake mu tuo siya apan dili mo hadlok. Ang espirito tigulang na ka-ayo. Daghan ang ilang manga na kita. Ug ma tawag ka kanila, mag ka hinumdum ka sa imong gi memoria sa kalibutan.**

ROSIE: *(Speaks with her, translating.)* **There are still some Filipinos who believe that there are spirits who live in the ground, in the stones, in the darkness beneath the trees. My grandfather believed in them, but he was not afraid of them. They are very**

old. They have seen many things. To call upon them is to call upon the memory of the very earth.

'Sus, Rosie, how powerful they are – and yet they cannot live where there is no belief. Here, you might find some who say they believe in God, but it is in the head, not in the heart. So, how much less are there who believe in spirits? But you come from the same country, Rosie – you can remember. You just have to reach beyond all memory of what you have known here. It is like a song being sung among many other noises. Block out the other noises, and listen for the song.

(Lights go down. Music. A young man enters, in a faded shirt and trousers rolled up to the knee, barefoot. He looks constantly over his shoulder.)

They say my grandfather Rosario came from nowhere, that there were no records of his birth, that no one remembered hearing of him from other towns. They say he was descended from witches.

He came to the town of Catmon, and being bright and strong, he attracted attention in the small fishing village. The mayor of Catmon took such a liking to him – some say he was bewitched – that he adopted him almost as a son and sent him to the University of Santo Tomas. The Spanish students looked down on him for not being fair, for not being Spanish.

(Two men enter, aristocratic students from Spain who attend the university.)

MAN 1: Look at that fellow – who let that monkey loose in the courtyard?

MAN 2: I believe he is the new "adopted" son of the Mayor of Catmon. You know, he is not the only one, either. I believe they have admitted other negritos like him to the university. Perhaps they have a point in letting them learn something, rather than just admit the children of colonists and Spaniards.

MAN 1: Oh, *(Yawns)* I suppose. And where is Catmon? And where did this mayor get the money to buy this monkey's place at Santo Tomas?

ROSIE: How mean!

MAN 1 *(Turning to her)* **And what does it matter what a little girl like you thinks? I'll tell you what I think. The Philippines is like the Garden of Eden – and you Filipinos have run around in happy oblivion in a land of unbelievable riches. But I tell you what. Your grandfather and many others after him will get their education. And you know what happens when your eyes are opened in the Garden of Eden. You leave.** *(The two men exit.)*

GRANDMA: It's okay, anak. It's only a dream.

ROSIE: No, I remember! *(Music)*

> **I remember walking in the streets. A rich lady was on my right, and a fruit vendor to my left. I remember singing the same song as I waved flowers – flowers that seemed to multiply, like the loaves and the fishes. I remember seeing the soldiers' shining guns. I remember pitying their nervous faces. I remember the word we chanted: la...ban. Laban!**

GRANDMA Once upon a time.

ROSIE: I remember crying when martial law was declared. I remember Uncle Manny who used to say what he wished. I remember one night he disappeared – I remember the next morning his brother had bruises on his face. I remember seeing Imelda's picture at my cousins' house. I remember she gave them forks and spoons plated in gold.

GRANDMA: I remember...

ROSIE: Once upon a time.

GRANDMA: Listening to the wireless radio. Running up to the American soldier and asking him for his k-rations.

ROSIE: Chocolate, Joe!

GRANDMA: We were so hungry.

ROSIE: Chocolate, Joe!

GRANDMA: Their food tasted so good.

ROSIE: Running from the Japanese.

GRANDMA: Our house burned down in the war. Once upon a time. I remember.

ROSIE: I remember seeing seven ships sailing into Manila Bay. A fleet of Spanish vessels sank into the bloody water.

GRANDMA: The Spanish were at war.

ROSIE: But we fought for the Americans.

GRANDMA: Spain surrendered, and so surrendered us.

ROSIE: After four hundred years of Spanish rule. We were the Americans' little brown brothers. I remember I was a poor little brown girl and I sat in the cheap seat of the balconies in the movie houses. I remember seeing the army officers below. I remember seeing rich white immigrants wearing silk and pearls.

GRANDMA: Once upon a time.

ROSIE: I remember picking root crops from the ground that had fed my fathers. I remember yielding the root crops to a fat conquistador, the lord of the estate.

GRANDMA: I remember he had sailed in from Mexico. I remember the day he took our land. I remember he raped me and gave me a mestizo son.

ROSIE: Once upon a time.

GRANDMA: I remember I wanted to be a nun. I remember a friar seduced me. Once upon a time.

ROSIE: I was a priestess to my tribe. And our chieftains stood proud and tall. And they, with their half-naked bodies and bolos and spears defeated the white men in armor. A man named Magellan, with a spear in his heart, lay dead on the bloody beach.

GRANDMA: Once upon a time.

ROSIE: I remember...running free in the land of the sun. *(Music rises.)*

SCENE 7: TWO FEMALES AND TWO MALES

Rosie, 12

Tessie, 42

Paolo, late 20s

Max, late 20s

Lights come up on young people dressed in the styles of 1957-58, frozen in dance positions. When the song starts, they dance a modified version of American rock and roll.

Rosie enters and asks the audience to imagine what it was like in the following weeks. Visions she dreamed at night danced in front of her eyes in the daylight. As much as possible, she says, she and Grandma explored their homeland through family experiences. She says she and Grandma couldn't predict all they would see; once chosen, it seemed, the visions took their own course.

Tessie and Ben, part of the dancers and dressed as twenty-year-olds, draw apart from the crowd. Each is with friends; each "is intent on checking each other out." Those with Ben push him into Tessie as the girls hide their faces behind their hands.

Ben tells Tessie he can't help but see that she not only is the brightest in her class but also has the brightest eyes. He asks her to dance.

When Grandma enters, the crowd disperses. Grandma speaks to Tessie of the differences between life in Cebu and in Brooklyn. She says that in Cebu, families take care of their old ones. In Brooklyn they give them away to nursing homes. Tessie tells her she will always be with the family.

Rosie asks Grandma if she would like to go for a walk. Grandma replies that she is too tired, that her mind is so filled with dreams that she doesn't sleep well. But there is a responsibility that comes with the gift and they must go on. She tells Rosie she has a present for her — she will show her who the princess is.

The lights comes up to reveal Grandma as a young woman adjusting the hem of someone's bridal gown. It is her youngest sister, Estrellita, and she is the princess in their dreams. Grandma tells Rosie she remembers this moment when she thinks of 1941, when Estrallita planned a December wedding. The lights fade as

Rosie whispers a thank you. When the lights come up again, Rosie is sitting on her bed looking at the photograph of Paolo.

1. In the first part of this scene, Rosie seems more typically a twelve-year-old. Why did Dizon write the scene this way? What differences are there that make Rosie seem more like a girl her age?

2. The scene here switches immediately from present to past? What would you do to make sure the audience is not confused by the abruptness?

3. Why do you think the playwright is showing this scene in a flashback rather than having Tessie explain it to Rosie?

4. Why does Rosie say Paolo would have liked her very much?

ROSIE: A picture...of someone who would have liked me very much. I tried to ask Mom more about Uncle Paolo.

TESSIE: Hmmph. But you are right. He does look a little like Albert.

ROSIE: More than that. What was he like?

TESSIE: Oh...

ROSIE: Was he smart?

TESSIE: Yes. Always reading. He also painted very well – no one knew that of course except the family. In many ways, he was really very shy.

ROSIE: Did he ever get married?

TESSIE: No.

ROSIE: Did women fall in love with him?

TESSIE: Oh, yes, all the time.

ROSIE: Did you like him very much?

TESSIE: Yes.

ROSIE: Who was he closest to?

TESSIE: So many questions, Rosie!

ROSIE: No, please, Mom, don't go yet.

TESSIE: Well. He did have a best friend. Max.

ROSIE: Max.

MAX: My brothers and sisters. We have all survived into 1947.

ROSIE: Max.

PAOLO: There goes Max, getting ready to work up a crowd again.

MAX: Give thanks to America. God bless America. Let us cheer for America.

TESSIE: Kuya, why does he get so excited?

MAX: But let us not forget everything we fought for: the loved ones we lost! Our homeland!

ROSIE: Max.

MAX: Let us not forgive the puppet government who ruled our country in the shadow of the Japanese. Those traitors should be put to death. Instead, a man like Roxas is put in office!

PAOLO: Max!

MAX: Yes, Paolo.

PAOLO: Have you met my sister, Tessie?

MAX: A pleasure. I see your brother has been bringing you to the rallies. What do you think of them?

TESSIE: I see that this is something he cares about very much.

MAX: Yes. As we all should.

PAOLO: Are you really going to use that speech at our next gathering?

MAX: What are you going to do, Paolo, interrupt me as you did the last time?

PAOLO: It wasn't an interruption.

MAX: I stop to draw a breath and suddenly you're talking. It's about another inspired idea, another prophetic dream.

PAOLO: You tend to get so extreme.

MAX: To achieve what we need to achieve, we need to be extreme. To counteract and overturn the violence done to us, we must use violence of our own. It is the dialectic. It is for our country.

Do you see, Tessie, what we could do if we all feel this passionate! We wouldn't submit to any kind of rule save our own. This is like fighting for my life. You know what I would do if I could no longer fight for my country? I have a silver revolver I keep in a velvet cloth. It is as ceremonial as the sword used by the Japanese in hara-kiri. I would point the gun at myself, shoot myself with it, put the barrel to my mouth, to ensure that I'm truly dead when my brain is blown to pieces –

PAOLO: Max! Stop it! You are too much! *(MAX looks at both of them.)*

MAX: My apologies, Tessie. *(He hugs PAOLO briefly.)* Paolo. *(He exits.)*

TESSIE: That's all. Max was his best friend.

ROSIE: Yes.

TESSIE: I've got to run, Rosie. Be good – I – think Daddy will be home for dinner tonight.

ROSIE: Yes, Mom. *(She stares at the picture of PAOLO.)*

SCENE 8: THREE FEMALES AND ONE MALE

Grandma, 65 or older

Rosie, 12

Tessie, 42

Ben, early 40s

Rosie wakes, startled by noises she hears. She gets out of bed and goes downstairs. Grandma comes from the kitchen with two lighted candles that she places on the table where there is a small supper for one. Rosie enters the light of the candles.

1. Why is Grandma preparing a meal for her husband?

2. Why does Tessie want Rosie to go back upstairs? Why does she tell Rosie not to worry about it?

3. Put yourself in Tessie's (or Ben's) place. Describe how you might react and what you would feel seeing your daughter screaming that someone she has never known is dead?

GRANDMA: Ay, anak, why are you awake still?

ROSIE: I heard noises.

GRANDMA: *(Arranging the things on the table)* No, I'm just warming food, because my husband has not eaten yet.

ROSIE: He...hasn't?

GRANDMA: No. I knew tonight he would not be home until very late. I could see in his face, when he was putting on his clothes this morning. And the shirt he wore, that I took so long to iron yesterday.

ROSIE: *(Reaching her hand towards her grandmother)* Lola...maybe we should put the food away. He...It can be eaten tomorrow.

GRANDMA: What are you saying? Are you saying he's not coming home?

ROSIE: No...

GRANDMA: I know he will come home. He comes home, he always comes home. He will come in the door, and not make any noise, hoping that everyone is asleep. He will turn around and I will see the anger in his face when he sees everything here, waiting for him. It makes him angry that I know he comes home late. But he eats the food, and I sit and watch him eat it. I sit and watch him eat it, and he says nothing to me. He does not even look at me, but I look at him. I see how his hair is a little bit wet, I can smell the clean smell of soap. I laugh inside, thinking how he takes care to wash himself before he comes home to me. *(She suddenly bursts into deep, devastated sobs. ROSIE runs to her and hugs her, trying to bring her over to the sofa. Once they are seated, she holds her grandmother's shoulders and rocks back and forth with her.)*

ROSIE: Lola, please stop crying. *(Pause)* Lola, we don't want anyone to hear you. *(Has an idea)* Lola, I made up a song for us. Do you want to hear it? *(GRANDMA continues to sob hysterically.)* Shh, here, shh, here I will sing it for you, okay? Are you listening? *(Suddenly — someone flips a light switch on in the living room and TESSIE and BEN descend the stairs quickly.)*

TESSIE: What's going on? What's this food?

ROSIE: *(Crying)* I don't know.

TESSIE: Rosie, go upstairs!

ROSIE: Why?

BEN: Nanay! Nanay! Can you hear me?

TESSIE: Ma? Ma? Unsa na man? Ngano man pag hilak ka?

GRANDMA: He will come home! He will!

TESSIE: Yes, he will come home.

BEN: I'll probably have to increase the dosage.

GRANDMA: Rosie!

BEN: We should bring her upstairs for now.

GRANDMA: Rosie!

BEN: And we'll have to keep watch.

ROSIE: I'll watch her.

TESSIE: You're right. It won't be easy.

ROSIE: I'll watch her!

BEN: *(Struggling to get GRANDMA up)* Will you take care of her?

TESSIE: Rosie, please go to sleep, darling. Don't worry about it.

ROSIE: I don't mind!

TESSIE: Rosie, there's nothing you can do. Grandma is sick. *(Helping
    BEN take GRANDMA away)* And you're not to trouble her at all
    tomorrow! *(All exit, except for ROSIE.)*

ROSIE: Grandma...sick.

    Did it drain her...to remember so much?

    And the stories must have been painful for her, having been
    touched by them already.

    I'm only a granddaughter with the gift.

    In an odd way, these memories can't touch me.

    (TATA suddenly appears, wearing a flowing white gown.)

ROSIE: It's only a dream.

    Hello...I know you. You're Rosamunda's sister, Estrellita.
    Tata. I'm Rosie. I'm Rosamunda's granddaughter. I remember
    you have a beautiful white bridal gown and your sister is
    taking it up at the hem.

    Are you lost?

    *(With a sharp groan, TATA's eyes roll upward and she collapses,
    blood pouring from her mouth. ROSIE screams. TESSIE runs on.)*

TESSIE: Rosie! What are you doing out of bed? Rosie...

ROSIE: *(Still seeing TATA'S body)* **Tata! Tata is dead! Tata is dead!**

TESSIE: All right, that's it. You and Lola can't spend any more time talking nonsense. This is a madhouse! Rosie...ssh... Rosie...

SCENE 9: THREE FEMALES AND FOUR MALES

Tessie, 42

Rosie, 12

Grandma, 65 or older

Albert, 19

Ben, early 40s

Max, late 20s

Paolo, late 20s

Tessie is fearful of her mother's talking to Rosie about dreams and spirits, and so tells Rosie and Albert about the fears of her own childhood in Camotes — spirits, witches, ghosts and ogres. Dreams, she says, are just backfires from the brain's cortex, not messages from the past or omens of the future. She came to America largely to escape such superstitions, she says, and she wants her children to believe they have been given brains to take control of their own lives.

1. Why do you suppose Tessie and Albert have different views of the relationship between Rosie and Grandma? What influenced these views?

2. Why do you think Tessie becomes angry at Albert?

3. Why does Tessie want Ben to leave? Why is she being so obstinate and difficult? Why does he finally give in?

4. What does Tessie hope to gain by talking to Grandma?

5. Much of the play deals with a clash of cultures? How is that apparent in this scene?

6. Why do you think Tessie keeps trying to explain away the dreams as imaginings?

7. What is the purpose of having Grandma and Tessie speak simultaneously in part of this scene? Do you think this an effective dramatic device? Why? Why not?

8. When Tessie asks Grandma why she doesn't know what happened to Paolo, why do you think Dizon shifted the time and setting so abruptly?

9. In this scene and other parts of the play, Dizon has characters talking in turn, but to the audience rather than to each other. Do you think this is an effective dramatic device? Why? Why not?

ROSIE: Can't I bring the tray upstairs at least?

ALBERT: I grew up with Mom at home all the time.

TESSIE: That's why I'm here.

ALBERT: It was Sesame Street in the morning, Flipper in the afternoon.

TESSIE: It's time for you to catch up on what you've been missing. Or I won't let you participate in those activities anymore. Now go. *(ROSIE exits.)*

ALBERT: We watched a kid's show once where they would hang donuts by a string and the contestants would see who would eat their donut the fastest with their hands tied behind their back. Mom and I tried it. We ended up getting powdered sugar all over the floor and mostly over my face.

Then, one day, I came home and Mom wasn't there.

ALBERT: *(Simultaneously with TESSIE)* She had to start working.

TESSIE: I had to start working.

TESSIE: Of course we needed the money, but I needed to get out of the house.

ALBERT: I thought it was because I was a smart-ass kid and she couldn't stand watching TV in the morning and TV in the afternoon. She never had to worry about Rosie, though. I made sure Rosie had someone to watch TV with, and play the donut game.

So, what's all this about Rosie, Mom? You shouldn't be so hard on her.

TESSIE: Maybe not. But you don't know the whole story.

ALBERT: What is the whole story?

TESSIE: *(Turning her back, fidgeting with the food)* Rosie and Grandma spend all their time together – and now Rosie is missing piano lessons, she doesn't stay for newspaper, and what do you think is happening to her studies?

ALBERT: I know what's happening. Rosie is having the best time of her life.

TESSIE: Albert –

ALBERT: I think it's great that there's someone home when she gets home from school...

TESSIE: **Albert...**

ALBERT: **...somebody to talk to, somebody to make dinner...**

TESSIE: *(Bursting out)* **I don't have time for this right now, Albert!** *(Turning back to the tray)* **Why don't you go visit what's-her-name for a while?**

ALBERT: *(Coldly)* **Heather, Mom, her name is Heather.**

TESSIE: **Whatever.** *(BEN enters.)*

ALBERT: *(Exiting)* **Don't bother trying, Dad. She's using the heavy artillery.**

BEN: **Alberto, you apologize to your mother! Albert!** *(Walking towards TESSIE)* **Tess –**

TESSIE: *(Holds up her hand.)* **Ben, it would really help right now if you went and played tennis.**

BEN: *(Not believing his ears)* **What?!**

TESSIE: *(With her back to him)* **You heard me. I would rather you go and –**

BEN: **I know, I would rather talk.**

TESSIE: **And I would rather not!** *(He still doesn't move.)* **Get out of here!** *(Pause)*

BEN: **Okay.** *(Starts retreating.)* **I will go play tennis. It doesn't MATTER, of course, that I don't have a PARTNER...but I will go.** *(He starts to exit.)* **Tess?** *(She shakes her head – she is adamant.)* **Okay – I'll play tennis.** *(Exits.)*

GRANDMA: *(Entering)* **Teresita? Why is there so much noise down here?**

TESSIE: **What noise, Ma? It's just the usual stuff. How are you feeling? Are you hungry?**

GRANDMA: **Ah...** *(Looking around, guardedly)* **...no...** *(She starts rummaging through her pockets and moves toward the kitchen.)*

TESSIE: **Where are you going?**

GRANDMA: *(Exasperated)* **I didn't want to make the bedroom smell. I'm going to go smoke there in the garden.**

TESSIE: **No, Ma – wait, before you go smoke – here. Why don't you sit here first?** *(Installs her on the couch.)* **I'll bring the food to you.**

GRANDMA: **Where's Rosie?**

TESSIE: Oh – she's making up a piano lesson. *(Hands her the soup.)*

GRANDMA: *(Between sips)* **Such a good girl.**

TESSIE: Yes.

GRANDMA: Bright.

TESSIE: Yes.

GRANDMA: **Smart like you. Still...your sister Lorna was prettier when she was younger.**

TESSIE: Yes, yes, Ma.

GRANDMA: Okay, I'm full already. I want to go smoke.

TESSIE: Wait! Wait! I took the day off to be with you. Don't you want to stay with me?

GRANDMA: Who is watching the store?

TESSIE: One of the managers is covering for me.

GRANDMA: Ay, Teresita, why did you do that? You only make yourself more nervous when you have nothing to do...

TESSIE: I do not!

GRANDMA: ...like you have tapeworm or something. Okay, I'm here, anak. What did you want to talk about?

TESSIE: Do you like it here?

GRANDMA: Yes, it's very nice.

TESSIE: You don't know any other old people. I was afraid you would feel lonely.

GRANDMA: Ay – never mind! There is plenty to do here in the house. There is the garden outside. Rosie and I are like barcada – old friends – already.

TESSIE: But Ma...

GRANDMA: Do you remember when it would rain and you were tired of playing on the floor, you would come and sit by me while I was sewing. And Paolo would sing to us and you would lean your head here, on my knee, and listen. *(PAOLO appears, strumming a guitar and singing "Dandansuy.")*

TESSIE: My favorite song when it would get dark.

GRANDMA: Do you remember?

TESSIE: Or when it was time to pick pebbles from the rice grains.

GRANDMA: Or when it was hot.

TESSIE: Ma – what happened last night? *(PAOLO disappears.)*

331

GRANDMA: Anak-what are you talking about?

TESSIE: Last night. Did you know you thought you were in Lahug, that Papa was not going to come home? This is my fault, for not staying home with you, for not making you happy.

GRANDMA: Tessie...what are you talking about? I am happy when my children are happy. Remember when we went to look for the pot of gold?

TESSIE: Ma...

GRANDMA: Remember? Do you remember Paolo and you and I followed the sun when it came out after the rainstorm? Do you remember...

TESSIE: ...how far we walked.

GRANDMA: How the leaves were shining from the rain.

TESSIE: The sun was setting behind the farthest hill of the city. When we walked up, the mist in the air was filled with golden light. We had found our pot of gold and we made ourselves a wish. Ma, all that happened a long time ago.

I must have been only five, maybe six years old at the time.

Do you remember what it was like later?

Do you remember Paolo and you spending more time by yourselves?

Do you remember?

Wasn't that when you started dreaming?

GRANDMA: What, anak?

TESSIE: It's all right. I know about it. Paolo told me. He even tried to show me once. "Sleep," he would say. "It is almost like – "

GRANDMA: Stop.

TESSIE: Ma, please tell the truth. Isn't that what you're really telling Rosie? You tell her it's called "the gift"? And she believes it?

GRANDMA: It is a gift. We do not dream because we are unhappy. We do it because we do it. It is a special power to see what we have seen.

TESSIE: Don't you think I know Rosie has an overactive imagination? I know I should be home more. I know I should pay more attention to her, but I have to work, that's just the way it is. So she starts making up fairy tales! At the age of twelve!

GRANDMA: Who said she is making fairy tales?

TESSIE: I know, Ma.

Just like Paolo. He didn't have a gift – he had his imagination. It drove him crazy. Waking up in sweats. Delirious about having to save the world. Save the world – you'd think someone so smart wouldn't believe in such nonsense. Next thing you know we'll be seeing the momo, the agtah, the wakwak flying from tree to tree.

GRANDMA: Are you ashamed of your brother?

TESSIE: I'm ashamed that I couldn't do anything! That nothing could be done, that dreaming was all you really could do.

GRANDMA: What are you talking about, Maria Teresita?

TESSIE: When I first noticed that Paolo and you had started this dream thing. Papa had begun coming home at three in the morning.

GRANDMA: You know nothing.

I have always had these dreams. It's only that you were too young to notice before. But you can remember when we had to move around so much during the war. You remember when we had to leave the house in the middle of the night and go to the cave in the mountains. It was December, 1944 – you were already seven. I had had a dream about that night, I already knew where to go, I knew that we were taking the right road. You thought your father was the one who knew. But I told him. It was a good thing he listened to me. You know my sister Estrellita, your Tita Tata, went with another group, to another part of the jungle. They were going to an American shelter. They died just near there. The Japanese put bayonets through their stomachs. *(Pause)* I knew that would happen too.

Do you think this is only something to do when I am unhappy?

TESSIE: I understand, Ma. I'm sorry.

But it also has nothing to do with Rosie. I don't even think she's old enough to know. And I don't want her to know.

GRANDMA: She wants to know her homeland.

TESSIE: She can know it. She's not supposed to save it.

GRANDMA: And what if that is what she wants?

(The juxtaposed dialog that follows is to be spoken simultaneously.)

GRANDMA: What are you talking about, anak?

TESSIE: I don't know, but neither does she. It's different for Rosie.

She is no longer in her mother's country.

We've worked hard to achieve this. My daughter wants for nothing and she can be anything she wants. There will be no talk of loyalties, she will not be dragged down by it, like him...to feel sick and powerless, thinking that you had somehow failed, because the land and the people you love have turned against you.

(Pause)

GRANDMA: What is she then? Is she not still part of the same people and language and struggle?

The Philippines is a beautiful land where one is not easily forgotten. Why must it give up all that is good and beautiful in its people because of troubles?

You cannot throw it away so easily, Maria Teresita.

It is your mother's country!

(Pause)

TESSIE: Paolo! I'm talking about Paolo! You say your dreams have told you so much! They didn't tell you enough to save Tata, they didn't tell you enough to save Paolo! If they told you anything at all, why don't you know what happened?

GRANDMA: Tessie! *(TESSIE rushes out. Blackout. We hear a gunshot. A man's scream.)*

(Lights up on MAX, holding in his hand a silver revolver, his other hand dripping blood. He is hysterical. He drags On-stage the body of PAOLO, also drenched in blood, a thin trickle streaming from his mouth.)

MAX: Oh, my God! Somebody help me! Help me! Oh, God!

SCENE 10: THREE FEMALES AND TWO MALES

Rosie, 12

Tessie, 42

Grandma, 65 or older

Ben, early 40s

Albert, 19

As the entire cast enters, Grandma begins to tell of "the long thread of a story that never breaks," a story that continues through the ages so long as there is a single voice to tell it. Again there is simultaneous dialog, which merges into one conversation, then separates and combines and separates once more before combining in this scene that ends the play.

Grandma talks of Max's telling her he heard a gunshot as he neared Paolo's apartment building. Paolo lay dead on the floor. That night, Rosie tells Grandma, you learned that you never need be alone again. The night he died, Grandma says, she heard his voice whisper, "Good night, Ma."

Tessie picks up the story of Paolo's death, that the police said no one knew who had done it. She remembers thinking that Max could have told the family anything, that he could have *said* he heard a gunshot. She says she kept the thought to herself and "felt dirty with secrets" the day Max saw her. Because she loved Paolo so much, she says, she tried to keep him intact. She tells of coming home one night when she was thirteen and discovering Grandma and Paolo "frozen in space." She thought they were dead, and she fell to the floor, heart beating. She brushed against Paolo's leg and he yawned as if awakening from a deep sleep. She was angry at being scared for nothing, at having "discovered a terrible nightmare."

We are suddenly in the past where Paolo is telling of a dream in which ballot boxes for the election are filled not with votes but with maggots. He tells her he has to find the spot where the ballot boxes fell from a truck and burst open. "And someone may kill me for wanting to find out," he tells her. "But promise me you'll never tell anyone what I saw."

Max appears and says Paolo was not "a political creature. He just happened to be involved in politics" and "truly loved his country." Max says Paolo told him of his dreams, his fears. Among

Paolo's things, Max says, he found unsent letters to Tessie, who didn't appreciate Max's giving them to her. Paolo wrote that he regretted not painting his visions.

Max talks about how the dreams affected Paolo's waking hours, and that he wanted to show Tessie that Paolo was going insane.

Ben mentions knowing that Paolo killed himself but Tessie never talked about it.

Albert talks about how happy Rosie is now and about how much he loved her and how his headaches disappeared when she told him stories. Grandma says they cannot forget the songs and stories of their ancestors. She doesn't want Rosie to be like Tessie, putting her heritage behind her. Albert argues that Rosie needs her living family, not ghosts.

Toward the end of the scene, the characters are speaking in short phrases or sentences. Grandma says they have to remember. Ben says they shouldn't dig up their ghosts. Grandma shouts, "They're not ghosts!"

The lights come up on Grandma and Rosie, "alone in the darkness." "Tata, how did you manage to find me?" Grandma asks. "Paolo, you've come to see your mother. Ay...my...children...where have you gone? Where are you?" The lights go to black.

1. Why is Tessie sending Grandma home now? Do you agree with her decision?

2. What is the significance of Grandma's speech that begins, "Ay, na'ako"?

3. Do you think the play ends appropriately? Why? Why not? Do you think this is a good play? Why? Why not?

(As lights come up, airport sounds. The family is waiting for GRANDMA's flight to board.)

ROSIE: Of course, she had to go back. Spirits can't live in Brooklyn. Neither can Grandma.

TESSIE: Ma, is there anything you want us to send you?

BEN: Tessie, you know she can't hear you right now.

TESSIE: I know she can — just...not right now.

GRANDMA: Ay – so many people here...

TESSIE: Yes, Ma, we're at the airport. You'll be leaving in fifteen minutes.

ROSIE: Grandma didn't seem to get it.

   The whole night before, we had spent packing her things.

   The whole morning, we had talked about her going back to the Philippines.

   We were at the airport for over an hour.

   Perhaps she didn't want to wake up, so that she wouldn't have to say good-bye.

ALBERT: Do you think we'll go visit her next year?

BEN: I don't see why not. Tessie?

TESSIE: Yes. I'd like that. That would be better.

ALBERT: Hey, they're starting to board. We better get her going...

BEN: Ma? Ma? Come on, now, Ma...let's bring your things. Here, hold this...

TESSIE: Here, Ma, let me fix your scarf.

ALBERT: Bye, Grandma. It was really good having you.

TESSIE: Albert, why are you saying good-bye? She's not leaving yet.

ALBERT: Mom, they're boarding NOW.

TESSIE: *(Realizing)* Oh my God...Ma, good-bye... *(In spite of herself, she starts sobbing.)*

GRANDMA: Anak? Why are you crying?

TESSIE: Because you're leaving, Ma!

GRANDMA: Ay, na'ako... *(She strokes TESSIE's head.)*

   My brave girl. Thank you, Maria Teresita, for this visit. You have become beautiful. You have become a wife and a mother. I am very, very proud and happy for you.

   Shh, shh...don't cry. Some families never get to touch each

other again. We are lucky in that we can.

ROSIE: Lola...

GRANDMA: Yes, Rosie.

ROSIE: I forgot to ask you...I wanted a picture of you as a child.

GRANDMA: *(Holding ROSIE's hands very tightly for a moment)* **Ay, Rosie. Of course. So now you know how to find a picture of me.** *(She starts to exit. They all call good-bye as the lights fade.)*

ROSIE: We went to visit Grandma for Christmas. She died soon after. I did find an old picture of her when she was thirteen. Grandma was right. I knew how to find a better picture. *(She runs over to a tableau of GRANDMA, PAOLO, TATA and MAX and in an instant is "captured" in a photographic, sepia light. She runs to a tableau of TESSIE, BEN and ALBERT, and is captured by a brighter light in the same way.)*

ROSIE/TESSIE: You see the Filipino woman – the Filipina – is descended from a long line of priestesses.

ROSIE/GRANDMA: And I could remember all my dreams as if I were dreaming them for the first time. *(As ROSIE exits through the audience)*

ROSIE/TESSIE/GRANDMA: Once upon a time, I was a little girl, with a secret and wonderful power. *(Blackout)*

Credits

ABOUT THE AUTHOR/EDITOR

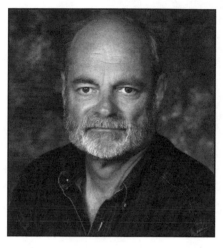

Marsh Cassady has written more than forty books including novels, short story and drama collections, haiku, biography, and books on theatre and storytelling. His audio and stage plays have been widely performed (including off-Broadway), and he has written and recorded a three-set audio tape on storytelling.

A former actor/director and university professor with a Ph.D. degree in theatre, Cassady has worked with more than a hundred productions. Currently fiction/drama editor of *Crazyquilt Quarterly,* he was editor of both a regional and a national magazine. Since 1981, he has conducted an all-genre writing workshop in San Diego and has taught various creative writing classes at UCSD and elsewhere. While teaching at Montclair State in the 1970s, he started a program of workshops, classes and special projects in playwriting. His own writing has won numerous regional and national awards.

ALSO BY MARSH CASSADY

Great Scenes From Women Playwrights

Characters in Action

The Theatre and You

Acting Games — Improvisations and Exercises

The Art of Storytelling

ORDER FORM

MERIWETHER PUBLISHING LTD.
P.O. BOX 7710
COLORADO SPRINGS, CO 80933
TELEPHONE: (719) 594-4422

Please send me the following books:

_____ **Great Scenes From Minority Playwrights** $15.95
#TT-B207
by Marsh Cassady
Seventy-four scenes of cultural diversity

_____ **Great Scenes From Women Playwrights** $14.95
#TT-B119
by Marsh Cassady
Classic and contemporary scenes for actors

_____ **Characters in Action #TT-B106** $14.95
by Marsh Cassady
Playwriting the easy way

_____ **The Theatre and You #TT-B115** $15.95
by Marsh Cassady
An introductory text on all aspects of theatre

_____ **Acting Games — Improvisations and** $12.95
Exercises #TT-B168
by Marsh Cassady
A textbook of theatre games and improvisations

_____ **The Art of Storytelling #TT-B139** $12.95
by Marsh Cassady
Creative ideas for preparation and performance

_____ **The Scenebook for Actors #TT-B177** $14.95
by Dr. Norman A. Bert
Great monologs and dialogs for auditions

**These and other fine Meriwether Publishing books are available at
your local bookstore or direct from the publisher. Use the handy
order form on this page.**

NAME: _____

ORGANIZATION NAME: _____

ADDRESS: _____

CITY: _____ STATE: _____

ZIP: _____ PHONE: _____

❏ **Check Enclosed**
❏ **Visa or MasterCard #** _____

Signature: _____   *Expiration
Date:* _____

    (required for Visa/MasterCard orders)

COLORADO RESIDENTS: Please add 3% sales tax.
SHIPPING: Include $2.75 for the first book and 50¢ for each additional book ordered.

❏ *Please send me a copy of your complete catalog of books and plays.*